CW01264086

WHAT AILS FRANCE?

What Ails France?

BRIGITTE GRANVILLE

McGill-Queen's University Press
Montreal & Kingston • London • Chicago

© McGill-Queen's University Press 2021

ISBN 978-0-2280-0680-0 (cloth)
ISBN 978-0-2280-0695-4 (ePDF)
ISBN 978-0-2280-0696-1 (ePUB)

Legal deposit second quarter 2021
Bibliothèque nationale du Québec

Printed in Canada on acid-free paper that is 100% ancient forest free
(100% post-consumer recycled), processed chlorine free

Library and Archives Canada Cataloguing in Publication

Title: What ails France? / Brigitte Granville.
Names: Granville, Brigitte, author.
Description: Includes bibliographical references and index.
Identifiers: Canadiana (print) 20200416146 | Canadiana (ebook)
    20200416219 | ISBN 780228006800 (cloth) | ISBN 9780228006954
    (EPDF) | ISBN 9780228006961 (EPUB)
Subjects: LCSH: France—Economic conditions—21st century. | LCSH:
    France—Social conditions—21st century. | LCSH: France—Politics and
    government—21st century.
Classification: LCC HC276.4.G73 2021 | DDC 330.944—dc23

This book was typeset in 10.5/13 New Baskerville ITC Pro.

Contents

Tables

Preface

A couplet from Paul Éluard's poem *Liberté*, written during the Nazi occupation of France in 1942, reads: 'By the power of a word [liberty]/I restart my life' (Eluard 1958, 217). While poetic flights are not to be expected, and would be ill-advised, from an economist like me, the fears and hopes that led me to write this book were spurred by the feeling Éluard expresses. My aim is to show – in an analytical rather than a poetic way – how the governance of contemporary France asphyxiates the country's potential to forge itself anew. I will also describe what I see as the most promising ways to cast off the restraints on a 'restart' of national life.

Any serious shock such as a pandemic will instil a sense that things cannot go on as they were. But the thirst for new approaches was already raging in French society before anyone had heard of Covid-19. It fuelled the 'yellow vests' (*gilets jaunes*) protest movement, which, when I began writing this book, had reached its first anniversary. In much media reporting and commentary, protesters' grievances were played down in favour of covering the violence that was often perpetrated by malicious infiltrators rather than true *gilets jaunes* and was met with a police response that left hundreds of protesters injured or even maimed. The yellow vests protests reflected a deep sense of grievance: feeling unrepresented and deceived by the political class, the *gilets jaunes* despaired for their own – and their children's – economic future.

The yellow vests movement was a distinctive backlash by a substantial section of French society against economic developments and their devastating social effects, which have become all too familiar throughout the advanced industrialised world. Since the 1980s, the arrival of new exporters, mainly China along with other emerging economies, and the start of the digital/information technology (IT) revolution have hit low-wage and low-skilled workers hard. The productivity gains from new technologies have not been adequately shared with workers, either directly through wages or indirectly via redistribution through government budgets. While financial liberalisation and freer cross-border capital flows have facilitated tax 'optimisation' on the part of the largest firms and their wealthy shareholders (the notorious '1 per cent' and '0.1 per cent'), governments have had to raise the tax burden on 'ordinary' domestic taxpayers – compounding their relative income losses.

The global financial crisis (GFC) and ensuing eurozone sovereign debt crisis amplified these problems in two ways. First, the unconventional monetary policy pursued by the central banks of advanced countries pumped liquidity into capital markets, inflating the prices of financial and real assets. Such assets are predominantly owned by the wealthy. The people responsible for such policies presumably reckoned on this wealth trickling down, but wages and living standards stagnated across the developed world – with unskilled workers, small savers, and retirees the worst affected – and inequalities widened. Second, fiscal austerity (especially in the eurozone) limited the ability of deficit countries to spend on social protection and redistribution policies, further worsening the situation of low-wage and low-skilled workers. This eroded trust in both national and European institutions, which for many appeared to be the unaccountable source of the sacrifices that millions had to endure. The political effects of such trends spread throughout Europe and North America. 'Brexit and Trump' became a shorthand summary of those effects that, in continental Europe, took the form of a rise in 'populist' parties with ominous echoes of the 1920s and 1930s.

The French version of this story, viewed from outside the country, may not seem so particularly egregious. The account of French problems in this book may, on the contrary, strike readers from around the world as variations, perhaps even relatively mild ones, on their own countries' difficulties. While I occasionally point to similarities and contrasts between France and other countries, my aim in doing so is to sharpen the 'French' analysis rather than attempt any systematic cross-country comparisons. The premise throughout is that, while many of the elements of French fractures are common to most industrialised (and especially European) economies, some features are highly distinctive and offer sharp lessons that deserve wide attention.

A prescient book – *Le Mal français* – published back in the 1970s by the minister and memorialist of General de Gaulle, Alain Peyrefitte (1925–99), argued that the 'ill' besetting France stems from the fact that the country has never been able to get rid of its absolutist heritage, which originated in the policies of the great ministers of seventeenth-century kings. Those policies entailed an uncompromising centralisation, making everything flow in favour of technocratic Caesarism (Peyrefitte 2006).

A relevant contemporary manifestation of this politicised technocracy is the establishment of the European monetary union. The Polish economists Stefan Kawalec, Ernest Pytlarczyk, and Kamil Kamiński recall the attitude of interwar politicians and financiers defending the gold standard at all costs as a warning against the danger of denial about the single currency's contribution to present-day economic and social crises (Kawalec, Pytlarczyk, and Kamiński 2020). By the time I had finished writing this book in 2020, crisis was naturally linked in the public mind with other and more recent causes, above all Covid-19. Such denial of underlying causes undermines the very European cohesion and values cherished by the deniers. These include many leading lights of the French 'intelligentsia', who have abandoned the typically radical enthusiasms of their youth: they are more disturbed by the disorder of the yellow vests protests than they are exercised about the causes of those protests. They may come to regret this complacency about the roots of widespread public anger and despair. In the face of such danger, there is no place for silence and indifference. Those who sympathise with the grievances of the *gilets jaunes* are routinely denounced as heretics, fascistically blaspheming against a proven formula for prosperity. Yet silence in the ranks and the injunction to remain silent on pain of being labelled a 'populist' spells not protection, but threat. My aim in writing this book is to make whatever contribution I can to breaking that silence, which I see as a precondition for freeing up the search for ways to escape stagnation and hopelessness.

While researching this book, I have been inspired by many scholars: Paul Collier, and his work on migration in particular; Daniel Kahneman, who reminds me to think hard before forming an opinion; Jonathan Haidt, whom I read thanks to my great friend Amy Boone, who taught me to look carefully at my own prior moral preferences; Deidre Nansen McCloskey, who, for me, provides a guard rail against bad economic thought; Branko Milanovic, and his pioneering work on inequality; and Jeffrey Sachs, who has the courage and integrity of his convictions.

I am especially grateful to my editor at McGill-Queen's University Press, Richard Baggaley, thanks to whom I have been able to hone the concept of this book. It would also never have been written without the suggestion, help, and friendship of Kamil Kamiński.

Life has blessed me with many friends from all over the world, and this book is for them.

WHAT AILS FRANCE?

Introduction

Go into any French bookshop and you will be greeted at the first display table by volumes dealing, often rather polemically, with present-day political and socio-economic controversies. It is rarer for such material to find its way into a hardcover in 'Anglo-Saxon' publishing, as they would say in France; an essay covering such topics will more often see the light of day in the form of an ephemeral pamphlet.

Well, you hold in your hands a long 'pamphlet' about the political economy of contemporary France, written at an intense pace to match the social and political storms raging in France at the mid-point of the five-year presidential term to which Emmanuel Macron was elected in the spring of 2017. From the outbreak of the yellow vests (*gilets jaunes*) protest movement in late 2018 to the Covid-19 pandemic in 2020, these events are the product of deep and chronic problems and/or hold up a mirror to such problems. No ephemera here, then: while crises and presidencies come and go, their underlying causes are far from fleeting. This means that, like other French economists of my generation, I have had years to think about the dysfunctions of France's political economy. There is, perhaps, a special propulsion to such thinking for those, like me, whose professional life has been spent outside France. The storms of the Macron presidency have spurred me to put these thoughts on paper.

Readers persuaded of this point – that my topical subject matter offers a sufficiently durable shelf for a book to sit on – might still expect such a book to be more even-handed, in the style of a traditional scholarly monograph, than this at times indignant tract. I should therefore start by laying to rest any suspicion that I am in some kind of denial about the economic performance of France and its human welfare indicators looking respectable compared with its peer group of advanced industrial countries. One reason for the critical focus of this essay is that the problems it describes make that performance, already mediocre in many respects, less sustainable. The more important reason for my approach, however, is that these problems highlight areas that are not captured by many conventional indicators.

The story I have to tell is, at heart, an economic one. It does not take the form of a litany of grievances or a list of recipes for making France great again. I truly believe that France is great enough already, but I wish that more of the country's potential for well-being rubbed off on the lives of the very substantial sections of the population that now feel alienated. The love of one's country felt by any patriot comprises a yearning for escape from all constraints and rigidities which stifle that country – from the top down.

Reflecting this spirit, much of the discussion in this book is critical of Macron's presidency. Deep-seated problems cannot, by definition, be blamed on a single president. It would also be unreasonable to expect even such a young, energetic, and ambitious political leader to make any more than modest progress in coping with so dubious a long-term legacy. Even now, plenty of people admire Macron's intelligence and youthful energy; perhaps such fans are galvanised by his detractors, who are becoming ever more numerous and vehement. My own unease about him dates back to the heyday of his political honeymoon in mid 2017, when he fired the head of the armed forces, General Pierre de Villiers, for insubordination. Here Macron first revealed, in public, an insecure edginess and difficulty connecting with people that is belied by the elegantly phrased scripts of his prepared speeches. These are filled with words that should resonate, inspiring respect and pride, yet the words as delivered seem empty of life and soul. The young president recites his speeches like the good pupil he was. A more substantive critique of Macron follows in chapter 1, but I should point out that it is in a spirit of self-criticism that I have begun here by highlighting this personal impression of the president as lacking necessary political gifts; I strive to prevent such impressions from clouding the recognition that I think is due to Macron on several counts.

One area where Macron scores well in my book is intellectual honesty. A good example of this quality allows me to introduce what may, to some readers, come across as another controversial theme that features prominently in what follows (in addition, that is, to my overall critical view of Macron). The theme in question is Europe's economic and monetary union (EMU), which, in its present form, I regard as harmful for France and for Europe. Macron's public position – expressed before coming to power in a speech he made in London in February 2017 – implied as much. He argued that the countries of the eurozone would need to become much more integrated, especially in the sphere of public finances, for the single currency to become sustainable. This integration would amount to a political union, of which Macron – judging by several of his speeches as president – also appeared to be in favour. Although I do not myself support such political integration, I must recognise Macron's sound logic. The problem, however, is not one of personal preference but of lack of realism. As Macron soon found out, Germany had no interest in following his lead; it took the coronavirus pandemic to shift the German position, albeit in a way that, at time of writing, remains highly ambiguous. More to the point, most people in France would be equally if not more resistant to the political union implied by Macron's positions than the German government and people. Ignoring the French people's voice will cause them to feel more alienated and to make their claim on their 'Frenchness' louder. The results of the first round of the presidential election in April 2017 showed that half of all participating voters supported anti-establishment candidates who had campaigned on platforms labelled by the mainstream media as 'extremist' for calling into question European integration and/or the North Atlantic Treaty Organization (NATO).

Here we meet another of my targets: the righteous consensus. There are many points of view that are regarded as 'beyond the pale' by French officialdom and those preaching from most media pulpits. I have found that criticising fixed exchange rate regimes such as the EMU falls into this category, especially as European politicians who are similarly critical of the single currency are generally regarded as dangerously populist. I support adjustable exchange rates and flexible government budgeting (meaning higher deficits in hard times to provide an indispensable economic 'oxygen supply' in the sense of fostering profitable opportunities that businesses can pursue). Contrasting as it does with official France's instinct to impose layers of complex regulation on all kinds of economic activity, such thinking is regarded by the high official caste as if it were agitation by undesirable dissidents. It is sometimes referred to as the 'brown plague' ('brown' as in the fascist Brownshirts). Jacques Attali, who shot to prominence as an adviser of President Mitterrand in the 1980s, even labelled 'sovereignist' sceptics of the euro as anti-Semites (Nadau 2019)! This lack of honesty and reflection on the part of these official intellectuals reminds me of one of Alain Peyrefitte's reflections on the May 1940 debacle: 'It is not the insufficiency of the material which lost, it is the shielding of mentalities' (Peyrefitte 2006, 39–48). Stuck in its rigid mindset, official France all too often ignores the surrounding dynamism of ideas and attitudes.

This is a good point at which to address the question of my 'priors'. In the heat of the unrest that gripped France in May 1968, 'D'où parles-tu, camarade?' was on many lips. To the literal translation of this question – 'From what standpoint are you speaking, comrade?' – the adjective 'ideological' should be added to bring out the underlying spirit. Rather than getting bogged down in pre-emptive introspection, I will leave my ideological biases to emerge from what follows, confident that any that are discovered may be found to lack internal consistency. A more useful first answer to this 'comrade' question, I think, is to trace some of the personal and family origins of my free-spirited instincts.

My paternal grandfather fought in what for France became the epicentre of World War I: the Battle of Verdun (21 February 1916–18 December 1916). He was among the minority of combatants to return home 'unharmed'. As with so many other survivors of that carnage, the absence of severe physical injuries belied lasting mental distress. I have childhood memories of vacations spent with my grandparents, and of how he would cry out loud during his nightmares. He would sleep with his hunting rifle by his bed ('just in case!'). Back in civilian life, he worked for the state railways; by the outbreak of World War II, he was a station supervisor, helping to ensure the smooth running of the railways in Occupied France by day, and – according to family legend – getting involved in sabotage attacks on those same railways by night.

I do not know that much about my father's history: for example, I was unaware of the various decorations he had received, which I discovered among his personal effects after his death. After the Fall of France in June 1940, my father, then aged nineteen, joined the Free French forces taking shape under the leadership of Charles de Gaulle and spent the war flying planes in various theatres from North Africa to the Middle East. My uncle, his brother, afterwards thought this was just as well. I remember the words he used to express that conviction: 'Otherwise, he would have joined the *Maquis* [Resistance], and you would not be here. He was as crazy as your grandfather!'

My mother was born in Haiphong to a family of merchants from Provence. They had settled in what is now Vietnam in 1885 – that is, in the early years of the French colony in Indochina. Her Basque maternal grandfather was killed in a duel that he himself initiated. At the age of twenty, she left the chaos of post-war Vietnam for France, but in her heart, she never really left Indochina. During World War II, one of her uncles was active in the Resistance while another rallied to the Free French Air Force, later joining the Normandie-Niemen squadrons that saw combat on the Eastern Front. Their response to the shattering defeat of 1940 had been to embrace sacrifice as the price of freedom.

These, then, are some of my own family's variations on the turbulent themes of French twentieth-century history. This family life as I experienced it in childhood was no loving idyll. Bringing up children 'correctly' according to the ideas of my parents' generation often felt, to me (on the receiving end), like harshness and indifference. My reaction against this family life was itself an anchorage. My upbringing unwittingly trained me to hone doubt and irony against prejudices, illusions and utopias of all kinds. It also instilled in me a spirit of contradiction: searching for new ideas, then shooting them down. Overall, I was left with what I have always thought of as a certain madness for freedom. This is, perhaps, why my friends at the World Bank, where I worked as a young researcher in the early 1980s, called me 'Little Friend of all the World', after the eponymous hero of Rudyard Kipling's *Kim*.

Family life also gave me some unusual exposure to the French political world. This was not because I had any relatives in politics as such – far from it. However, my father's military career ended with a period of service in an Air Force wing responsible for flying ministers around on official trips (the Groupe de liaisons aériennes ministérielles – GLAM). The definition of 'official trips' was flexibly interpreted, most notably by an interior minister in the 1950s called François Mitterrand, who would use GLAM planes for Christmas getaways. After an early career highlight of 'surviving' a fake assassination attempt against himself in the Avenue de l'Observatoire in Paris, Mitterrand would go on to be president of France for fourteen years.

Like many of the original Free French, my father did not care for the likes of Mitterrand who, in 1940, had started out as collaborators. It would be years before I learned of this, however, as my father only spoke of it in reaction to my youthful leftist enthusiasm about Mitterrand's presidential election victory in 1981. I was struck by these revelations, as my father was no raconteur (this reserve may have been a typical war veteran's aversion to raking up the past). I was thereby alerted to the hazard of deception in politics.

These family tales may help to give a sense of why I find Macron's presidency disappointing. Instead of using the power of the state to support and encourage people, Macron has never shown any interest in healing the deep divisions in French society revealed by the presidential election campaign of 2017. Instead of appearing empathetic towards people voicing discontent, he has reacted to most such expressions as if they were a personal affront. Macron's insecure and tense response to public grievance has unleashed a vicious circle of mutual alienation between state power and the people.

My next introductory concern is to counter any initial impressions that this essay belongs to the genre of 'declinism': a pejorative term from the arsenal of, for example, the detractors of *La France qui tombe*, a work published in 2004 by journalist and writer Nicolas Baverez (Baverez 2004). Baverez was accused by his critics of excessive pessimism about the French economy and unwarranted nostalgia for past glories. I feel no such nostalgia. As for pessimism, and contrary to the way that much 'declinist' literature deplores protest, I see the yellow vests movement as a salutary jolt to the blockages in French society caused by the country's stagnant, self-perpetuating, and self-congratulating governing class. At it stands, this class is caught between its aspiration to lead a bright nation shaping the destiny of the world and its present reality of presiding over an old, out-of-breath, and rudderless state.

At an election fundraising event in September 2016, the US Democratic Party's presidential nominee, Hillary Clinton, notoriously described half of the supporters of her general election opponent, Republican nominee Donald Trump, as a 'basket of deplorables'. Her sentiment would be echoed by many well-to-do French urbanites, who are often squaring their conscience with the rationale that they object to violent protests; this is despite ample evidence that much of the violence occurring around the yellow vests demonstrations was perpetrated by unrelated troublemakers as well as circumstantial evidence that some troublemakers were, in reality, *agents provocateurs* being used to discredit the *gilets jaunes* (Willsher 2019).

Another reason why I see the yellow vests as deserving dignity and respect has to do with the importance of rediscovering the rich potential of small-town and rural France. Many of the problems in contemporary French political economy highlight the need for radical decentralisation, institutional simplification, and more 'horizontal' social and corporate structures. The yellow vests movement is a symptom of these problems and, as such, makes for a common thread that runs through much of what follows.

The movement's distinctiveness was not limited to its longevity, with regular, large weekly protest events continuing across France for well over a year after the *gilets jaunes* first burst onto the scene in November 2018. It was also unprecedented in several other ways. Perhaps most striking of all was its spontaneous bottom-up organisation, unrelated to any existing structures such as trade unions, political parties, or civic associations. The grievances of the yellow vests – about lack of well-being, confidence towards institutions, and openness towards the rest of the world – were difficult to locate on the conventional left–right spectrum (Boulo 2019). This complicated government efforts to respond with traditional structural reform proposals.

Research has found that the one element uniting the diverse yellow vests is that their life satisfaction rates are very low (Perona 2019). They have a profound sense of malaise and dissatisfaction with their lives and their future opportunities. This sense of misfortune is strongly linked to level of education, work, and revenue. However, it does not only touch the poorest: a relatively high level of malaise can be found among an important part of the population situated at the juncture between the working and the middle classes. They, too, feel forgotten by the Parisian political elites. Their purchasing power has suffered from increasing taxation, yet they are not benefitting from France's generous welfare state; this is because they are often neither unemployed nor destitute, and they mostly live in the peripheral areas of France, where many public services have been scaled down. This has generated a strong sense of unfairness.

'Grumpiness' (*morosité*) has become a well-worn description of the French public mood in standard press articles. I do not see this tag as being useful in explaining or understanding contemporary protest movements. For one thing, caution should be exercised when interpreting visible signs of cheerfulness. I am quite sure that if somebody on the street were to ask me, 'Are you happy?', I would probably shrug and walk away as I replied, 'None of your business'. In any case, such grumpiness might be better viewed as a cultural trait than as a reflection of specific political economy trends. Speaking from my own youthful experience of being peer pressured to read books by the likes of psycho-philosopher Jacques Lacan and modish novelist Philippe Sollers, alongside regular doses of gloom and despair from watching Alain Resnais films, I expect few people would escape such an environment without any symptoms of depression. In my student days, we were taught by example and implicit precept to be unhappy, or at least to appear miserable, lest any cheerfulness be interpreted as a sign of stupidity, unworthy of an intellectual. At the early age of seventeen, I realised that I was not going to be the next Arthur Rimbaud. In despair, I chose Anglo-Saxon exile, where I found respite from having to take part in heated debates about the meaning of life, the unconscious, and the non-existence of God (religion being generally regarded as an intellectual disease).

Yet the French do have objective reasons to feel downhearted (other than French films and new philosophers). Scholars have observed that the French are unhappy, and this is despite a 20 per cent decrease in average annual hours worked per employee in the past thirty years. In a 2014 survey, respondents attributed their unhappiness to having inadequate voice ('democracy'), poor institutions, an overly hierarchical society, a lack of autonomy in the workplace, excessive state regulation, a persistently high rate of unemployment, problems with the education system, and changing cultural attitudes (Senik 2014).

The rulers of this Republic govern from behind the heavy gates of Parisian palaces, built for princes and dukes, with large private gardens, thus rationing the green space available to ordinary Parisians to a few pocket handkerchiefs such as the Luxembourg Gardens. Strong disenchantment has resulted from years of top-down economic mismanagement, official corruption, and internal political bickering. These long decades of political mismanagement have weakened French institutions such as the justice system, the independence of which tends too often to actively fighting its own campaigns rather than passively and impartially arbitrating the disputes of others.

Despite the importance I have placed on the yellow vests movement as the most relevant backdrop for the themes of this book, my first impulse to write it came after the murderous terrorist attack on the editorial offices of the satirical weekly newspaper *Charlie Hebdo* on 7 January 2015. The possibility of ethical renewal in the media and public sphere seemed to exist for a time after the *Charlie Hebdo* massacre. The kind of truth-telling thinkers usually shunned by the mass media were suddenly invited to appear on TV and radio. However, this period of hope proved short lived: the approaching national elections in 2017 dictated a return to political business as usual, with the normal pundits back in the limelight to bloviate in their stilted language. This circus was interrupted by the next season in hell, when, on 13 November 2015, jihadi gunmen slaughtered 130 people in Paris's Bataclan theatre as well as nearby cafes and restaurants. The mayor of Paris switched off the Eiffel Tower's lights as a mark of respect for the victims, but this kind of symbolic gesture wears thin in the face of the sadness and despair created by such an attack. President François Hollande declared that 'France [was] at war', but it was the fact that, in the wake of the Bataclan outrage, no elected official saw fit to resign – not even the interior minister, the most senior official in the French state directly responsible for domestic law and order – that made a stronger impression on public opinion. This lack of accountability is at odds with politicians' habit of rushing to TV studios after each rebuff in successive elections to declare that they have heard the voters 'loud and clear'. Even those among them who may be sincere are deluded about the viability of the strategies and policies to which they cling. None seems able to occupy the moral high ground.

Another mass slaughter took place on Bastille Day (14 July) 2016 in Nice, which was followed soon after by a known jihadi on parole slitting the throat of a eighty-six-year-old priest as he was saying mass at the altar of his church in Normandy. After Nice, Prime Minister Manuel Valls declared that France must be prepared for more deadly attacks and would have to 'learn to live with the threat' (LesObservateurs 17 July 2016). What was presumably meant as a call to embrace a wartime spirit of endurance was lost on a public that interpreted it as a sign that terrorist attacks were becoming the norm and part of the French landscape. Valls also introduced some tough security measures, but these have failed to prevent further periodic terrorist outrages: just as I was putting the finishing touches on this book in autumn 2020, in fact, we learned that a fanatical Muslim youth had beheaded a schoolteacher before broadcasting the appalling spectacle on social media. The track record since 2015 suggests that new horrors such as this will only trigger posturing, rather than effective policy responses.

These attacks have raised questions about the right balance between counterterrorist measures and civil liberties. The underlying problem here was powerfully stated nearly two centuries ago by the liberal economist Frédéric Bastiat: 'If the natural tendencies of mankind are so bad that it is not safe to permit people to be free, how is it that the tendencies of these organisers are always good? Do not the legislators and their appointed agents also belong to the human race? Or do they believe that they themselves are made of a finer clay than the rest of mankind?' (Bastiat 1998).

I regard economic stagnation and widespread public discouragement, often verging on despair, as resulting from a failure of democratic representation. This sad state of affairs stems above all from the tradition of political centralisation, the entrenchment of bureaucrats at the pinnacle of a top-heavy state, and the conformist and careerist political class educated at the elite *Grandes Écoles*. My focus on Emmanuel Macron reflects the way that he is at once an exemplar and a hostage of this order; this will become clear from my discussion of his pension reform project, which, even before the outbreak of the coronavirus pandemic, eroded much of what remained of his political capital during the winter of 2019–20. In his search for an answer to this question of balance that was more responsive to, and representative of, the public mood, Macron found himself increasingly at odds with the policies promoted by his former colleagues, the top officials of the finance ministry (known as 'Bercy').

The power of this thin layer of high-level technocratic bureaucrats to determine policy has altered the functioning of democratic representation. In making this case, I draw on a rich body of economic, sociological, and historical studies (Genieys and Joana 2015). This research has demonstrated how, under François Mitterrand, those high-level civil servants developed a policy combination of fiscal retrenchment and economic internationalisation (Jobert and Théret 1994). This policy formula was enshrined in the 1992 Maastricht Treaty and subsequent legal foundations of monetary union.

In his critique of this century's political economy developments in advanced industrial countries, economist Paul Collier contemplates a new class of well-educated, highly skilled people who forged their ties at schools and universities, and who feel themselves to be morally superior to the less well educated. He refers to this group's WEIRD label – Western, Educated, Industrial, Rich, and Developed. They are elites who seem more loyal to one another than to their communities, and who often show a greater interest in distant humanitarian causes than in people suffering a few miles away in economically depressed small towns (Collier 2018). People like the *gilets jaunes* feel that the world is being changed and that their decline in living standards and loss of dignity are of no concern to those with power and influence. This 'higher France', to borrow a term coined by geographer Christophe Guilluy, encompasses the urban upper-middle class, which has benefited from globalisation and which therefore supports the mix of economic policies that has prevailed since the 1980s (Guilluy 2019, 4). While the WEIRD are keen to preserve the status quo, they also believe that only they have the knowledge and authority to shape social change. Their network is composed of business people, academics, the media, government officials, and the 'chattering class' of think-tankers and other so-called thought leaders. They meet at clubs, conferences, and ideas festivals, sponsored by the largest and most affluent corporations, where their values are shared, strengthened, disseminated, and translated into action (Denord, Lagneau-Ymonet, and Thine 2011).

Angel Gurria, secretary-general of the Organisation of Economic Co-operation and Development (OECD), compared the typical stance of today's global elite to that of the maxim of Tancredi Falconeri, the aristocratic hero of Giuseppe Tomasi di Lampedusa's novel *The Leopard*: 'If we want things to stay as they are, things will have to change' (di Lampedusa 2007). Gurria contends that the global elite, faced with a worldwide backlash against globalisation, has found myriad ways 'to change things on the surface so that in practice nothing changes at all' in the hope of protecting an order that works so well for them (Gurria 2017). This famous line from *The Leopard* offers a perfect description of those situations where what seems like a political upheaval turns out to be nothing of the kind. The novel is set in Sicily at the time of the unification of Italy in the 1860s. Since that episode saw the disappearance of whole states and ruling dynasties as well as their replacement by a new country and governmental regime, it would appear to qualify as a political upheaval. In many key respects, however, the economic and social order remained unchanged. Even if a leopard *could* change its spots, that does not make it any less of a leopard.

This trick does not look to be repeatable now. In France and other advanced industrial countries, the social and political reaction against the dislocating impact of globalisation and technological change on the ever-widening margins of rich societies will not be stilled by the mere appearance of change. Instead it spells true upheaval. The only question is whether the process will take the form of a violent revolt, threatening material progress and peace (both internationally and domestically), or, much more desirably, of a concerted determination to call into question present socio-economic and political arrangements. The arrangements in question – such as top-down oligarchic political regimes relying for their fraying legitimacy on a veneer of democratic procedure – are those that produce ever-greater concentrations of wealth that result from what might be summed up as a case of 'non-diffusion'. The combination of weak competition and inadequate redistribution has resulted in today's technology-driven productivity gains failing to improve the lot of broad swathes of society: this very much includes the increasingly squeezed 'middle' as well as, more obviously, the lower-income groups. The political turmoil caused by rising socio-economic inequality, which started in the 1980s, has prompted much research and thinking on policies to promote 'inclusiveness', that is, a society in which the benefits of the wealth generated by globalisation and technology are more widely shared (Piketty 2019). A perception of greater fairness would boost the legitimacy of globalisation and, in general, set society and the economy more firmly onto an evolutionary path of development with less risk of revolutionary upheaval. For Jean Tirole, a French economist who won the 2014 Nobel Memorial Prize in Economic Sciences, a first step would be to ask the French people to reflect on the kind of organisation in society that they would favour (Tirole 2016). To some extent, Emmanuel Macron attempted such a dialogue when he launched the *Grand Débat* in January 2019 in response to the yellow vests movement, but this did not lead to any democratic reforms. Instead, the French state charges ahead like a runaway horse. This is a Leviathan state that tends to stifle autonomous action and initiative, distort incentives, and, in doing so, accumulate potentially dangerous financial liabilities.

While this style of governance sits uneasily with the ideal of freedom that crowns the motto of the French Republic, signs of renewal are apparent. These include business dynamism in the teeth of bureaucratic and fiscal pressure, a trend towards pooling of resources, and, in general, innovation and creativity. Both having a voice and being accountable are conditions for sustaining such positive trends in the evolving knowledge economy. Although widely regarded as backward, the yellow vests protesters in effect campaigned for precisely these conditions: in addition to lobbying for improved living standards, the yellow vests focused on getting a better hearing for people routinely ignored by bureaucrats (in their case, because of physical segregation and economic marginality, but it should be remembered that tech entrepreneurs are equally marginal from bureaucrats' point of view). This demand for improved 'voice' is particularly relevant as regards taxes and other decisions of the centralised vertical technocracy.

The difficulty of flexibly responding to people's aspirations and concerns is compounded by layers of bureaucracy and regulation that extend to the rules and institutions of the eurozone. These realities tend to alienate citizens and weaken democratic legitimacy. Another contributory factor here is that most political parties are filled with career politicians whose lifelong *raison d'être* is to get themselves elected while lacking any qualifications or vision. This age-old problem is particularly acute in the modern context of ever-increasing complexity. Political leaders are neither trained nor assessed for the jobs they must do in government.

Many voters react against the political class by either abstaining from voting or voting systematically against established political parties (i.e. those that traditionally alternate in government). The representatives of these parties are increasingly perceived as useless or corrupt. As regards economic models, most economic policies are designed in total ignorance of their overall effect. The design of economic policies should consider not only the direct consequences of a particular measure (such as fiscal consolidation on the budget deficit) and the direct trade-offs (such as, in this fiscal policy example, the equitable sharing of present 'pain' for later 'gain'), but also its deeper structural consequences – e.g. for the labour market and the 'supply side' of the economy (Naidu, Rodrick, and Zucman 2019). This mention of fiscal policy takes us back yet again to the eurozone, which constrains fiscal manoeuvre at the national level while leaving a blank at the European level.

Another dimension is that evoked by Lawrence Summers in his account of the 2018 road trip he took across the United States. I must admit that my first thought on reading this travelogue was how good a thing it is that, as an old French saying goes, ridicule never killed anyone. My reaction soon switched, however, to admiration for Summers's honest admission that until he undertook this trip, his understanding of the diversity of American society was rather limited. It made him recognise – disarmingly – Americans' strong attachment to their families' way of life and their remoteness from the preoccupations of the international globalised elite. With the enthusiasm of a convert, he then criticised policymakers for failing to see what he had just seen: namely that citizens, whether from the United States or France, have many different preferences about how to live. As he sums up: 'Perhaps more appreciation of that on the part of those who lead our society could strengthen and unify our country at what is surely a complex and difficult moment in its history' (Summers 2018). Many researchers are interested in the growing desperation felt among large parts of the population in high-income countries. These scholars are not toiling in studious isolation, as this theme has come to dominate politics and wider public life in North America and Europe. One of the few uncontroversial conclusions for now may be that this socio-economic problem will lead, one way or another, to major reforms or, failing that, disorderly upheaval.

In a press interview in 2017, American sociologist Joan Williams spoke about the broken relationship between elite whites and working-class whites (wwc), the latter of which account for the 'middle 53 per cent of American families' and are regarded by their social superiors as 'an outdated class of fat, stupid, sexist racists, doomed for the dustbin of history' (Kuper 2017, 18). The same contempt can be observed in other advanced economies, notably France. During the first eighteenth months of his presidency, Emmanuel Macron voiced many 'little pronouncements' that betrayed a scornful attitude mixed with insecurity towards the wwc; then the yellow vests protest movement burst onto the scene. In answer to a question about what Donald Trump was perceived to be offering the wwc, Williams's one-word reply was 'dignity'.

My recommendations do not pretend to settle with a magic wand all the challenges facing contemporary France. However, I do find myself, like the high Victorians, on the side of optimistic modernity in the sense of taking advantage of our digital age's many innovations to bring about a more representative democracy and, therefore, a fairer society. My hope is to brighten the French gloom by pointing out ways to create a more supportive environment for thriving individual creativity. All breakthroughs in economic policy are shaped by major historical episodes, where policymakers' learning trajectory is streamlined by dramatic events such as hyperinflation, chronic unemployment, and financial and – to use a topical example – pandemic crises. Such breakthroughs occur at irregular intervals and at considerable human cost. The experience of and lessons from such shocks become part of a country's collective memory, so they inform policymakers' choices as they re-apply those lessons to different circumstances, times, and states of knowledge. But this learning process now seems to be hampered by an ideology that is more powerful than any religion fought by the French state in the two centuries since the 1789 revolution. A powerful dimension of this ideology is called Europe, where the mantra is that, thanks to the European Union (EU), peace has replaced war and that, therefore, what is needed is 'more Europe'. True lovers of Europe and supporters of European harmony and effective cooperation can only be disturbed by the way that, as a result of the French governing class ignoring people's values, needs, and voice, mistrust toward the EU and its institutions is growing.

The French tradition includes the thoughts of Frédéric Bastiat, Alexis de Tocqueville, and Raymond Aron – freethinkers who shaped France much more than is often acknowledged today. This essay makes a case against the populism of both the governing oligarchy and radical demagogues. It is the populism of elites, endlessly trying to buy off public discontent while leaving problems untouched at their roots, that is the enabler of the populism of radicals. This book's opinions are offered in the Free French spirit that has always stood up against public intellectuals becoming court jesters.

This introduction is followed by five chapters, each examining aspects of the French political economy. In every chapter, I identify a blockage that, in my view, should be addressed. All of these blockages share the same underlying feature of a rigid ideology made more hidebound by administrative conditioning and entrenchment: in short, a Parisian groupthink and 'group practice'. These chapters offer a critique of aspects of the French state and society, which is all too often seen as overweening and conformist. The tax system, complex and burdensome, exemplifies the stultifying effect of the French order – i.e. the country's political economy in the broadest sense – on entrepreneurial dynamism. These core arguments are fleshed out in critical surveys of other aspects of French life, including the education system and the failed assimilation of immigrants from the country's former colonies in Africa. Each chapter ends with a 'solution' that some readers may find superficial but which I hope will still be seen as underpinning the general tenor of my argument – that if freedom could be allowed to flourish, and if the state could be reformed to play a much more effective role, the French might rediscover their *joie de vivre*.

1

The 'Republic of the Technocrats'

Il est temps peut-être que les rois d'aujourd'hui soient mis à la marge. Ceux qui croient que Paris est le centre, comme un conglomérat de vainqueurs. Ceux qui regardent les "marges" comme des réserves ténébreuses de plaintes et de révoltes à venir.

[Perhaps it's time to have done with our contemporary kings – the people who, like a conglomerate of victors, reckon that Paris is the centre and view the periphery as dark pools of looming grievance and revolt.]

Christian Bobin (Maurot 2017)

The Fifth Republic (1958–present) was labelled by historian and economist Jean-Pierre Dormois as the 'Republic of the Technocrats', where 'technocrat' is used to describe an elite 'whose superiority comes from their expertise' (Dormois 2004, 80). That distinction of *expertise* being attributed to this administrative elite may raise an eyebrow, given the poor results of French governance over the past half-century. These experts seem always to search for a way to reheat old approaches, as if they were still fighting the last war (Gobry 2019).

Julian Jackson, a biographer of General de Gaulle, attributed to his subject's political handiwork – that is, the Fifth Republic – this phenomenon of an expanded technocratic elite. De Gaulle more than quadrupled the number of technical advisers surrounding the political leadership in the Fifth Republic compared with its predecessor (the Fourth Republic). Each of these forty-five advisers who served four-year stints in what de Gaulle called 'the household' (*la maison*) had specific skills (economics, education, diplomacy, press), and most of them were young civil servants who had graduated from one of the elite educational institutions known as the *Grandes Écoles* (Jackson 2018, 376–7).

This style of governance was distilled in one such school: the École Nationale d'Administration (ENA), established by Michel Debré soon after the 1944 *Libération*. Debré, who would later become the first prime minister of the Fifth Republic, was then in charge of administrative reform for the purpose of training the administrative elite. The mission of this elite was to serve the general interest with loyalty and discretion (Birnbaum 1977; 1998). The class of high-level officials that emerged in this framework after the war was motivated by a desire to modernise and to serve France in the reconstruction effort. Their image, including of themselves, was as builders of the state (Genieys 2010). The ethos of these high-level civil servants in that period was reflected in the integrity and asceticism of, for instance, the diplomat François Seydoux de Clausonne (Schumann *et al.* 1981).

Already at that time, however, warnings were being sounded about the danger that this caste might pose for democracy. One such voice was that of socialist and one-time member of the Free French, André Philip: 'The danger of President de Gaulle is the orientation towards an authoritarian technocratic socialism; he risks surrounding himself with experts and top administrators who are both efficient and authoritarian, and finding himself being used as a form of propaganda by which the masses are made to adopt the decisions by those who know best' (Baruch 2008, 102–3, quoted in Jackson 2018, 640).

Today these builders have been replaced by gravediggers of democracy (Galbraith 1967). According to British economist Dennis Robertson, the ultimate scarce resource in political economy is 'love' (by which he means morality and public spirit) (Robertson 1956, 154). To this, Albert Hirschman adds that the supply of public spirit is neither limited nor fixed, but, at the same time, there will always be a tension between increasing that supply and the instincts of self-interest and preservation (Hirschman 1984, 93–4). Thinking themselves arbiters of the nation's destiny, these high officials have ended up undermining the machinery of the state and the democratic process. In 2019, Pascal-Emmanuel Gobry, a Paris-based commentator on public ethics, came up with a powerful formulation of this problem: 'The national collapses – 1789, 1940 – were always preceded by a generation of elite stupidity, cowardice and greed. Whatever their faults, the yellow vests have correctly identified France's biggest problem' (Gobry 2019).

In *Le Mal français* (*What Ails France*), published in 1975, the lead-ing memorialist of the de Gaulle era, Alain Peyrefitte, blamed the *Mal* of his title on the highest bureaucratic echelons of the state administration. He traced this disease back to the seventeenth cen-tury (known in France as the Great Century) and the reign of Louis XIV, about whose most famous chief minister, Jean-Baptiste Colbert, Peyrefitte wrote that, when speaking of the state, 'he [Colbert] does not mean the nation ... but the royal bureaucracy' (Peyrefitte 2006).

Writing over a century earlier, Alexis de Tocqueville – a central figure in the tradition of liberal political thought in France in the nineteenth century – perceived that the apparently cataclysmic French Revolution in 1789 had ended up changing little about the way that France was governed. He saw the Revolution as reinforc-ing rather than destroying the centralising drive of the French state under the overthrown monarchy: everything still revolved around the central power and its hierarchically organised agencies (Toc-queville 1985). Nothing symbolised this better, perhaps, than the French railway system imagined and conceived by Alexis Legrand, an engineer and director of public works under King Louis-Philippe (1830–48). The railroad track was laid out like the spokes of a wheel, with Paris at its hub and six main lines to Lille, Strasbourg, Marseille, Bordeaux, Nantes, and Le Havre. No economic or tech-nical imperative justified this scheme; on the contrary, it would have been logical to start the main railway routes from the ports and the first industrial regions, and to link the natural communications of the major rivers. The entire structure of the rail network was not guided by economic considerations but by political concern to link Paris to each prefecture. Harvard sociologist Frank Dobbin sums up this bleak picture: 'By refusing to allow municipal and provincial governments to promote railroads, and by refusing to allow private parties to build the railroads they desired, the French state brought railroad development to a virtual stand-still for over a decade, and by most accounts it slowed the development of railroads through the end of the century. ... The paradox that resulted was this: rather than blaming the state for slowing rail development, the French gave credit to the state for whatever lines it did authorize' (Dobbin 2004, 39).

Peyrefitte's vision of the danger that this technocratic elite being close to power represented for democracy was prophetic. If the cor-poratism of the high-level civil service (the so-called *grands corps de l'Etat*) was already a threat to democracy fifty years ago, this seems even more true today, its power having been considerably strengthened over time.

A plethora of top positions, whether in the public or the private sector, with their privileges and very comfortable remuneration, are the reserve of the Grands Corps. These positions cover a wide spectrum, from heading prestigious cultural institutions, such as the Villa Medici in Rome and the Grand Palais in Paris (the monument built for the 1900 universal exhibition, the current function of which is to host prestigious exhibitions and fairs), to governing the Banque de France, even if this is now, in effect, a mere branch of the European Central Bank (ECB) in Frankfurt (Jauvert 2018, 49). Comparing the training of these bureaucrats with that of a doctoral student in the social or natural sciences, it is not clear what superior equipment or accomplishments might justify their exclusive right to draw the handsome salaries attached to these positions, with their accompanying perks and perquisites. The only rationale for this state of affairs is the absurd one that intelligence and talent in France is limited to this stunted little group; by all accounts, the training received by successive graduates of the ENA (énarques – anglicised from here on as 'enarchs') is characteristically mediocre (Saby 2012).

The philosopher Pierre Bourdieu depicts this high bureaucratic caste as a state nobility that uses its calling of public service as a façade behind which it serves its own corporate interest and strengthens its power (Bourdieu 1989). The shared cultural capital that comes from having similar backgrounds provides a conformist mould (Hartmann 2000, 250). The consanguinity that prevails between the business, state, economic, and media elites leads to the overall mismanagement of the affairs of the state and the economy. They develop a groupthink, labelled by Bourdieu in his *Outline of a Theory of Practice* as a *doxa* (Bourdieu 1977b). This mental structure is articulated and disseminated by the 'public intellectuals' – the journalists, pollsters, and lobbyists in orbit around this oligarchy, who constitute its outer rim.

While campaigning for the presidency in 2016, Emmanuel Macron signalled his wish to undertake a major reform of the high-level civil service (Macron 2016). However, the only instrument at his disposal for implementing this course of action were the very enarchs (those ENA alumni) who embodied the system he was looking to reform.

For sociologist Louis Chauvel, what really undermines French democracy is what he calls the 'constitution-within-the-constitution', that is, the role played by the non-elected state bureaucracy that, Chauvel argues, amounts to state capture (Chauvel 2006). Therefore, unless Macron could somehow manage a 'coup' against his own tribe, his plans to transform the state apparatus would be blocked by the technocratic administration. The high bureaucratic caste will serve a president only so far as their own vital interests are not threatened. In other words, a would-be reforming president like Macron will end up being a prisoner of the technocracy.

The enarch establishment has three distinctive features. First, it appears immune to the 'circulation of elites' pattern spotted by Vilfredo Pareto, whereby an underperforming elite, however buttressed by heredity or class, is supplanted from below (Pareto 1964). Second, this is an oligarchy in the literal sense of being a small group counting no more than 6,000 individuals (that is, a bit less than 0.01 per cent of the country's population) (Bennhold 2006). Third, this oligarchy acts in the shadows behind the government, which plays the 'front of house' role. Its power is therefore strong, insidious, and difficult to counter. The persistent, excessive influence of this small clique of *hauts fonctionnaires*, particularly the *inspecteurs des finances* at the summit of the whole system, underlies many French citizens' sense of hopelessness and the impotence of democratic representation in the face of economic stagnation.

The foundation of top civil servants' power was laid in the constitution of the present Fifth Republic, which was drafted in 1958 by the same Michel Debré who, as we saw, established the ENA a decade earlier. No previous French constitution since the Second Empire had so increased the powers of the executive branch at the expense of the legislature. A range of articles (40, 44, 49) in the constitution allow the executive to ignore parliament. While France is a democratic republic, with an elected president and a bicameral parliament consisting of the Senate (Sénat) and the National Assembly (Assemblée nationale), the president can bypass law-making procedures and also call a referendum on any legislation or on any constitutional change he or she favours. Under Article 16, the president can declare a state of emergency and rule as a near-dictator for a period of months. Government-initiated bills take priority over legislative proposals coming from the parliament itself. Civil servants are given preferential treatment relative to elected members of parliament: the latter must resign their seats before joining the executive, whereas the former can be elected to parliament or appointed to government posts without resigning from the civil service. Moreover, the moment they quit politics, civil servants are allowed to resume their former jobs – or, if no suitable vacancy is available, to draw the equivalent salary in any case – along with full social benefits (Gurfinkiel 2007).

This is the institutional framework in which the ruling technocrats have enjoyed free rein to implement a flawed dirigiste style of economic management. It has extended into the private sector, too, in the many scandalous cases where members of the high caste have passed through the revolving door to wreak havoc as the heads of large companies. An investigative report into public administration published in 2005 by the Institut Français pour la Recherche sur les Administrations Publiques (iFrap), an independent institute, took stock of the destruction left in the wake of such members of the elite corps of 250 *inspecteurs des finances* (by 2019, their numbers had risen to about 300): the collapse in the 1990s first of Crédit Lyonnais, a large commercial bank with losses of €100 billion, and then of the utility-turned-media company Vivendi (€72 billion of losses), before the black holes in the balance sheets of France Télécom (€68 billion) and Alstom (€3.2 billion) needed plugging during the 2000s. Their low integrity and lack of accountability have undermined the trust of the French people in the institutions of the Fifth Republic.

Two recent events highlight the tense relationship between this oligarchy of technocrats and the broad French public, and they offer cause for concern about the state of the democratic process. The first was the high caste's critical reaction to protesters' use of violent symbolism recalling the French Revolution: this came in the form of effigies of President Macron's head being carried on a spike along the streets of Paris. In January 2020, while taking part in a France 5 TV network programme marking the seventy-fifth anniversary of the liberation of Auschwitz, lawyer Robert Badinter, who in 1981 piloted legislation abolishing the death penalty and went on to become minister of justice under François Mitterrand, condemned the parading of such symbols of hatred. On the social networks, Badinter's intervention provoked anger because his haste to condemn the symbolic violence directed against Macron was not balanced by any criticism of the actual physical violence that the forces of law and order had inflicted on the yellow vests and other demonstrators in the preceding months. The second took place on 28 January 2020 during a protest in the streets of Paris by uniformed firefighters, who got into a scuffle with some of the police officers in charge of policing that demonstration. The widely circulated images of these clashes must have left viewers torn between several emotions: astonishment at seeing representatives of these two bodies in charge of public safety involved in a violent public confrontation; nervous amusement at witnessing a spectacle worthy of the punch-ups in the Gaullish village of the immortal *Astérix* comic strip; and, in the end, anxiety about the implications of this incident for the functioning of the state as provider of the most basic public goods.

The main line of argument used against the likes of the yellow vests characterised their protests as undemocratic, since, it was said, Macron had been duly elected on a platform of reforms, and the only legitimate recourse for citizens disliking those reforms was to await their chance to vote him out of office in the election at the end of his five-year term. In the establishment mindset, anyone failing to see and act on that principle needed to be educated.

These two incidents in early 2020 highlight how the foundational legitimacy of periodic elections must be complemented in practice by a more dynamic consent of the governed. When such consent to proposed reforms is lacking, and all expressions of dissent that might pass muster with the likes of Robert Badinter have been met with only indifference and contempt on the part of the authorities, people will resort to violence. In his book *Démocratie et totalitarisme*, liberal political philosopher Raymond Aron (1905–83) focused on what he saw as the key question of the openness of ruling minorities. The danger, Aron argued, lies in corruption by excess of oligarchy, where the ruling minority maintains its position by closing itself off to social demands (Aron 1965).

Reigning supreme, the top echelon of the state administration enjoys unchecked power that, given the complexity of world affairs, can be neither effectively exercised nor held properly accountable. To address the problems of contemporary French society, much more diverse inputs – of expertise and experience – will be needed than are possible from a hermetic oligarchy living and working in the space of a few Parisian hectares. The recruits to this oligarchy are young people in their mid twenties whose lives since they completed high school have been dominated by demanding competitive examinations. By the age of twenty-five, these young masters will find themselves working in the eighteenth-century palaces that house the offices of the Republic. Such beneficiaries of the inadequate control of public expenditure that has been a hallmark of the Fifth Republic must be susceptible to having their heads turned – or, to use the French expression, to *folie de grandeur*. Danger stems from what has become a zero-sum struggle between unchecked administrative power and the counter-power of increasingly widespread protest.

This rest of this chapter explores in more depth how the Republic of Technocrats has become a threat to the democratic process in France. First, I show that the creation of the Fifth Republic led to a mistrustful environment in which the oligarchy could thrive. I go on to demonstrate how these technocrats amassed ever more power, notably through their control of the parliament, without counterbalancing accountability. I then consider this oligarchy's track record of poor results, for all their confidence and power. This raises the question of how far the contemporary protest mood may be attributed to Emmanuel Macron's own failings rather than his happening to be president at a time when public patience with this system, having just about held together during the terms of previous ineffectual presidents, finally snapped. The chapter ends with a review of the latest proposal to abolish the ENA and the Grands Corps as well as suggestions of ways to give more 'voice' to the mass of French citizens.

GREAT EXPECTATIONS

Frans de Waal, a Dutch–American biologist, once called chimpanzees 'the honest politicians we all long for' because they, at least, do not hide their desire to get to the top (de Waal 2000). This sentiment is seemingly endorsed by sociologists Emiliano Grossman and Nicolas Sauger, who, in their book *Why Do We So Hate Our Politicians?*, identify politicians' hypocrisy as a main cause of public distrust (Grossman and Sauger 2017).

Many observers have traced the chronic distrust characterising French society back to the post-war break with what was then perceived as the 'liberal' pre-war order. That break may be seen as a reaction to the debacle of 1940, taken as proof that the institutional arrangements and policy strategies that existed up until then must have been flawed. The outcome was the emergence after the liberation of a new policy consensus founded on planning, the nationalisation of banks and industries, and universal welfare (though, ironically, it was the Popular Front governments of the 1930s that laid the foundations of the future welfare state) (Jackson 2018, 368–9). This social model, built on corporatist and statist foundations, transformed family capitalism before 1940 into bureaucratic capitalism after 1945.

France gave the world Jules Verne, whose visions inspired many generations of entrepreneurs worldwide. Yet the personalities buried in the secular mausoleum of the Pantheon in Paris include soldiers, politicians, resistance fighters, writers, and scientists, with no representatives of the long tradition of successful entrepreneurs and engineers that have propelled France to many technological and commercial frontiers. What about Jean-Baptiste Say (1767–1832), who, although remembered as a pioneering economist, was also an entrepreneur? After a stint as manager of an insurance company in England, Say founded a cotton factory at Maubuisson in the Oise department, which he later transferred to Aulchy-les-Moines in the Pas-de-Calais; here, he faced 'uncooperative workers, a hostile environment and adverse natural conditions which must have shaped his theoretical conceptions' (Koolman 1971, 286). Say is typical of many entrepreneurs in having had several strings to his bow – for entrepreneurs' ventures often stem from their problem-solving accomplishments in one or another field of endeavour, where their initial interest and motivation was unrelated to any business plans.

Family-owned businesses have played a major role in French economic development, even if they often get bad press. This type of ownership allows firms to take a long-term view when making investment and other strategic decisions: a sharp contrast to the short-term objectives dictated by diffused stock market ownership (Sraer and Thesmar 2007). Founders of major industrial dynasties include Jean-Martin Wendel (1711, steel industry), Eugène Schueller (1909, L'Oréal), brothers Jean-Pierre and Jean Frédéric Peugeot (1815, Peugeot), and brothers Édouard and André Michelin (1889, Michelin). A more recent example is the Mulliez family, who not only founded (in 1961) what has now become the retail giant Auchan, but still own it outright (i.e. the company has not been listed on the stock market).

Unfortunately, under the Fifth Republic, in order to be popular, a leading French politician like Jacques Chirac (president from

1995 to 2007) need only declare – as he did in 2005 – that 'liberalism would be as disastrous as communism' (de Ménil 2007, 191). In 2018, the World Bank's annual 'Doing Business' survey, which ranks countries by the quality of their business climate, reported that it was easier to start a new company in Kazakhstan or Ukraine than in France (The World Bank 2018). Criticism of this anti-business approach is usually dismissed in France as a sign of 'ultra-liberal' ideology opposed to the 'social model' that the French nation has embraced. The Scandinavian model, which combines a generous welfare state with pro-business policies and traditions, invalidates such claims. Thanks to this hostile environment comprising a burdensome and labyrinthine tax system, regulatory thickets, and risk-averse bankers, many young entrepreneurs with the will to build inspiring companies emigrate to destinations like London or Silicon Valley, where they find it easier to embrace the technological revolution of Verne's imagination.

All countries are marked by their collective memory, as, for example, Germany is by its hyperinflation episode in the 1920s. The equivalent traumas for France are John Law's Mississippi Bubble – the result of an early eighteenth-century speculative state-backed venture – and, at the end of that century, the hyperinflationary experience generated by the revolutionary printing of paper money (*assignats*). These account in part for the slow development in France of the banking sector and capital market (Murphy 2005). An adventurous Scottish economist and financier, Law gained the confidence of the Duke of Orleans, who, after the death of Louis XIV in 1715, had become regent of France during the minority of the new king, Louis XV. Faced with a colossal royal debt amassed in the financing of Louis XIV's long and futile wars, the regent benefitted from Law's astute management of his financial predicament. This success gave Law the stature and influence that underlaid the launch of the Mississippi Company and secured his place in pecuniary history. Were it not for the losses suffered by that company's stockholders, 'Law's grandiose attempt to control and to reform the economic life of a great nation from the financial angle … would have looked very different to his contemporaries and to historians' (Schumpeter 1997, 295). Instead, this experience led the French to regard banking and finance with suspicion and to retard considerably the development of their financial system. At the same time, this collective memory fuelled an almost mystical vision of the state. In a report for a governmental economic policy advisory body (Conseil d'analyse economique), French economist Jean-Jacques Laffont characterised what he called the 'Benevolent Jacobin' state as transcending mere utility (such as administering the provision of public goods) and incarnating the people's will (Laffont 2000).

This attachment to the paternalist state was rekindled in modern times by de Gaulle as the architect and first president of the Fifth Republic. Many of the politicians who subsequently expressed nostalgia for de Gaulle's presidency had been quick to criticise him at the time for authoritarian, even dictatorial, tendencies. Given the expectations that such a paternalist political system will tend to create about itself, the kind of public disenchantment seen today is not surprising. In its January 2020 evaluation report, the Group of States against Corruption (GRECO) stressed that the persistence of the yellow vests movement highlights citizens' growing intolerance of the lack of integrity among government officials. Established in 1999 by the Council of Europe to monitor its member countries' compliance with the organisation's anti-corruption standards, GRECO called on France to improve the effectiveness and practical application of the framework in place to prevent corruption within the executive branch as well as in the police and *gendarmerie* (GRECO 2020). The origin of public distrust of law enforcement and justice may lie partly in the prevailing 'us-versus-them' culture in the education system: this ranges school pupils against teachers as authority figures, making the former fearful of being judged as 'collaborators' by their peers as opposed to being open to exercising delegated authority and leadership themselves. Table 1.1 shows higher levels of trust in France for the public service and less trust in the political system, the police, and the legal system (relative to the EU average). This relative distrust of fellow citizens is ominous. Nobel Prize-winning economist Kenneth Arrow wrote that 'much of the economic backwardness in the world can be explained by a lack of mutual confidence' (Arrow 1972, 357).

The importance of benevolence has long been recognised by economists, from Adam Smith through to modern-day thinkers such as Becker (1974) and many others. The expected benefits are mutual – that is, the benefactor as well as the beneficiary should gain. There are problems, however, in applying the ideas of Smith's *Theory of Moral Sentiments* (first published in 1759) when the largest, and decisive, benefactor is the state. In short, the distrust in the political system is fed by the expectations the French have of the welfare state (*l'Etat-providence*).

In his report from which I have already quoted, Jean-Jacques Laffont concluded that the role of the state should ideally be that of a guarantor of social cohesion. He contended that voters had inadequate opportunities to exercise democratic control, leaving too much discretion to politicians and, therefore, to the influence of interest groups. He argued that welfare spending was skewed to state insiders – a problem that called for additional constitutional constraints on government to limit the exercise of discretion for personal gain. This report was badly received by high-level civil servants, politicians, and academics, and it was conveniently ignored (Tirole 2016, 207).

Studies based on values surveys such as Aghion *et al.* (2010) bring out a characteristically French distrust of market mechanisms as persisting through successive generations and stemming from a tradition of state control. The tenacious notion of the state as saviour may be traced to widely held values and ideals based on notions around the intrinsically exploitative nature of economic relations (Dormois 2004, 44) or to the heroic civilising mission of public service (Hazareesingh 2015, 8). Table 1.2 displays the findings of surveys conducted in the period 2005–12 by the international polling firm GlobeScan, which gathered responses from people in different countries to the following proposition: 'The free enterprise system and free market economy is the best system on which to base the future of the world.'

Only 36 per cent of respondents in France assented to this proposition in 2005 compared with the sample average of 61 per cent. By 2012, this number had increased by 3 percentage points, but it was still far behind those of other countries – except, that is, for Spain, which during the eurozone sovereign debt crisis was the only country with a worse opinion of free markets than France.

Combining the results of tables 1.1 and 1.2 shows that French distrust of free markets is combined with a relatively low level of trust in others and a high level of trust in the civil service relative to its European counterparts, as 'distrust fuels support for government control over the economy' (Aghion *et al.* 2010, 1016).

Scholars working in this area have shown that people who are distrustful of the market are attracted by public sector employment. Thanks to the civil service statutory codes, the public sector offers job security (Saint-Paul 2010). This is not to deny that many will

Table 1.1   Average rating of trust by domain and trust in the public service 2008–13.

	Police*	Legal system*	Political system*	Others*	Public service†
EU (28 countries)	5.9	4.6	3.5	5.8	42.60
Germany	6.4	5.3	4.9	5.5	54.20
Greece	5.0	4.1	2.0	5.3	26.27
Spain	5.4	3.1	1.9	6.3	38.80
France	5.6	4.5	3.0	5.0	62.16
Italy	5.8	3.6	2.1	5.7	35.09
Sweden	7.1	6.7	5.6	6.9	50.60
UK	6.4	5.5	3.8	6.1	40.55

*Rating (0–10). Data compiled by Eurostat in 2013 among the population above sixteen years of age. †Percentage of people that have 'quite a lot' or 'a great deal' of confidence in the civil service. Here, 2013 corresponds to fieldwork conducted between 2008 and 2013. Germany (*n* = 2,046), Greece (*n* = 1,500), Spain (n = 1,189), France (n = 1,501), Italy (*n* = 1,519), Sweden (*n* = 1,206), UK (*n* = 1,561).
Sources: Eurostat and European Values Survey (2008–13).

choose public service employment to do good for others and to serve the state, but the lure of job security is likely to have more weight in an economy where unemployment is chronic, as it is in France (about 30 per cent higher than in Germany since 1991). The feeling of insecurity associated with unemployment may also fuel distrust of markets (Frey and Stutzer 2000).

A study using data for twenty-six countries drawn from the 2005 Work Orientations III survey highlighted that job security for lower income and lower education levels is a significant consideration in opting for public sector employment. Another factor, applying typically to France, is that public employment is career rather than position based, with high-ranking civil servants enjoying particular social prestige (Van de Walle, Steijn, and Jilke 2015). The French civil service is organised as a lifetime career structure. This means that entrants are recruited not for specific jobs but into a corps that represents both a profession and an occupation. On passing relevant entrance examinations, civil servants are given permanent contracts enshrining their status as 'office-holders' (*titulaires*). They then benefit from a framework defined by tenure and status, independent of the political process (Audier *et al.* 2012). Others holding civil service jobs while not being members of this lifetime cadre (about 18 per cent of the total in 2017) are known as *contractuels* and have ordinary employment contracts (Donzeau and Pons 2019).

Table 1.2   Belief in the free market system versus trust in global businesses, selected countries 2005–12.

	Belief in the free market system, 2005[*]	Belief in the free market system, 2012[†]	Reject the free market economy, 2005
Average	61	57	28
China	74	72	20
US	71	71	24
Germany	65	62	32
UK	66	57	27
France	36	39	50
Spain	63	14	28

'Belief' indicates a response of 'strongly agree' or 'somewhat agree' to the statement: 'The free enterprise system and free market economy is the best system on which to base the future of the world.' [*]In 2005, the international polling firm GlobeScan with the Program on International Policy Attitudes of the University of Maryland consulted 20,791 individuals from 20 countries ($n = 1,000$ in most countries). The 2005 GlobeScan Report on Issues and Reputation was conducted between June and August 2005 by research institutes in each participating country, under the leadership of GlobeScan. (A full list of participating institutes, with contact details, is available at www.weforum. org.) Each country's findings are considered accurate to within 3 percentage points, 19 times out of 20. Fieldwork was conducted in China, Indonesia, Canada, Germany, Kenya, South Korea, India, Nigeria, Brazil, the UK, Mexico, France, Spain, Argentina, Italy, Poland, Russia, Turkey, Philippines, Nigeria, and the US. [†]In 2012, GlobeScan, in partnership with the BBC, consulted 12,000 individuals. Fieldwork was conducted in China, the US, Indonesia, Canada, Germany, Kenya, Peru, South Korea, India, Nigeria, Brazil, Australia, the UK, Mexico, France, and Spain. *Source*: GlobeScan.

Regardless of motives, a survey of French people in the eighteen- to forty-year-old age bracket conducted in 2000 showed that 47 per cent of respondents would prefer to work in the public rather than in the private sector (Culpepper 2008). During the Fifth Republic, France has ended up with more civil servants than any other European country (5.5 million in 2017, that is, about 20 per cent of the French labour force) – and that is even after allowing for distortions in such international comparisons caused by different definitions of civil servants (a category that in France – unlike, say, the United Kingdom – includes soldiers, local government workers, public sector nurses, state schoolteachers, and certain categories of police officers). Compared with 1980, when the number of civil servants stood at 3.9 million, by 2017 the overall size of the public service had increased by 46 per cent, giving it a growth rate twice as fast as that of the population over the same period (Donzeau and Pons 2019).

The thin uppermost layer of this army of civil servants constitutes the ruling caste of technocrats. In the wake of the yellow vests movement and other expressions of public discontent, they have faced an unprecedented challenge to their legitimacy.

THE UNTOUCHABLES OF THE REPUBLIC

This strapline is a literal translation of the shared title of two separate books by journalists about the concentration of power among the most senior civil servants, known as the *grands commis d'État* (Ottenheimer 2004 and Jauvert 2018). In the modern French idiom, 'untouchables' signifies members of a remote super elite. The sense of this image is not necessarily that such individuals are above the law (although, at times, they may be); rather, it signifies that they enjoy entitlements exceeding what the general public regards as reasonable and, above all, that they are exempt from scrutiny. This last point, concerning weak accountability, distinguishes this super elite at the top of the state machine even from their counterparts among the lavishly remunerated top management of multinational corporations.

The use of this label 'untouchables' is ironically symmetrical with its perhaps more familiar use in the Hindu caste system, where it denotes members of the lowest caste, who are excluded from normal social circles by a boundary that should not be crossed. As if breathing a hermetically inaccessible air, the *grands commis* might better be described as 'untouching', in the sense of necessarily having lost touch with the proper spirit of public service that survives in much of the middle ranks of the apparat (Jauvert 2018).

This French version of the 'untouchables' caste emerges from the highly selective *Grandes Écoles*. These include the École Polytechnique, the top school for engineers founded in 1794, and the already-much-discussed ENA, the top civil service school. The ENA's official mission is to foster dedication to public service by attracting talented students who are intellectually well trained but socially diverse. Its focus is on administrative practice through internships. Students are admitted to the ENA either via competitive entrance examinations or through an internal competition reserved for civil servants of all ranks.

The creation of the school took place in the context of the transition from a rural to an industrial model. During that post-war period, the state remained the primary force for social change, supported by the French Communist Party (PCF) within the resistance movements that shared with Gaullism a mystique of the State.

The proportion of ENA graduates among senior civil servants grew relentlessly during the post-war years (Rouban 2002, 20). By the time Valéry Giscard d'Estaing (ENA, class of 1951) became president in 1974, the post-war ENA classes had reached maturity, dominating in particular the elite Financial Inspectorate to which Giscard himself belonged. Of the seven presidents of the Fifth Republic who have succeeded its founding president Charles de Gaulle, four were enarchs, as were half of the prime ministers (table 1.3).

In the context of the emerging Cold War, the approach to economic planning in post-war France was to steer a new path between Soviet central planning and Vichy corporatism, with a strong element of welfarism. This led to a profound transformation in the role and political behaviour of the state elite in charge of ensuring the implementation of planning policies. As the architects of those policies, the technocrats straddled the nationalised industries and the Grands Corps. They thoroughly penetrated most areas of the state-dominated economy and altered the functioning of democratic representation.

The French version of the Soviet Gosplan, the central planning agency (CGP) created in 1946, developed successive five-year plans with quantified output targets, their ambit widening beyond *core* industries to nearly all sectors of public and private activity via control of the financial system, boards of directors, and industrial relations. Exchange controls were imposed, and capital markets had a minimal role in channelling finance to businesses. This environment of centralised state-directed economic development and management was propitious for the status and power of the technocratic administrative elite that dominated the process of formulating and implementing public policies (Thoenes 1966). Their group spirit helped these top officials imprint their outlook on the political class and wider civil society (Genieys and Joana 2015). This influence was underpinned by legitimising economic growth and rising living standards. The three post-war decades (1949–79) were described by economist Jean Fourastié, who worked at the Planning Commission, as 'The Thirty Glorious Years' (*Les Trente Glorieuses*) (Fourastié 1979). This was the golden age of the technocrats, who basked in the reflected glory of modernisation policies symbolised by the deployment of flagship technological breakthroughs such as the TGV (high-speed train) and Concorde (supersonic airplane) (Suleiman 1987).

Table 1.3   List of presidents and prime ministers (June 1969–February 2020).

Presidents	Prime ministers	Date of taking office	Duration (months)
Georges Pompidou	Jacques Chaban-Delmas	20 June 1969	36
	Pierre Messmer	5 July 1972	23
Valery Giscard d'Estaing	Jacques Chirac ENA	27 May 1974	27
ENA	Raymond Barre	25 August 1976	57
François Mitterrand	Pierre Mauroy	21 May 1981	36
	Laurent Fabius ENA	17 July 1984	20
	Jacques Chirac ENA	20 March 1986	25
	Michel Rocard ENA	10 May 1988	36
	Edith Cresson	15 May 1991	11
	Pierre Beregovoy	2 April 1992	12
	Edouard Balladur ENA	26 March 1993	26
Jacques Chirac ENA	Alain Juppé ENA	17 May 1995	24
	Lionel Jospin ENA	2 June 1997	59
	Jean Pierre Raffarin	6 May 2002	37
	Dominique de Villepin ENA	31 May 2005	24
Nicolas Sarkozy	François Fillon ENA	17 May 2007	60
François Hollande ENA	Jean Marc Ayrault	15 May 2012	22
	Manuel Valls	31 March 2014	33
	Bernard Cazeneuve	6 December 2016	6
Emmanuel Macron ENA	Édouard Philippe ENA	15 May 2017	26
	Jean Castex ENA	2 July 2020	—

Such rapid growth was not unusual after World War II in Western Europe. France was catching up with the technological frontier, increasing productivity by mobilising rural labour to support the expansion of urban manufacturing. This period of extensive growth repaired war damage, replaced capital stock, and made use of a series of US innovations developed in the 1920s and 1930s that were ripe for commercialisation.

But while this vertical paternalist policymaking was conducive to technological catch-up in the post-war reconstruction period, it began to obstruct the diffusion of technology underpinning the subsequent period of intensive growth. This rapid technological change driven by a new global division of labour exposed the difficulty faced by the institutions of the Fifth Republic in managing the transition from post-war mass production to a model based on internal innovation and the development of services requiring a higher degree of cooperation and individual initiative (Eichengreen 2006).

Modernisation and technological change slowed down with the liberalisation of trade and capital flows. The 'national champions' of the 'glorious' period started to run out of steam. Lower growth rates in industrial production and in real per capita incomes gave rise to industrial conflict. Faced with rapid globalisation, the French Gosplan failed to counter economic stagnation and chronic unemployment. Both trade and budget deficits increased. A favourite idea was that unemployment could be reduced by curtailing labour supply, which spawned various schemes to delay the entry of young adults into the workforce and to encourage the early retirement of workers. This fashion culminated in the landmark thirty-five-hour week policy of the Socialist government elected in 1997. As can be seen from France's relentlessly high unemployment rate, none of these schemes achieved the desired effect.

Against this background of deteriorating economic performance, the technocrats' role and legitimacy started to be questioned. They became a frequent target of criticism from parts of the political class. Conventionally labelled as 'neoliberal' (a pejorative term in French political speech), these critics trenchantly denounced the responsibility of the top bureaucratic cadre, as it ever more completely took over the reins of the Fifth Republic (Birnbaum 1977), for causing economic underperformance, the bureaucratisation of society, and the alteration of the functioning of representative democracy. A large body of sociological research analysed this governing caste's self-perpetuation strategy and cast doubt on claims about the meritocratic nature of the process by which it is recruited (Genieys and Joana 2015).

To survive, this administrative super elite had to adapt and reinvent itself. The stagflation of the 1970s prompted a shift in economic strategy away from dirigisme and towards a pragmatic version of the rising alternative agenda of liberalisation (Prasad 2005). Under François Mitterrand, the high-level civil servants were transformed into 'state economists', occupying strategic positions in the Ministry of Finance and imposing a policy of fiscal rigour while pursuing the internationalisation of the economy (Jobert and Théret 1994). This led the technocrats to concentrate on reducing the state budget deficit, with the stated goal of ensuring the sustainability of the 'French model' of welfare and complying with the external legal constraints on domestic fiscal policy that flowed from France being part of Europe's monetary union. The practical result has been to strengthen the prerogatives of ministers and the administration at the expense of the legislature and 'social partners' (a stock phrase denoting corporate management and trade unions). The technocrats were thus reinvented as custodians of state policies (Genieys 2010).

In its 2005 report, iFrap contended that the enarchy running France was inadequately trained for the task. The report reminded readers how the constitution of the Fifth Republic had constrained the power of the legislature through two provisions – articles 40 and 44 – which, as we have already noted, were introduced by Michel Debré in the 1958 constitution at the behest of de Gaulle (iFrap 2005). The practical effect of these provisions is that the executive can overcome the resistance of lawmakers, whose only recourse is to pass a vote of no confidence in the government – a cumbersome procedure and, in political terms, a last resort that is generally disproportionate to the process of detailed scrutiny of specific draft legislation.

The number of enarchs in the National Assembly is relatively low: in 2017, they accounted for only 17 out of the total complement of 577 deputies in this lower house of parliament (down from 29 a decade earlier). The enarchs' power, therefore, is not exercised directly in the parliament, but rather through the government – with the help of articles 40 and 44, and because the deputies do not have the information they need to carry out their role effectively. The domination by the executive (the government) is especially strong during parliamentary debates on the budget, when the government and, in particular, the finance minister impose their decisions. The ruling caste formed by the ENA, from its position in the ministerial offices and the high administration of Bercy (the Ministry of Finance), succeeds in monopolising the exercise of power and foiling any attempts by the parliament to wield any real influence. Lawmakers have no chance of overcoming their disadvantage of being less well informed than the minister of finance. Parliament is unable to verify the data put forward by Bercy. Deputies often discover that they are being invited to approve hundreds of new measures in a hurry, without having more than a few days to assess them.

The precondition for a properly functioning representative democracy is an informed parliament. Yet the enarchy monopolises and sterilises information, thereby stifling the parliament, whose initiatives are in any case blocked or worked around by the implementing decrees (secondary legislation) that lie within the sole competence of the government. The executive thus governs in a solitary fashion in its technocratic ivory tower, surrounded by a well-staffed administration providing it with ample informational and administrative support. In these conditions, the parliament has lost part of its proper prerogatives.

An attempt to redress that imbalance was made in 2008 in the form of constitutional amendments. These gave the two houses of parliament greater scope to control their own agenda and increased parliamentary checks on executive actions such as curtailing the time made available for considering draft legislation and enacting legislation by executive decree (i.e. without formal parliamentary approval). The core parliamentary sanction remains the ability to pass a vote of no confidence in the government and, thereby, force the government to resign.

In contrast to the opacity that is so typical of the executive, the parliament has made some serious efforts to improve transparency (and gets a better transparency score than other public bodies). For example, the authors of parliamentary reports must annex a list of persons consulted. While there are requirements for tracking the consulted interest groups at the parliamentary level, the potential of this control measure has not been fully realised, since it fails to provide an exhaustive list of all consulted interest groups at the final stage of legislation. The physical circulation of lobbyists in the Palais-Bourbon (seat of the National Assembly) is now controlled by means of a register, but such controls are virtually non-existent in other institutions and state agencies. Outside parliament, most other places of public decision making remain in the shadows or out of bounds as far as efforts to lift the veil on lobbying are concerned (Transparency International 2015).

If the parliament has minimal influence, the same goes for members of the government. Ministers are appointed not for their relevant expertise but to satisfy political balances. Therefore, most of them arrive in office without prepared projects or even adequate briefing. To advance their political career, a newly appointed minister needs media exposure. The best way for a minister's name to be seen and heard is for them to become the official originator of a piece of reformist legislation that will carry their name. For this, the ambitious minister will need the help of the high-level civil service.

In practice, the only member of the executive that is able to take a policy initiative not vetted by the enarchy is the president of the Republic, because they have a staff and an adequate time horizon thanks to their mandate (reduced from a seven- to a still substantial five-year term under Jacques Chirac in 2000). Yet even this degree of presidential independence is relative, unless there were to be a thoroughgoing purge of personnel at the highest level of state administration. At time of writing, Alexis Kohler – the secretary general of the Elysée (that is, the president's right-hand man) – is a typical representative of this technocratic caste, as are his chief of staff, Benoît Ribadeau-Dumas, and the prime minister, Jean Castex.

The debate on reforming the ENA began in the 1960s, an early theme being the desirability of recruiting more students from the broad existing ranks of the civil service and, connected with that change, making practical performance records a more important selection criterion than competitive examination. One of the first such proposals was included in the Socialist Party's political programme in 1972, only to be shelved at the behest of young enarchs who were by then rising in the ranks of the party apparat. One reform was finally introduced in 1981, creating a third entry route to the ENA from the private sector. Such initiatives were based on evidence that enrolment through professional competitions – both internal, for existing civil servants, and external, for non-civil servant professionals – appears to result in greater social diversity than that through conventional examinations. In 2002, a bill was proposed to abolish the ENA, highlighting the cost carried by taxpayers following enarch-caused financial disasters such as the Crédit Lyonnais.

But such reform efforts fell flat, and ENA enrolment became ever more selective, socially and professionally, with one study showing that the level of cultural and financial capital required to get into the ENA (in the sense of being equipped for the competitive entrance examinations) had increased between 1951 and 2000 (Rouban 2015). Researcher Luc Rouban estimated that the share of students from the higher socio-professional categories was around 70 per cent in the 2010s, compared with 15 per cent in the overall labour force. This distribution reflects the social range of the student intake at Sciences Po in Paris – a school that remains the most common route to success in the ENA's external competitive entrance examinations. The preparatory classes open to candidates from disadvantaged backgrounds launched at Sciences Po in 2001 and at the ENA itself in 2009 have produced disappointing results, with only 8 students admitted to the ENA out of the 142 candidates who followed those courses (CP'ENA) between 1999 and 2019 (Rouban 2020).

ENA students are paid a gross monthly salary of €1,682 during their two years of study on condition that they commit to a decade of work in the civil service after graduating. The annual expenditure per ENA student is €82,900, while that of the average student in France is €11,700 (2016 data) (Schneider 2017). ENA students acquire the status of trainee civil servant upon entering the school, which gives them access to the full range of civil service perks including official travel expenses and, above all, pension contributions (since their years of study thus count as employment for pension purposes, this benefit allows ENA students to retire two to three years earlier than other graduates). Each year, the ENA spends €1.5 million on travel, meals, and overnight stays, which are granted to students when they are in the field (e.g. for an internship in the prefectures). Embarking on the senior civil servant career path is no longer a sacrifice, as the 'payback' commitment to public service for a certain number of years is not rigorously enforced. Enarchs leaving the civil service for private sector jobs before the end of that period are supposed to repay to the state a proportional share of their tuition costs, but the process is not clear in practice.

In 2017, the number of participants in the ENA's three admission competitions reached 1,368 candidates for a total of 80 places (with another 37 places going to foreign students). Students admitted through the internal competition (existing civil servants) and the competition open to private sector professionals each amounted to a little over 10 per cent of the intake, with another 8 per cent entering through the external competition (open to graduates holding first degrees). For the eighty French students enrolled annually, their final graduation rankings will be the most reliable predictor of their future career paths. Only those ranked among the top fifteen graduates are offered careers on the most prestigious path, that is, one of the three Grands Corps: the State Council (Conseil d'État), the General Financial Inspectorate (Inspection générale des finances) and the Court of Auditors (Cour des comptes). Promising futures await these gilded young enarchs – a *jeunesse dorée*

– sailing into the uppermost echelons of the state administration. From here, several then move on to top jobs in business or government, while also in effect controlling the legislative branch, as we have seen. They will fill nearly 80 per cent of the director posts in the Ministry of Finance as well as 75 per cent of the head posts in both the ministerial private offices and the presidential administration (Nouailhac 2015).

Certain qualities seem to be lacking in their education. For instance, the training offered by the ENA appears to stifle passion and creativity. Every year, after reading candidates' essays and conducting interviews, the ENA admissions committee publishes a report. The one for 2017 was typical of recent years: the general intellectual level of applicants was considered 'good, even very good', but the overwhelming majority had trouble thinking for themselves. They 'recite talking points' and are unable to 'offer true reflection or a personal point of view'. The committee said that it had to 'hunt down originality as if it were a rare treat' (Valeursactuelles. com 2018). Such failings were aired as far back as 1967 in a pamphlet entitled *L'Énarchie*, which was authored by a certain Jacques Mandrin – a satirical collective pseudonym for Jean-Pierre Chevènement, Alain Gomez, and Didier Motchane, all three of whom had been contemporaries at the ENA (class of 1966). They denounced ENA graduates as an oligarchy, duly coining the term *énarque*. This trio of critics saw the ENA not as a school but as a competition. Here is a flavour of their sharp satire: 'To fight inflation, what are you going to do? Answer: I am setting up a study group. And foreign exchange problems? I am forming a study group. What about the housing problem? I am creating a study group.'

They also observed that the typical enarch does not get out enough (Mandrin 1967). Instead, they are taught to control, regulate, and distribute (Saby 2012). Their training provides scant feel for the calculated risk taking that underlies effective wealth creation.

The ENA selection process and training model have remained essentially unchanged since the school's inception. Under the banner of republican meritocracy, it has become an instrument for elite selection with social filters that undermine that very meritocratic principle. By playing such a central role in the training of its own elites, the state has closed in on itself (Suleiman 1974, 1976, 1978). In what follows, I explain why this enarch caste is now facing its biggest legitimacy crisis.

MISMANAGEMENT: 'L'OLIGARCHIE DES INCAPABLES' (USELESS OLIGARCHY)

The irony of this 'useless oligarchy' barb (taken from the title of a 2012 book by two political commentators) seems ever more topical in the years since that book was published (Coignard and Guibert 2012). The contemporary enarchy is fronted by a young president, who, apart from a few episodes where he spoke with a slightly hallucinatory air, has acquired a reputation for having superior intelligence and related qualities. Anna Cabana, a comment journalist at BFMTV, had this to say about him during a studio debate in February 2020: 'The President of the Republic impresses everyone around him. He impresses both advisers and ministers.' However, the problem, according to Cabana, is that this impressive aura does not generate 'a beautiful and healthy emulation' but rather 'paralyzes the system'. 'They are all basically stricken by amazement ... so exceptional is Emmanuel Macron', she explained. Cabana also evoked 'his temperament, his intelligence and the rather exceptional chemistry of his being' (Piquet 2020).

Unfortunately for her, and for France, reality has proved less impressive. 'Super Macron' successfully triggered one of the country's deepest social crises in the form of the yellow vests movement. The trigger in question was the so-called diesel blunder. To demonstrate his commitment to the environmental cause, Macron approved a 23 per cent hike in diesel fuel duty. Nearly two-thirds of all cars in France run on diesel (a result of the policies of successive previous governments), with a particularly high concentration in small towns and rural areas where people are most dependent on their cars (Gurfinkiel 2019).

The diesel tax caused a large-scale backlash, with thousands marching in protest. Although alarmed, the government refused to back down, failing to grasp how serious the situation was to become. The diesel protest, by giving rise to the yellow vests movement, transmuted into a formidable political crisis stemming from the way that France is governed. What began as a drizzle of dissenting voices was soon galvanised by animus towards Emmanuel Macron and his government, then led by Prime Minister Édouard Philippe. Never had the very legitimacy of the authorities been attacked so fundamentally: the May 1968 disturbances certainly diminished de Gaulle's personal standing, but not that of the prevailing state system. The yellow vests movement stands out in other ways too, in the (weekly) regularity and longevity of its protests; the fact that its organisation did not depend on any existing structures such as trade unions, political parties, or associations; and the broad socio-economic categories it represented. Far from being habitual protesters, the vast majority of the *gilets jaunes* were people in work: these were usually low-income workers, but many who could be classified as middle-income workers also joined the cause. There was a feeling among the latter group that they were just scraping by in an environment where taxes paid to the state were not matched by public services received in return, and a bleak perception that their children could only look forward to further declines in living standards.

In the yellow vest mindset, the positive concept of the nation stands opposed to the negative concept of an authoritarian European empire. People's allegiance to either of these poles is determined by perceived well-being, confidence in institutions, and openness towards the rest of the world. The result is a sharp confrontation between the lower and middle classes, who aspire to restore the national fabric, and the upper classes, who are more drawn to a post-national universalism.

With opinion polls showing that around three-quarters of the public sympathised with the yellow vests' grievances, the protesters enjoyed a certain legitimacy from a democratic perspective compared with the official representatives of democratic institutions, who were seen as having discredited themselves by dint of their perceived corruption, nepotism, arrogance, and ignorance of how most people really live. As for violence, there was plenty of that to go around on both sides. Minister of the Interior Christophe Castaner enflamed rather than appeased the mood by criticising only the violence of the yellow vest protesters and not acknowledging the contribution of the frequently disproportionate use of force by the police. Castaner's silence on this last point went unquestioned in virtually all media coverage until it was exposed by David Dufresne, an independent journalist who became the main chronicler of police violence against the yellow vests through his project *Allô Place Beauvau*, the Place Beauvau greeted by this 'hello' being the Parisian square in which the Ministry of the Interior is situated (Solano 2019).

Perhaps the most striking feature of the yellow vests story is the complete unpreparedness of the president and the government when the movement started. This was a result of the technocrats' cocoon: to foresee the risks they were running, they only needed to peruse a fraction of the recent academic studies, journalists' essays, and social media posts to sense the swell of public disgust at their indifference to people's priorities.

The results of the 2017 election should also have acted as a warning: in the first ballot, Macron came first with 24 per cent of the vote, closely followed by the national populist Marine Le Pen, the conservative François Fillon, and the hard-left candidate Jean-Luc Mélenchon. In short, Macron's real political base amounted to about a modest quarter of the vote; this was not reflected in the more tactical two-thirds majority support he received from voters in the second-round run-off against Le Pen, who, for most people (though this is a diminishing majority), hails from a political tradition regarded as morally repugnant.

Nevertheless, once the election was over, public opinion appeared willing to hope for the best from the new young president; that, at least, was the constructive attitude implied by the victory in the following month's parliamentary election of Macron's newly minted political party. The name of that party – *En Marche!* – captured a spirit of resolute advance. In those heady days of the first flush of his power, based on having a solid parliamentary majority as well as the presidency, Macron styled himself as Jupiter. Spurred on by this edgy Olympian in the Élysée Palace, the new government got to work on a series of reforms that most previous governments had avoided because of ideological blockages, or for fear of unpopularity. To encourage investment in businesses, the wealth tax (ISF) was replaced by a more limited tax on real estate; High Commissioner for Pensions Jean-Paul Delevoye started working on simplifying the retirement system; Minister of Education Jean-Michel Blanquer addressed sensitive questions about the school curriculum; and Minister of the Interior Gérard Collomb had a 'Right to Asylum and Immigration Act' passed by parliament that was less lenient than previous legislation. These flagship early measures relaxed labour market regulations to encourage hiring and thereby reduce unemployment. At this initial stage, protests were sporadic and ineffectual, indicating that public opinion was broadly in tune with the young president and his *En Marche!* majority. Unfortunately, what the Parisian elite failed to recognise was how many people would lose out due to some of these early measures (such as increases in the carbon tax and the general social security tax (CSG) along with a Ministry of Finance decision to cut the housing benefit on which many poor families and students depend). Implemented in the first six months of Macron's presidency, such measures contributed to a broader perception that the standard of living was falling for many French people. Before long, Macron came to be widely seen as the 'president of the rich' (a perception fuelled in particular by the abolition of the old wealth tax), and his numerous clumsy public comments increased disenchantment about him personally.

At the start of the second year of his term (spring 2018), this Jupiter ran into a storm of scandals, which, despite his being personally implicated in various ways, he attempted to brush aside, driven by his strong sense of being *untouchable*. The scandal involving Alexander Benalla, a young operative in Macron's personal security team who had been filmed illegally beating May Day protesters, could have been resolved if the president had responded rapidly by dismissing his wayward bodyguard (Garrigues 2019). Instead, and after a long silence, Macron came out with some combative remarks, including that Benalla was not his lover – a statement that was unprompted by any question from a journalist or even a social media rumour. This insecure defensiveness was remarkable, as French political culture has always shielded politicians from sex scandals. The notorious behaviour of the former finance minister and presidential hopeful Dominique Strauss Kahn only caused political problems for him when he continued in the same vein while living in the United States in his capacity as Managing Director of the International Monetary Fund. The first exception to this rule that French politicians are immune from public scrutiny of their private lives only came two years later, with the case of Macron's candidate for the Paris mayoralty, Benjamin Griveaux (BBC News 2020).

The Benalla affair was followed in August 2018 by the resignation of Nicolas Hulot, the environment minister, and of Gérard Collomb, the interior minister. The young Jupiterian monarch, meanwhile, riled opinion with his almost unerringly insensitive reaction to ordinary people making complaints: most of his remarks boiled down to suggesting that complainants had only themselves to blame and that many of his fellow citizens were inadequate. By now, he had begun to be portrayed in the media as the new Louis XVI, with his wife as the new Marie-Antoinette (Valeursactuelles.com 2020).

After the outbreak of the yellow vests movement in November of that year, it was only after several weeks of apparent disorientation that President Macron and his government decided, in December 2018, to cancel the fuel price hike, announcing at the same time increases in the minimum wage and other benefits designed to boost the purchasing power of the working and middle classes. Macron accompanied these concessions with the launch of a three-month 'great national debate' for the purpose of 'listening to the public' and sealing 'a new national contract'. The transparent aim here was to neutralise the *gilets jaunes* until the European Parliament elections the following May (Delwarde and Lough 2019). But the yellow vest protests continued week after week. Even if the number of demonstrators decreased, this persistence and endurance showed the depth of resentment concerning the lack of recognition their community was receiving.

Later in 2019, a proposed reform of the country's byzantine pension system was met with strikes on railway and subway systems; these were joined by teachers, nurses, lawyers, and many other eager protesters. Then, on 16 December 2019, Jean-Paul Delevoye (as noted above, the top official dealing with this reform) was forced to resign. This came about following revelations on omissions in his declaration of interests to the High Authority on Transparency in Public Life (HATVP) and, above all, on his continuing to hold remunerated positions after entering government. Such accumulation of different sources of income is prohibited by Article 23 of the constitution. Trust in the youngest ever president of the Fifth Republic plummeted in the face of his increasingly evident failure to bring in the new age evoked by his campaign promises. The old world had proved resistant. A hefty twelve of the sixteen ministers appointed by Macron who resigned during the first half of his five-year term did so because of economic wrongdoing or, at least, malpractice (Guillot, Lecaplain, and Rivet 2019).

Corruption scandals have always been par for the course in successive French Republics: the presidencies of François Mitterrand and Jacques Chirac were littered with them. One of Mitterrand's foreign ministers (Roland Dumas) and Chirac's first prime minister (Alain Juppé) received criminal convictions. More recently, in October 2014, Thomas Thévenoud was dismissed from his post as Secretary of State for Foreign Trade, for failing to declare taxable income during the previous three years. In 2013, Minister of the Budget Jérôme Cahuzac was brought down by press revelations that he illegally held Swiss bank accounts. Unusually for a wrongdoer of this rank, Cahuzac served real prison time (Garrigues 2019). How is it that so many top public servants behave as an unscrupulous oligarchy? A part of the answer must be the arrogance of power. Unchecked power generally leads to abuses and failures, and the more power that the enarchs accumulated over the years, the more they ran the country in their own interest. As with any monopoly, the enarchs' exclusive grip on public policy boosted their own margins to the detriment of investment, productivity, growth, and wages.

Another cause of the rot is caste solidarity in the face of challenges from the outside. A good example of this can be found in the form of Sylvie Goulard, whom Macron first appointed as defence minister, then nominated for the new European Commission (EC) formed in 2019. Her candidature was rejected by the European Parliament because of a scandal over fictitious jobs created using official financial allowances received by the European parliamentary caucus of the MoDem party (allied to Macron). Goulard was then promptly 'resettled' as a deputy governor of the Banque de France. Agnes Saal had to resign from her position as CEO of the National Archives Institute (INA) after a press revelation that she had run up taxi expenses of €40,000 in a year. A month later, and despite remaining under investigation, she was offered a job at the Ministry of Culture (Jauvert 2018; Garriges 2019). Top French officials have a reliable safety net that often has brushes with impunity. Such cases highlight the double standard that exists in France: a small entrepreneur at the first sign of difficulty will face prosecution, putting their personal property in jeopardy, while an enarch can be confident of continuing to receive lifelong, generous compensation despite their faults and failures.

The tentacles of the upper bureaucratic caste reach deep into the business worlds of finance and industry. Ever since the left-wing Popular Front government came to power in 1936, there has been an intermittent but essentially one-way trend towards nationalisation. The companies brought into partial or outright state ownership cover many different sectors – from banks and insurance companies to railways and airlines, from mining companies to the steel industry, from radio, TV, and media agencies to aviation and cars. The post-1958 Fifth Republic went much further, embarking on large-scale industrial schemes that blurred most distinctions between state-run and private companies. The latter became so dependent on government contracts as to behave like de facto divisions of the former.

As late as the 1960s, service sectors such as transport (air, road, sea, and rail), banking and retail, health care, and legal were fully protected from foreign competition. Access to many professions was restricted by *numerus clausus* arrangements: examples here include medical practices, pharmacies, public notaries, driving schools, and locksmiths (Dormois 2004). The nationalisation programme of the first years of the Mitterrand presidency saw the state taking control of most leading industrial and financial firms. The state's grip began easing with the 1984 financial deregulation (end of subsidised credits and quantitative credit restrictions), the growing capitalisation of the stock market relative to gross domestic product (GDP), and some limited privatisation. Employment in the public sector declined from about 10 per cent to 5 per cent of the active workforce between 1985 and 2000 (Culpepper 2008). The power of the French state was somewhat curtailed by the 1992 Maastricht Treaty and the resultant launch of the European single currency in 1999, while the development of the EU's single market had the benefit of bringing more transparency and competitiveness through the European Commission's Directorate General for Competition.

This overlap between the worlds of state administration and business creates acute conflicts of interest. Top civil servants routinely move to heading up public bodies or large business organisations that they were previously responsible for regulating, supervising, or financing. For example, starting in the early 2000s, at the instigation of *inspecteurs des finances*, governments on the left and right set about privatising the operation of the country's arterial toll roads (*autoroutes*). The government's independent auditor later found out that the bidders may have underpaid by as much as 40 per cent, with average tolls since increasing in real terms by 20 per cent, despite the absence of any corresponding increase in the quality of the infrastructure. Most of the bidders were large conglomerates whose business depends on government contracts, and who routinely hire ex-civil servants (Monin 2019). Another conflict of interest concerns civil society organisations subsidised because of decisions taken by one or more high-level officials, who then pop up as these associations' leaders.

There is no reason why *inspecteurs des finances* should be successful company managers, but the lack of competition masks their incompetence. It should therefore come as no surprise that public institutions and enterprises under their leadership are often mismanaged. In its 2005 report, iFrap laid out a shockingly long list of failings that it had uncovered in state-owned companies (iFrap 2005). I have already noted two of the most notorious disasters – Crédit Lyonnais and Vivendi – but this feels like the right place to review this dismal scene in the round. In addition to Vivendi, other large non-financial companies that have fallen victim to enarch-induced financial failures include France Télécom and the engineering group Alstom. The guilty men in these cases were not just any old enarchs: without exception, they came from the ranks of the super elite – namely, the financial inspectors. Most successful French business leaders have had nothing to do with the ENA. The country's richest man, the head of the luxury goods group LVMH Bernard Arnault, did attend one of the *Grandes Écoles*, but this was Polytechnique, not the ENA. Serge Kampf, the founder of the IT sector leader Capgemini, was an unsuccessful candidate for the ENA. Vincent Bolloré went from taking an ordinary law degree to transforming his family-owned conglomerate, while Martin Bouygues, head of the eponymous telecommunications and construction group, dispensed with higher education altogether. This is not in itself a criticism of the ENA, the mission of which is to train civil servants rather than provide business education. The problem is that the French oligarchy allows those civil servants to run serious businesses.

The scandal of Crédit Lyonnais in the 1990s is worth looking at more closely as a prime example of this problem. In 1988, Jean-Yves Haberer was appointed CEO of this large state-controlled bank by the Socialist government under President Mitterrand. Haberer had the impeccable credentials of the high oligarch caste. After graduating from the ENA in 1959, he became a financial inspector, rapidly rising to the rank of a director of the Treasury; he then took on various ministerial private offices before running another bank, Paribas, in the mid 1980s. Upon arrival at Crédit Lyonnais, Haberer embarked on an acquisition spree that after only four years made the bank the seventh largest in the world by assets. It was precisely then that the trouble began, triggered by one especially disastrous loan (financing the acquisition of Metro-Goldwyn-Mayer Studios in Hollywood, which went bust). The subsequent rescue measures revealed many other holes in the bank's balance sheet. By the time it was completed at the end of the 1990s, the bail out of Crédit Lyonnais had cost French taxpayers around €20 billion, which was about 0.5 per cent of the country's GDP at that time.

The oligarch technocrats also defend their position by presenting the system of centralised dirigisme over which they preside as a benevolent deliverer of welfare. This paternalism is a component of the conscious distinctiveness of French public policy compared with peer group countries – what has traditionally been referred to with pride as the *exception française,* along with other nationalistic platitudes that contrast the generosity of the French social model with the supposedly harsher Anglo-Saxon form of competitive market capitalism.

This statist approach leads to funding for engineers and scientists to develop the perfect vaccine or the best-performing airplane, and to always thinking 'big' and 'national' rather than relating innovations to consumers' needs and their changing preferences (McCloskey 2016, 523). This approach constitutes the very *raison d'être* of the technocrats and goes a long way towards explaining the damaging economic choices seen since the 1980s. One such sad and comic episode reflects the unbridgeable cultural gap between statism and innovation: a meeting that took place between François Mitterrand and Steve Jobs at the initiative of journalist and politician Jean-Jacques Servan-Schreiber. He believed that France should enhance its computer industry along the lines pioneered by Macintosh. Mitterrand ignored this initiative, opting instead for a national IT strategy devised by Thomson, a large French electronics company. At the heart of that strategy was the provision to all households of Minitel, a paper-saving device that hosted an electronic database version of the traditional telephone directory (Benchoufi 2011). This central planning version of the IT revolution was made rapidly redundant, and its wastefulness laid bare, by the technology tide that surged in the following years.

In this Mitterrand–Jobs meeting and its consequences, we see the *exception française* in action as an arrogant French statesman, with all his courtly accoutrements and elegant turn of phrase, faced off against all-out entrepreneurial creativity, imagination in all its modes, the permanent reformulation of a world to come. We see the bureaucracy of the state apparatus versus the imagination of the innovator, who puts his livelihood and entire being on the line as he develops his prototype in a small studio. The clash of two worlds was total: Steve Jobs explained to François Mitterrand during a visit to the United States in 1984 that Silicon Valley was not made by first-class students but by real risk takers.

This clash is still visible. After the war, state-led research through the creation of specific public research organisations (PROS), such as the Alternative Energies and Atomic Energy Commission (CEA) and the French Space Agency (CNES), was 'planned' around sectors. Created in October 1945 by General de Gaulle, the CEA typifies the excellence of government-led French research collaborating with public agencies on projects of national interest (such as nuclear, renewable energy, defense, cybersecurity, IT, and health care technology) as well as with private firms. In 2016, the CEA came first in that part of the Reuters's 'Top 25 Global Innovators' ranking that identifies the publicly funded institutions doing the most to advance science and technology as measured by the number of filed, granted, and cited patents compared with other government research institutes. However, while large research projects seem to benefit from these state grants and subsidies, this approach is not sufficient in itself to produce innovation. Cooperation between firms, universities, *Grandes Écoles,* and PROS, while encouraged, is subject to multiple supervisory authorities, resulting in unnecessarily high costs. In 2014, the OECD described French public research (mostly overseen by those PROS) as 'the most rigid in the world in terms of thematic orientation' (OECD 2014, 31).

The French state's predilection for pumping funds into whatever technology is favourably viewed at the time generally peaks at the start of political cycles. In 2018, while still in the first year of his presidency, Macron promised €1.5 billion over five years to support research in artificial intelligence (AI). He hoped by this to entice French AI researchers working abroad (mainly in the United States) to return home. But this goal may prove unattainable. The lack of openness and transparency of the French research system together with its burdensome and unpredictable taxation deter international research and development (R&D) investment and researchers from settling in France.

Back in the 1950s, economic geographer Jean-François Gravier was already denouncing the expensive and generally useless 'innovations' preferred over less grandiose but more useful improvements such as the aerotrain, which was to link La Défense (the new business district on the western edge of Paris) to the new town of Cergy-Pontoise without stopping (Gravier 1972). The aircushion hovertrain (*aérotrain*) design, spearheaded by French engineer Jean Bertin in the late 1960s, almost established itself in France as a widely used mode of very high-speed transport. Launched in March 1971, the project was canned by the government a little over three years later. Objections had to do with the reliability of the technology and over-long development timescales; an additional reason was the death of President Georges Pompidou, who was succeeded by the enarch Valéry Giscard d'Estaing (VGE), for whom this frontier technology apparently seemed too far adrift from bureaucratic certainties.

Some modes of the *exception française* boil down to economic patriotism blurring with nationalism. The 'patriotic' agenda revolves around protecting employment, especially in manufacturing, from being transferred abroad. It is not only the French subsidiaries of foreign-owned companies that have been vulnerable to the practice known as *délocalisation*. French multinationals have also expanded through foreign acquisitions and have 'unpatriotically' created proportionally more new jobs in those foreign subsidiaries than in their domestic operations. France has also attracted considerable inwards foreign direct investment (FDI), and it is in this area that economic patriotism turns more nationalistic.

At the end of the Chirac presidency, for example, the government led by Prime Minister Dominique de Villepin (2005–7) opposed cross-border mergers such as the acquisition of the Danone dairy group by America's PepsiCo, and of steelmaker Arcelor by Anglo-Indian company Mittal Steel, while it pushed for a merger between water utility company Suez and the national gas company GdF to prevent Suez being acquired by the Italian energy concern Enel. Yet this economic nationalist agenda has not always prevailed against the will of shareholders and management. In the 1990s, for example, the government tried unsuccessfully to block the merger of Banque Nationale de Paris (BNP) and Paribas (Miwa *et al.* 2016).

In February 2012, during his successful presidential election campaign, François Hollande promised the steel workers in Florange (a town in the eastern region of Moselle) that their jobs would be protected if he were elected president. Once elected, he initiated what became known as the Florange Law; this was piloted through both government and parliament by combative Minister for the Economy and Industry Arnaud Montebourg, with a contribution from the young deputy chief of staff in the Elysée – a certain Emmanuel Macron. The main measure in this law was to double the voting rights of company shareholders of more than two years' standing (as opposed to speculative investors) unless two-thirds of all shareholders passed a resolution in favour of retaining the 'one share, one vote' system. The large number of French state shareholdings in major companies would, by definition, meet the criterion for enhanced voting rights, and they would always be likely to enjoy those super rights by contributing decisively to the minority required to defeat any attempt to block such rights. The goal here was to favour holders of large portions of stock, tie management hands, and block acquisition bids. An immediate consequence was that shares of the affected firms were traded at a discount to the market valuations of peer group companies.

Montebourg advocated deglobalisation and 'temporary nationalisation'. In 2012, he declared: 'We no longer want Mittal in France because they haven't respected France' (Melchiorre 2012). Comparing himself to Louis XIV's centralising and dirigiste chief minister Colbert, Montebourg used to appear in public in a sailor t-shirt (*marinière*) or in his other favourite costume, complete with a beret and a baguette, to convince French people that he only bought French goods. This same Montebourg enrolled in October 2014 for a four-week long Advanced Management Program at the prestigious business school INSEAD, aimed at 'transforming senior executives into great business leaders'. As he disarmingly explained to *Le Monde* newspaper: 'I've decided to take classes because running a business is a real job. I've realised that in the past two years' (Pietralunga 2014). (Another politician catapulted to high office who might benefit in many ways from announcing such a move would be Emmanuel Macron himself.) Before the 2017 election, Montebourg repositioned himself in a book called *L'Alternatif*, in which he castigated what he called *economic sarkhollandisme* (meaning the policies pursued by the establishment, i.e. the enarchy), regardless of whether the political leadership hailed from the right (Sarkozy) or the left (Hollande). He presented himself as 'a social Gaullist. ... A synthesis between Colbertism, love of business, the entrepreneurial freedom, the taste for innovation and the protection of working people'.

In 2018, the Florange blast furnaces were definitively closed. The 629 workers made redundant were either offered jobs in other plants or made to retire. The Florange Law was also one of the reasons for the trouble in Nissan's alliance and shareholding relationships with Renault and the French government. That law, combined with the aggressive stance of inexperienced Minister of the Economy Emmanuel Macron, set in motion the arrest of the company's long-standing CEO Carlos Ghosn by a Tokyo court in November 2018 (Pechberty 2018). Macron's pursuit of double voting rights in French carmaker Renault put Ghosn in a difficult position by unsettling the balance of power with Renault's other main shareholder, Japan's Nissan. Eager to maximise the opportunities offered by the Florange Law, Macron enlisted the help of Deutsche Bank to facilitate a raid by the state's shareholding agency (EPA) in April 2015, in which the government spent €1 billion on acquiring an additional 4.7 per cent of Renault's capital. Ghosn refused to support the Florange Law, arguing that if Renault applied it, the French state would have nearly a fifth of the votes, while Nissan would have zero. With the French state doubling its voting rights in Renault, Ghosn lost any room he had for management manoeuvres based on balancing the shareholding interests of the group's two base countries, France and Japan.

The French government's raid on Renault's share capital produced a string of negative consequences. The share price fell, and Macron's approach led Nissan to blame the French state for disturbing the delicate balance between Renault and Nissan. After Macron had become president, the government unsurprisingly continued with the strategy that he had initiated as economy minister. When his contract came up for renewal in May 2018, Ghosn was asked by French officials to study options for a 'consolidation of the alliance between Nissan and Renault' (code for Renault swallowing up Nissan). Nissan took this as a declaration of war (Bayart and Egloff 2019). The verdict on the handling of this whole affair must be deeply negative. Macron undermined an effective defensive alliance in a sector (automotive) facing deep structural challenges and, in the process, humiliated Renault's Japanese partners. The only silver lining was the entertainment value of the brio displayed by Ghosn in organising his extraordinary escape from Japan and its judicial system.

As if meddling in corporate governance was not enough, the bureaucracy has frequently structured government procurement contracts to help favoured private companies beat their competitors. While enarchs maintained their grip on the central state administration, some other enarchs – or the same ones – would periodically surface in leadership positions at large private companies. This notorious 'revolving door' practice (already noted earlier in this chapter) became increasingly common during the 1980s. The result has been a multifunctional unified elite (Dogan 2003). This revolving door further weakened the slender democratic foundation of technocratic policymaking dominance. As the post-war Thirty Glorious Years slipped into subsequent decades of weaker growth and high unemployment, the top technocrats continually switched jobs between the most powerful ministries (budget, economy, finance) and the corporate sector. They had the best of both worlds: unlike their true private sector counterparts, they could spend a few years drawing the higher salaries on offer in the private sector with the assured safety – if things went wrong or for any other reason – of being able to return to the 'home sweet home' of the civil service. It is no surprise that this has become a popular way of life. Barely a fifth of the superior enarchs who have the status of financial inspector actually work in that capacity. As a result, state elites collude with corporate elites. This unified oligarchy veers between public service roles and management or supervisory board positions in companies, both state controlled and private.

A report on the Grands Corps and the enarchs published in 2018 by the Senate found that the three elite institutions – the Council of State, the Court of Auditors, and the Financial Inspectorate – employed just 923 people between them (out of the 48,500 high-paid civil servants) (Sénat 2018). This minority of the minority – only 12 per cent of all enarchs – are the most likely to migrate temporarily or permanently to the private sector. A total of 33, 45, and 75 per cent of the super-elite enarchs based in the Council of State, the Court of Auditors, and the Financial Inspectorate, respectively, have made this move. Of the three-quarters of financial inspectors who move into business, 34 per cent have spent more than half of their careers outside of the administration, and almost 50 per cent return to the public sector after having worked in the private sector (with many of these making multiple round trips) (Denord and Thine 2015).

Over the long term, only 8 per cent of enarchs permanently leave the public service. There is no mystery as to why the majority prefer the alternative option of going on temporary leave. This makes their decision to move from the Grands Corps to the corporate sector risk-free, since they can fall back on the lifelong employment guarantee that they enjoy under the civil service statute (Guay 2014). The only obligation for ENA graduates in return for their state-financed studies is to remain in the civil service for four years. Attempts to extend this compulsory service period to ten years have failed due to the resistance of the interested parties. A compromise, however, was reached in 2017. This allows enarchs to continue leaving for the corporate sector after four years, but if they wish to retain their status as lifetime civil servants, they must return within four years to the public sector; once there, they must remain for six years before accepting another business job (Jauvert 2018, 15–20). During those four years serving in the Grands Corps, the top civil servants build up a solid professional network, which serves them well throughout their careers. The financial inspectors see themselves as final arbiters rather than as senior civil servants accountable for implementing the policy decisions and strategies of their democratically elected political masters.

Companies welcome the political connections of these high-level civil servants who have served in the private offices of government ministers. They frequently move into jobs in sectors they once regulated or for which they used to develop policy. The revolving door leads to unbalanced lobbying. Before former public officials can lobby their former colleagues, the law requires a cooling-off period of three years between the end of a public service mandate and the transition to a company that the person was previously responsible for in terms of surveillance or control activities. This prohibition applies to all public officials, including cabinet ministers and advisers of the president.

Since the enactment of the transparency law in 2013, this requirement has also applied to members of the government and key local authorities. The Public Service Ethics Commission and the High Authority for Transparency in Public Life are responsible for monitoring the implementation of that law. In practice, monitoring is a complex business. Although these two institutions are independent, there is concern about the proportionality of the powers and resources they have been given to carry out their respective missions. For example, the Public Service Ethics Commission is responsible for all public officials, but its recommendations are only mandatory if there are indications of outright conflicts of interest. Further, the Commission has no means of monitoring compliance in cases where it has approved a revolving door job move with conditions – such cases account for 42 per cent of all recommendations. It should be emphasised that the required cooling-off period does not apply to elected lawmakers, who are a primary lobbying target, and is not explicitly intended to cover lobbying activities.

The lack of effective monitoring and enforcement of the revolving door safeguards is illustrated by the scale and effectiveness of the financial lobby. The French banking system is highly concentrated, with five banks (Credit Agricole, BNP Paribas, Société Générale, BPCE, and CIC-Crédit Mutuel) dominating the sector (OFCE 2015). The proximity of the banking sector to political power results in financial firms wielding extensive influence, allowing the banking industry to exercise effective lobbying strategies that undermine the effectiveness of new regulations. The banking system went from being the government's investment arm to becoming an intermediary in a more capital market-based system. The share of financing for companies in the form of bonds traded in the financial markets as opposed to bank loans increased from about one-quarter in 1978–83 to over three-quarters of the total by the time of the GFC. This path started to be taken in the 1980s as the capital market became a funding source for increasing public and corporate debt as well as privatisations (Bazot 2014).

Jean-Paul Pollin and Jean-Luc Gaffard exposed the close ties between the banking sector and part of the high public financial administration, as seen in the former's successful lobbying to water down a new law on the separation and regulation of banking activities designed to reduce some of the risks exposed by the GFC. The final text fell far short of the original draft, which had been heralded as ambitious and would have gone a long way towards creating a stronger barrier between banks' investment and trading activities on the one hand and regular commercial and retail banking on the other, thus protecting taxpayers from having to bail out banks from the consequences of excessive risk taking in a future financial crisis. The law, as it was eventually passed, has been criticised as 'of minimal impact and essentially cosmetic'. Close links between the financial sector and the Treasury, including the obvious pattern of many former Treasury officials moving directly into lucrative jobs in the banking sector, have been seen as a major factor contributing to the weakening of the law (Pollin and Gaffard 2014).

The decision-making process in public policymaking remains closed and opaque. Although policymakers often set up consultative commissions or public consultations to prepare a draft law or regulation, such mechanisms remain optional, with no guarantee of transparency or balance in their composition. As for the Economic, Social, and Environmental Council, which is supposed to represent the various socio-professional categories and advise the government and parliament on these subjects, its reports and opinions are not always taken into account; when they are, the way recipients use them is not always made explicit. There is no culture of reporting or spontaneous desire for transparency, and such improvements as have been made in this area have only come after major crises.

France stands out among mature economies for the number of senior civil servants running 'blue chip' companies (whose shares are included in the CAC 40 stock index). Most of these top executives are *Grandes Écoles* graduates, with half of them being products of the ENA, Polytechnique, or the business school Hautes Études Commerciales (HEC) (Dudouet and Joly 2010). The impact of these civil servant top managers on corporate performance has been negative overall. Researchers have found that the bad performance of a firm does not lead to its ex-civil service directors and CEOs being replaced. The compensation these managers receive is also about 50 per cent larger than that offered to other CEOs (in large part due to the stock options that former civil servants are more likely to receive), and acquisitions made by civil service-connected CEOs are less value creating than those made by non-connected bidders (Kramarz and Thesmar 2013).

Their influence started to be tempered in the late 1990s with the increase in importance of the stock market and in foreign ownership of listed shares (and, hence, in the overall share capital of French firms such as the power utility Électricité de France (EDF) and the bank Société Générale). The reaction against civil servants in senior corporate management positions stemmed from the poor decisions of such managers. This was the case for EDF, whose shares consequently declined in value so much that they were excluded from the CAC 40. The takeover of Alcatel-Lucent by Nokia in 2015 signalled a weakening of the traditional French policy of protecting strategic companies from foreign takeovers. The internationalisation of ownership led to the appointment of foreign directors and increasing cross-border mergers such as the takeover of the cement maker Lafarge by Swiss company Holcim. Roughly 45 per cent of listed shares on the CAC 40 are owned by foreign investors – a larger percentage than can be found on any other big European index. These companies conduct over two-thirds of their business and employ over two-thirds of their workforce outside of France (Granville, Martorell Cruz, and Prevezer 2018).

A survey conducted between 2013 and 2015 that garnered responses from 2,485 foreign managers with 96 different nationalities working for 20 French multinationals, such as BNP Paribas, Danone, EDF, L'Oréal, Renault, and Total, aimed to assess what these foreign managers made of French management culture (Suleiman, Bournois, and Jaïdi 2017). For 63 per cent of those questioned, the management culture within French multinationals was 'unique', characterised by a subtle alliance between concern for performance and concern for people, thoroughness, and innovation. French companies were seen as hierarchical and dominated by a network of graduates of the *Grandes Écoles* – although, given their bosses' perceived performance, very few of the foreign-born executives could see why people with this background continued to hold so many of the top jobs. In practice, the influence of this network meant that most key decisions were not made in the open forum of formal meetings. Many of the foreigner managers said they felt excluded, unable to decode unspoken meanings or the context behind important discussions. However, they also found things to praise in the French corporate culture. They pointed to a working environment that enables people to grow and develop both professionally and personally. They also felt that formal commitments regarding training, benefits, and bonuses were generally honoured and that there was a focus on the overall well-being of employees. This is helpful in engendering loyalty to an organisation and creating a genuine sense of community. The survey respondents also said they were given a significant degree of freedom and flexibility – within broad guidelines – which resulted in a high level of job satisfaction. Finally, despite questioning the prestige of the *Grandes Écoles*, most foreign managers had a high opinion of their French colleagues and superiors, remarking on their intelligence, the quality of their education, and their dedication and professionalism in the workplace. With a little more simplicity and transparency, it seems, French-style management is not far from becoming a source of inspiration.

THE OVERLAP WITH THE MEDIA

France is proud of being the homeland of liberty. The *liberté* that comes ahead of *égalité* and *fraternité* in the troika of core Republican values signifies emancipation from royal despotism. Yet this value is now facing increasingly serious threats. For writer, lawyer, and technocrat François Sureau, the repressive atmosphere that has settled in this country of *droits de l'homme* (human rights) since 2018 testifies that liberties are no longer a right but a concession granted by the powers that be: a faculty liable to be restrained, restricted, and controlled as much in its nature as in its extent (Sureau 2019).

People in positions of power, and those who identify with them, never doubt that they are right thinking. Contemporary French *bien pensants* have taken to labelling as malign disinformation ('fake news') any contrarian view that challenges their opinion. Yet the twentieth century showed us that greatness in journalism does not come from conformity, but from intellectual courage and going against the crowd. In 1944, George Orwell was shocked by the way the British press had covered the bloody suppression of the Warsaw Uprising by Nazi Germany, and by the indifference of the Red Army, who waited on the banks of Vistula for the Germans to finish the slaughter. This drove him to write one of the most memorable passages in the history of journalism in his column for the *Tribune* newspaper: 'First of all, a message to English left-wing journalists and intellectuals generally: Do remember that dishonesty and cowardice always have to be paid for. Don't imagine that for years on end you can make yourself the boot-licking propagandist of the Soviet regime, or any other regime, and then suddenly turn to mental decency. Once a whore, always a whore' (Orwell 1944).

Orwell was also one of the few British intellectuals who voiced his moral disagreement with the way in which Poland, an ally of Britain and France in their war against Hitler, was handed over to Stalin. The contrast between Orwell and so many of his peers – who compromised their intellectual and moral integrity by supporting policies that stemmed from France's wartime alliance with the Soviet Union – is relevant to the present-day controversies in which the United Kingdom and other Western democracies are still mired; but the burden of conformism hangs particularly heavily on France. The role of intellectuals is to be critical, not slaves to the prevalent political nostrums on any topic, whether that be geopolitics, monetary unions, migration, or the welfare state. Free expression becomes particularly sensitive in covering international affairs, especially where governments have chosen to join armed conflicts. Public criticism of government policy is widely perceived, and sometimes openly denounced, as treasonous; and the media often tends in these situations towards self-censorship. While this is a problem for all democratic countries (the US media's uncritical coverage of the 2003 invasion of Iraq being a case in point), the French style of government propaganda is particularly pernicious when backed up by public intellectuals. These self-appointed preachers of French public opinion hand down pronouncements from their pulpits on questions too numerous and diverse for any single person, however learned and astute, to be qualified to answer. When the most prestigious of these intellectuals cheer on governments, dissenting arguments are muffled. The phenomenon has become known as *prêt-à-penser* or *la pensée unique* (ironical labels that signify stock prefabricated thinking in a conformist straitjacket).

Although the tradition of politicians being held accountable by the press is particularly associated with Anglo-Saxon democracies, it is a good old French tradition as well – but not one that Macron likes. After his election, while on his first visit to the United Nations General Assembly in New York, Macron declared: 'Journalists do not interest me, it's the French that interest me, that's what you have to understand' (Kucinskas 2017). This attitude was already apparent during his presidential election campaign, when Macron's team took to criticising media that presented his stories in ways that deviated from the team's official versions. In February 2018, Macron even moved the Elysée press room, which overlooked the courtyard of the Elysée Palace, to an annex where journalists could not observe him (Barjon 2018). First established in 1974, this press room was permanently manned by representatives of the major news agencies, with a select group of eight journalists holding access passes that were valid 24/7.

In his message of New Year's greetings to the press in 2018, Macron announced that the government was working on a law against the manipulation of information. He cannot have been pleased when the Senate voted to reject this 'fake news' bill in July that same year, especially since the bill had previously been passed by the lower house of parliament at first reading. It also cannot have helped that this rebuttal came in the middle of the Benalla affair, which turned into a political firestorm. Macron then threw down the gauntlet to the journalists and members of parliament who had criticised his handling of the affair with a combative colloquial phrase that signifies the speaker is spoiling for a fist fight (Miner 2018).

Speaking to members of his party's majority parliamentary caucus in July 2018, Macron castigated 'a press that no longer seeks
the truth, a media that wants to become a judiciary, [and] journalists who have decided that there is no more presumption of
innocence in the Republic'. Agence France Presse (AFP) is regularly
rebuked by the authorities for story headlines that are deemed too
critical. In January 2018, magazine *Le Nouvel Observateur* strongly
denounced Macron's policy on immigration, with a cover that fea-
tured a close-up of the president's face surrounded by barbed wire.
As if this were a crime of *lèse-majesté*, the wrath of Jupiter fell on the
journalists responsible, who were thenceforward blacklisted from
any meetings with Macron (Chaffanjon 2018).

Since a free press and the right to information are at the core of
any democratic society, these principles are duly reflected in French
law. Pluralism in the media was pointedly enshrined in a raft of legislation introduced by the liberation government in 1944, which was
designed to 'create the conditions for the expression of a diversity
of opinion and voice in the production and distribution of political
content' (Kuhn 2015, 171).

However, the legally guaranteed pluralism of the media is countered by the system of state aid. The ban on commercial advertising
on public television channels has made television networks reli-
ant on state subsidies and private media owners. Upon scrutinising
these subsidies to media organisations (including newspaper publishers), which amounted to about €5 billion in 2009–11, the Cour
des comptes found that such support lacked both transparency and
efficiency, and tended to help already prosperous newspapers while
new publications did not qualify. The subsidies neither helped to
counter the fall in circulation nor encouraged new online strategies
(Cour des comptes 2013). The Open Society Foundation's report
on digital media also mentions this lack of independence of the
media from the state. By law, the various regulators (the Conseil
supérieur de l'audiovisuel (CSA), the Commission Nationale de l'In-
formatique et des Libertés (CNIL), the Autorité de régulation des
communications électroniques et des Postes (ARCEP) and the Haute
Autorité pour la diffusion des œuvres et la protection des droits
d'auteur sur Internet (HADOPI)) have the status of independent administrative authorities (*autorité administrative indépendante* – AAI).
In practice, these bodies are not really at arm's length from the
state. In the case of the CSA, for instance, three of its nine board

members are nominated by the president of the Republic, with the right to appoint the other six being divided equally between the Sénat and the Assemblée nationale. Public television channels hold one-third of the audience, and public broadcasters maintain a dominant position in radio broadcasting. This closeness to the state affects the slant of news reported by public broadcasters, while causing agenda-setting biases and, judging by standard journalistic criteria, surprising omissions in the coverage.

French TV during news hour tends to focus on human interest stories (*faits divers*) rather than impartial reporting of important political news. There are few investigative journalists and they are constrained by libel laws that, on balance, favour complainants over defendants. Contrary to many countries, the law does not prohibit political actors from acquiring broadcast licenses, nor does it impose obligations of political impartiality on broadcast organisations. The state owns Radio France (composed of seven national networks such as France Inter) and France Télévisions, which includes the France 2 and France 3 channels (Villeneuve 2013). A study conducted in mid 2016 for the European Parliament's Committee on Civil Liberties, Justice, and Home Affairs (LIBE) compared seven EU member states – Bulgaria, France, Greece, Hungary, Italy, Poland, and Romania – that were 'specifically selected on the basis of previous research results that showed political pluralism at high risk, accompanied by heavy state interference in the media, or close economic ties between the political sector and private media owners' (Bard and Bayer 2016, 8). Several non-media companies (such as telecommunication and financial and insurance services) have moved into the traditional media sector following the decline in advertising revenues. While the ownership of media outlets often remains opaque, it is less concentrated in the national than in the regional press, which is controlled by just six groups. These regional newspapers' aggregate circulation of about six million is higher than that of the national press (under two million) (Bard and Bayer 2016, 101).

While ethical standards are high among journalists, impartial coverage of media outlets owners' interests is difficult to envisage without some form of self-censorship taking place. *Le Parisien*, for instance, which is owned by Bernard Arnault (the major shareholder and CEO of luxury goods group LVMH), did not report on François Ruffin's documentary *Merci Patron!*, which pits a pair of unemployed workers against Arnault (Rédaction du HuffPost 2017).

Other media properties owned by the Groupe Arnault include the newspapers *Aujourd'hui en France* and the leading business daily *Les Echos*. Other owners of major media outlets have business empires concentrated in various industries. These tycoons include Martin Bouygues, François Pinault, Patrick Drahi, Xavier Niel, and Vincent Bolloré.

In short, the media is firmly in the hands of the state and the business establishment. This helps the government influence public opinion in the desired direction (Bove 2020). To obtain alternative perspectives and information not tasting of powerful business and political interests, the public must resort to either *Le Canard enchaîné* in the print media or the online world of social media, blogs, and tweets. Alongside *Le Canard enchaîné*, *Mediapart* – an independent news website run by a former *Le Monde* journalist – plays an important role in breaking major political stories that prove embarrassing or damaging to the authorities.

The proposed law against fake news came in a context where the public was already distrustful of the media and the political class. The bill caused considerable unease on 'Orwellian' grounds: one of its provisions allows the courts to suspend a website or require the removal of any part of its content during election campaigns if it is deemed to be peddling fake news, while another empowers judges to close Twitter and Facebook accounts. Social networks will be subject to an 'obligation of cooperation', particularly to prevent sponsored content from spreading false information – but it is still up to the courts to determine what constitutes fake news. The argument put forward by the Minister of Culture in support of this proposal was that 'citizens no longer have sufficient discernment', making it essential, therefore, to 'educate citizens'. In other words, French citizens should not dare to stray on the web to check the information handed down to them by official news channels, as they are too stupid to distinguish truth from falsehood. Here we see the repressive instinct of the French state in reaction to the worldwide impact of the digital revolution on the media sector. In France, as everywhere else, print media has declined in line with advertising receipts, which plummeted in the aftermath of the recession of 2007–9. With the expansion of social networks, sources of information have multiplied on the internet – much to the alarm of all those who have traditionally controlled public opinion and are in fear of 'their' truth being under permanent assault.

Yet France already had a law on fake news: enacted in 1881, it was designed to provide legal remedies against the spreading of malicious rumours or slander. Article 27 of this 1881 law allows punishment even if there has been no specific infringement of the physical or moral rights of an individual, and no defamation or invasion of privacy. It is the state, the nation, its institutions, and the public mind that are the designated victims of fake news. While evidently restrictive, the norms enacted in 1881 seem liberal compared with the 2018 proposals for regulating fake news: the 1881 definition of this concept was a precise and detailed fact, not yet disclosed, the false character of which could be demonstrated. The fake news regulation proposed in 2018 does not require trifles such as evidence to deny the public access to a website. The other difference between these two pieces of legislation, highlighted by Etienne Gernelle, publisher of weekly news magazine *Le Point*, stems from Article 1 of the 1881 law, which states that 'printing presses and bookstores are free'. Gernelle recommended that Macron learn from the debates that preceded the 1881 law and the wisdom of the legislators of that distant 'old world'. He saw Macron's instincts pointing in the opposite direction – towards a thorough overhaul of the media, with the president dreaming of a tutelage programme that would make journalists' reporting consistent with some official standard of truthfulness (Gernelle 2019). Macron seems troubled by freedom of expression: he may do well to recall the words of Georges Clémenceau, a champion of equality, liberty, and secularism, who declared during the discussion of the 1881 law: 'The Republic lives off freedom.'

Censorship is already taking place on the international scene, as illustrated by the government's press release advising journalists to avoid certain areas of conflict. In a note sent to all editors in March 2018, the Foreign Ministry (Quai d'Orsay) urged media organisations not to send journalists to report developments in what were then the main hotspots in the Syrian conflict (eastern Ghouta and Afrin). Besides its request 'to kindly give up any possible project of [going] to this country', the document also recommends exercising caution before using 'the reports of independent journalists'. According to the journalists' unions, this official 'request' was designed to encourage newsrooms to keep their distance and, worse, to encourage them not to acquire and broadcast the reports of freelance journalists covering the conflict on location. In other words, they were being asked not to communicate a range of information about the conflict, lying as it did at the heart of a global geostrategic contest. This was a striking request, given that the media are, in principle, free to cover the topics they want to cover without worrying about the injunctions of any government (Ouest France 2018).

Foreign policy is the constitutional prerogative of the head of state, who is not subject to any day-to-day parliamentary (or other) accountability for his or her strategic decisions and alliances. One such instance took place at 4 a.m. on 14 April 2018. A tweet from Emmanuel Macron relayed the statement he had just published, in which he had announced that 'on Saturday, April 7, 2018, in Douma, dozens of men, women, and children were massacred by chemical weapons, in total violation of international law and United Nations Security Council resolutions'. Citizens had no grounds for questioning their young president's affirmation that 'the facts and the responsibility of the Syrian regime are not in doubt. The red line set by France in May 2017 has been crossed. [I,] therefore, ordered the French armed forces to intervene tonight, as part of an international operation ... directed against the clandestine chemical arsenal of the Syrian regime.' The tone is the one favoured by leaders positioning themselves as defenders of the innocent victims of tyrants.

The strange thing was the mainstream media's silence about the results of a laboratory analysis of samples collected by representatives of the Organisation for the Prohibition of Chemical Weapons on the ground in Syria. Here is the relevant finding of that analysis, published on 22 May 2018: 'No organophosphorus nerve agents or their degradation products were detected, either in the environmental samples or in plasma samples from the alleged casualties' (Organisation for the Prohibition of Chemical Weapons (OPCW) 2018). As it turns out, the reports of the Syrian regime carrying out a fatal chemical weapons attack on civilians in Douma were fake news. It follows that the motives for the 'retaliatory' armed attack by France on Syria, fraught as it was with the risk of wider conflagration in the Middle East and beyond, may have been less pure than those advertised and, what is more, fuelled by geopolitical considerations. At any rate, the media were complicit in the lack of accountability for this military action.

The contemporary debate about fake news was inflamed by allegations that it had been 'weaponised' by Russia and other foreign powers interfering in the US presidential election campaign in 2016.

A sceptical study of the real impact of any such fake news makes two points that are relevant to countries outside of the United States, including France. The first is the ever-greater influence on voters of television coverage and advertisements, relative to online information, that are closed to any purveyors of fake news (whether they be suspected malign foreign powers or domestic private agents). This is the case in France as well, where most information is obtained from the main television channels (Bard and Bayer 2016, 109). The second comes from Gallup poll findings, which reveal a continuing decline of 'trust and confidence' in the mass media 'when it comes to reporting the news fully, accurately, and fairly'. Voters are conscious that news can be 'captured'. If captured, the immediate question is, by whom: the state, a foreign state or private entity, or some combination of all of the above (Allcott and Gentzkow 2017)?

The French state is pursuing its own style of the wider official reaction among Western democracies against purveyors of messages that call into question the prevailing socio-economic and political order. In general, the regulatory changes described above suggest how information providers are being pressured to conform to a certain vision of the world and the economy. Any discordant messages can easily be muted by prevalent media outlets defending their own interests, and leaving the beaten track to conduct investigative reports is becoming increasingly risky for journalists.

The law on fake news finally enacted in December 2018 brought these trends to a head. The provisions of the law are applicable only during the three-month period preceding a national election. Most commentators agree that it is one of those laws that is a quick-fire reaction to circumstances and, as such, is unlikely to be effective. In this case, the new law brings nothing to the legal structure; it would have been better to simply update the 1881 law. That old law strikes a balance between press freedom and protecting citizens from defamation (whether or not they happen to be well-known politicians running for office). One of the reasons for doubting the effectiveness of the 2018 law is that it does not recognise the social media platforms owned by giant tech companies like Google and Facebook as publishers – a status that would subject them to the same obligations as media organisations.

More sinister are the new powers that this 2018 law grants to the CSA. The CSA may exercise these powers by sending a series of recommendations to operators of online platforms – including Facebook and Twitter – to fight against false information. The CSA can suspend the operation of any media organisation owned or influenced by a foreign government if the latter puts out, in a deliberate way, false information likely to alter the integrity of the election. The clearly intended targets here are the French-language operations of *Sputnik* and *Russia Today*, which are seen to be disseminating Russian state propaganda in France. The first elections to occur after the enactment of this law were for the European Parliament in May 2019, but the CSA did not see fit to use its new powers on that occasion. This suggests that the French state wants to keep this option of censorship in reserve as a last resort.

The yellow vests movement held up a mirror to the limitations of the French media and, in so doing, catalysed some constructive developments. Established media outlets were initially disorientated by this groundswell of a large section of French society emerging from the neglected and depressed periphery and demanding to be heard and seen. The yellow vests offered none of the usual props to conventional news reporting: they had no identifiable leaders – whether individual or in the form of some collective organisation – and their grievances and demands were inchoate and difficult to categorise in a conventional way. The initial bent of much media coverage was to depict the *gilets jaunes* as representing the grassroots of the national populist political force led by Marine Le Pen, but this was soon abandoned: it became clear that this was a mass social movement of the working poor, whose broad socio-economic grievances transcended 'normal' politics. The media were themselves an object of the yellow vests' grievance, since they were seen as complicit in, and hence partially responsible for, the failure of the ruling establishment to pay attention to 'peripheral' France.

During some of the yellow vests' early protest marches, that sense of grievance erupted into physical aggression, which was directed at reporters from media organisations perceived to be apologists for the government and condescendingly indifferent to the hardships of ordinary folk. Those scuffles naturally dominated media reporting, which thereafter concentrated on violent clashes between demonstrators and the police. Many yellow vest protesters faulted the media for paying more attention to eye-catching clashes and outspoken, often unrepresentative, rhetoric than to the movement's core concerns and wellsprings. The yellow vests countered with their own media coverage in the form of video reportage of their demonstrations, which was disseminated on Facebook Live. By this means, they also expressed their determination to be seen – not only by those with political power and their compatriots in general, but also by each other – as such footage served to weave the fabric of fellow feeling and mutual encouragement that sustained the movement for many months. This media technique had first been seen in early 2016, when the subject was the French equivalent of the Occupy Wall Street movement. With the yellow vests, this style of coverage came into its own, and it was also taken up by some professional, if marginal, media organisations, both domestic and foreign. The latter included the French-language service *Russia Today*, which thereby achieved its editorial goal of highlighting problems in Western countries like France (that tend to be critical of Russia) without laying itself open to the standard charge of falsification, since the content consisted of unedited, hours-long videos of the yellow vest protests.

As the long months of those protests continued, however, the coverage of the mainstream French media gradually opened out into a more enquiring mode, exploring the movement's roots and portraying its aspirations. This constructive shift carried with it an implicit acknowledgement: that editors and reporters had long been turned in on themselves and the familiar world of centralised political decision making rather than exploring the real life of the country. One notable example of this acknowledgement was the launch of a new current affairs discussion show, broadcast at weeknight prime time by the CNews network, which soon attracted a large audience. Thanks to the disarmingly open and benevolent style of its anchor, Christine Kelly, the show offers clear and frank discussions of questions that would be considered taboo on the main networks, such as whether France should remain in the European monetary union, or how French national identity had been affected by mass immigration. Such debates would have conventionally been regarded as 'rightist', especially as the show's most prominent permanent panellist, Éric Zemmour, is a French essayist known for his controversial nationalist positions. Instead of its ideology, however, it was the breath of fresh air that this new style of media debate provided – covering sensitive and neglected areas from varied perspectives – which attracted public interest.

IS MACRON WORSE?

The picture of the presidential election a full decade before Macron's victory offers a revealing contrast. In 2007, the two finalists for the top job, Nicolas Sarkozy and Ségolène Royal, were both relatively young by French political leader standards – but that is where their similarity with Macron ends. Unlike Macron, Sarkozy and Royal had solid experience in public politics requiring constant engagement in dialogue with people of all sorts. In contrast to the paternalist arrogance of their predecessors, François Mitterrand and Jacques Chirac, both of the 2007 contenders sought reform based on a strong political contract between the government and its citizens.

Sarkozy rode to victory on a clear public appetite for change. The fact that the French economy had been performing respectably enough relative to its peers could not dispel the widespread public perception of stagnation compared with the post-war decades, when people – especially the younger generation – could be confident of rising living standards. But change came in a vastly different form to the one desired – namely, the GFC. In France, as elsewhere, the effects of that shock rippled into the politics of subsequent years. As the incumbent tarnished by the effects of the GFC, Sarkozy lost the next presidential election to his Socialist opponent, François Hollande. Another five years of ineffectual government elapsed under Hollande before voters signed up for the politically inexperienced Macron as president and handed a parliamentary majority to his newly minted *En Marche!* party.

As already noted, within weeks of being elected, Macron characterised his presidency as 'Jupiterian'. The official photograph of this young Olympian, with his fixed and icy gaze, gives me cold sweats every time I set eyes on it in the mayor's office of my small village in northern Burgundy. Unlike the official portrait of his predecessor, which depicts Hollande strolling in the gardens of the Élysée Palace, the formal image of the leader of *En Marche!* shows him not so much advancing as looking petrified – or was it France that was supposed to be petrified of its new monarch? The photo leaves no detail to chance: from the sleeves of Macron's shirt to the tip of the flags in the background, everything is set to the nearest millimetre. Yet the overall impression is one of trying too hard. The photograph's effect is suffocating and it provokes anxiety, crowded as it is with symbols that are hard to decipher: the wide open window may be taken to signify Macron's openness to the world, while the few clouds in the blue summer sky may denote problems that the president will quickly dispel. What of General de Gaulle's *War Memoirs* lying open on the desk to his right, while two canonical literary treatments of youthful transgression – Stendhal's *The Red and the Black* and Gide's *The Fruits of the Earth* – sit stacked and closed on his left?

Who is this president? On the night of his election, he walked alone towards his victory rally in the courtyard of the Louvre to the sound of the EU's anthem: the *Ode to Joy* finale of Beethoven's ninth symphony. What image was he trying to project? Could it be a French version of Barack Obama, or perhaps JFK?

In the construction of his media image in the run-up to his successful campaign, Macron was portrayed as a dynamic figure, either alone or accompanied by his wife, Brigitte, and dressed in either sportswear or shirt sleeves. *Paris Match*'s cover story for August 2016 – 'A romantic vacation before the offensive' – was accompanied by a photo of Macron in a polo shirt with Brigitte paddling at the water's edge on the beaches of Biarritz (*Paris Match Rédaction* 2016). This media campaign was run by a leading exponent of celebrity coverage in the French media, Mimi Marchand. The international impact was impressive, as a 'Macronmania' craze swept through the 'Anglo-Saxon' press. British Europhiles traumatised by their Brexit referendum defeat found consolation and inspiration in Macron. Breathless columnists would take to the pages of the *Financial Times* or the *Guardian* to rhapsodise about the need for a British Macron. In the United States, *Time* gave similarly rapturous coverage to the new French president.

While there is nothing at all unusual about political stars crashing to earth, the Macron version of this has a force that demands particular attention. An answer favoured by several commentators to the question of what went wrong for Macron is that, rather than there being anything wrong with the man himself, there is everything wrong with the French people, who are seen as well-nigh ungovernable (Rougier 1955). With street protests being the national sport, as soon as a new president gets elected, the fun (re)starts.

Of course, a proper explanation must be deeper and more complex. That is a story worthy of Balzac, with *Lost Illusions* serving as the most fitting of titles from his great *Human Comedy* cycle of novels. Our tale opens in provincial France, in the town of Amiens, where an impatient, handsome, and ambitious young man, confident in his high opinion of his own talents, decides to move to Paris. Once there, he is taken up by legendary courtiers of power, ancient denizens of the Elysée – the opinion-former Alain Minc, and counsellor to presidents (starting with Mitterrand) Jacques Attali. The latter is reported to have said of Macron: 'I discovered him; I invented him' (Bénilde 2017). With economic stagnation and social fracture discrediting the mainstream political class, Macron's propulsion to the top of the Republican monarchy was seen by such power brokers as a gambit that would preserve the proper order in the face of 'populist' reactions against an elite benefitting from global trends while leaving much of the country behind and feeling, with a sense of despair, that their voices remained unheard.

Révolution is the title that Emmanuel Macron chose for the political platform book which he published ahead of his 2017 presidential campaign (Macron 2016). This title positioned him as the bearer of hope for renewal and grandeur in a new era: it was a promise that people's voices would be heard, whatever their origins, and that political scandals would soon become a vague memory. His vision – *la macronie* – was presented as an antidote to conventional ideological frameworks by championing transparency, openness, and optimism. In this book and during his subsequent campaign stump, Macron promised economic reforms, 'horizontality' (meaning a break with the culture of policy decisions being taken and implemented from on high), and clean politics. This pitch was successfully presented as a rallying point against the dark forces represented by his opponent Marine Le Pen and her National Front party (since renamed National Rally). Yet the success of this novice politician, unknown to the general public before 2014, owed much to the failings of the alternatives on offer to voters: a potentially formidable challenge from centre–right candidate François Fillon was felled by a well-timed corruption investigation, while Le Pen was hampered by her inadequacy as a communicator and her limited grasp of policy substance and strategy. In this context, it is worth highlighting the corollary of the subsequent parliamentary election victory of Macron's *En Marche!* party, which won an absolute majority in the National Assembly with 308 of the 577 seats. In other words, the two traditional governing parties – the centre–left Socialists and the centre–right Republicans – imploded. Although it is positioned as a kind of post-modern political party, free of conventional baggage and tired shibboleths, *En Marche!* and its parliamentary caucus mostly consists of eager and loyal political neophytes ready to applaud Macron's accomplishments on cue.

While much of Macron's support was negatively motivated (i.e. to stop Le Pen), many voters clearly projected various strong hopes onto him. As a result, the public disappointment has been all the greater. After three years in office, the right epithet for him would seem to be *Macron the Ill-loved.* During one of the street protests against his pension reform plan in early December 2019, a man arrived at the Place de la Bastille with a big pink heart on which he had written the following sentence: 'Macron, I hate you with all my heart.' Some slogans were more threatening: 'We're coming to get you.' Meanwhile, images of the president in the costume of the guillotined king Louis XVI floated above the columns of demonstrators. Macron had previously been the target of eye-catching physical aggression during the yellow vests movement. A year earlier, for example, he was taken to task in Puy-en-Velay, a town in central France, as demonstrators besieged his car – an episode that Macron, by his own account, was traumatised by. It is true that France is used to hard, uncompromising political conflict, and this is often focused on the incumbent president, in whose hands the powers of the Fifth Republic are concentrated. Equally undeniable is the country's tradition of regicide nurturing a revolutionary climate. But this fever pitch of public animosity against Macron still seems striking.

The rejection of Macron's person and his policies are linked. Opinion polls carried out in early 2020 (before the coronavirus pandemic) showed that large majorities viewed Macron's policies as ineffective (62 per cent), with a similarly solid majority expressing personal dislike for the man himself (63 per cent) (Herreros 2020). Such survey responses highlighted the public's loss of patience for a government regarded as hapless. Popular demands focused on increased purchasing power. The government's room for manoeuvre remained limited not only by the rules of the eurozone, especially as regards fiscal policy, but also by the internal constraints of the traditional assumptions and prejudices of the governing class. Macron is a member of this class, but he is also its prisoner, and this has made his goals – and his government's programme – that much harder to achieve (Jauvert 2018).

Shortly after his address to a joint session of the two chambers of the national parliament at the Palace of Versailles in July 2017, caricatures of Macron dressed in full monarchical regalia appeared. We have already seen how the caricature of Macron as 'president of the rich' became entrenched early on; it seems it remained to be shaken off, despite various increases in social spending targeted at the poor and in areas such as education and support for people with disabilities.

Another reason for the meagre political dividends from such policies was the president's arrogant style. A product of French Caesarism, Macron was a brilliant technocrat turned investment banker (and hence millionaire) before rising to power as a political appointee: this is an alienating profile, far from the background many French people would consider likely to promote national flourishing. Once in office, the moderniser candidate quickly adopted a 'technocratic authoritarian' style, signalling his wish for the executive to reign supreme over other branches of government (Schwartz 2018). His grandiose self-image was combined with the technocrat's characteristic dismissive impatience when confronted with obstacles and objections, and a dramatic lack of empathy for the plight of the working poor. Robert McNamara, reflecting on his career as the head of Ford Motors, US secretary for defense at the height of the Vietnam War, and president of the World Bank, concluded that the worst state blunders are rooted in a lack of empathy (Mulgan 2018, 158).

The hallmark of this monarchical republic is hubris that goes together with condescension and sometimes poorly disguised contempt for ordinary members of the public. In December 2018, when Gilles Le Gendre, leader of the *En Marche!* caucus in the Assemblée Nationale, was asked on the current affairs show *Territories of Info* about what the government should have done differently, he answered: 'We were probably too intelligent, too subtle.' This response seemed to capture 'Macronism', a notion of society as a kind of raw material, consisting of some elements that are valuable and dynamic and others that are worthless. There was no sense here of being at ease in a national community with all of its positive potential as well as its failings. Macron's idea of fostering social cohesion turned out to be convening a public debate (*Grand Débat*), at various sessions of which he delivered three-hour monologues. While it is reasonable and right for an elected figurehead to coax his or her community on to better things, the figurehead should also cherish and reassure that community's members with compassion and forbearance – consistent with the Christian foundation of French society and culture. The role of the president of the Fifth Republic was conceived by its founder, Charles de Gaulle, as an office in which to lead the nation with grand visions but also in a spirit of service and duty. Macron, despite his desire to be seen as a reincarnation of the youthful de Gaulle, is far from possessing the ascetic characteristics of the general (Jackson 2018).

Macron started out by convincing many that he represented hope and change: a hope that France might embrace modernity in its governance and economic performance, and a change from the complacent political class that had governed the country during the preceding decades. However, by the halfway point of his presidential term, that hope was on life support. His non-ideology was, in reality, a meta-ideology, reclothing the country's legacy system in a new, colourless centrism. Macron presented himself as the centrist's centrist, the sensible superhero, the moderate who could save the masses from obscurantism and who would reinstate France as the pivotal global champion of multilateralism. He promised to put France at the centre of a more coherent and coordinated Europe. The whole act seemed mistimed: it might have played better amidst the wave of optimism brought about by the collapse of the Soviet communist system and empire three decades earlier. That early hope has since been drowned by the effect of globalisation in heightening inequality and bringing about the relative impoverishment of the middle and lower middle classes in advanced Western economies.

Macron directed much of his starting political capital towards the ambitious project of reshaping Europe. This task was compromised by a combination of his own arrogance and German intransigence. Instead of building alliances, Macron opted for a go-it-alone diplomacy, pursued in what was often a hectoring style that has alienated his European counterparts. A headline in the *Financial Times* in October 2019 read: '"Imperious" Macron tests patience of EU partners'. Some colourful, anonymous quotes accused him of being 'drunk on power' like the bad guy in *Star Wars* (Mallet and Peel 2019). This criticism is unfair to the extent that Macron did set out a coherent vision of the flaws in the eurozone and required reforms such as the introduction of pooled insurance of household deposits in the eurozone's banks, of a large collective budget to be used for countercyclical fiscal management, and of a eurozone finance minister to run this budget. But his stance came to seem quixotic in the face of obstructionism from Germany, France's historic partner in the post-war construction of Europe. In the absence of German leadership, Macron seems to have felt that it was his job to assert leadership (Kluth 2019). As we will see at the end of the next chapter on the euro, the Covid-19 crisis precipitated a change of heart in Germany; but it remains to be seen how lasting this will be.

In light of the coronavirus pandemic, the assessment of Macron given here might need modifying; however, at time of writing, there is scant evidence of any change in Macron's approach. Even a sincere turn away from his off-putting style would leave Macron hard-pressed to overcome the climate of mistrust built up during his first years in power; on top of which, he remains up against the fundamental problem discussed from various angles in this chapter – the unsuitability of the entrenched high bureaucratic caste as an instrument for implementing any serious change.

RESTORING FAITH IN DEMOCRACY

Each presidential election in France highlights the ever-widening divide between the technocrats and the people. As the protest vote grows, the leaders of all political tendencies are affirming that they have heard the message, that things will change, that they will continue to listen, and that measures will be taken. But as successive lacklustre reform efforts peter out, the fracture looks increasingly like an abyss, while the oligarchy remains deaf. We have seen in this chapter the reasons for the congenital deafness of successive cohorts of enarchs. With their uniform educational conditioning and complacent mindset, characterised by unreflecting confidence in their own rectitude, these technocrats dominate positions of power in government and public administration, in the media, in culture, and in large swathes of industry and finance. It is hard to imagine a more effective anti-recipe for empathy towards middling and poorer groups in society than the present entrenched system, whereby new members of the upper caste are co-opted from a minute pool of graduates with a lifetime guarantee of high-flying careers and privileges.

The solution – or, at least, a necessary first step towards a solution – may seem obvious: to unplug the clone-making machine. The marathon three-month *Grand Débat* that Macron launched in response to the yellow vests movement allowed him to hear numerous criticisms aimed at the elite and, in particular, grievances against obstacles to equal opportunities in the school and higher education systems. Perhaps those conversations helped Macron recall his campaign promise to fight the 'injustice of a society of orders, statutes, castes, social contempt where everything conspires – and for what result! – to prevent personal fulfillment' (Macron 2016, 18). In April 2019, he announced a number of measures in response to the *Grand Débat*, including the closure of the ENA, a structural reform of the civil service that would supersede the Grands Corps, and a mild version of the idea of holding referendums at the initiative of citizens (*Référendum d'initiative Citoyenne* – RIC).

To start with his eye-catching proposal to abolish the ENA, at least in its present form: this announcement came against the background of some useful public service reforms that were already in progress. One such reform, which became law in July 2019, strengthened the mechanisms for upholding standards in public life, with a particular focus on the conflicts of interest associated with the revolving door between the civil service and business. The main practical change moved ethical supervision of civil servants from a committee in the prime minister's office to the arm's-length body known as the HATVP: this, as we saw earlier, has a wider remit, covering everyone in any position of authority or responsibility in the public sector (Garrigues 2019). Continuing this reform drive in the direction of the ENA, in April 2019 the government appointed Frédéric Thiriez, a former president of the Professional Football League, to come up with proposals on how to reform the training of future high-level civil servants. His specific remit was to think of ways to make the top tier of the civil service more diverse in terms of its members' social and geographic origins. Thiriez submitted his final report to prime minister Édouard Philippe in February 2020.

A core proposal was to establish twenty preparatory schools (one in each region) to train high school graduates interested in a career in public administration, with participants selected to ensure social diversity. The students completing these courses could then enter special competitions for entry to one of the various (higher education) public service schools for training law enforcement officials, health care administrators, etc. A tenth of the places were reserved for candidates from underprivileged social backgrounds. The transformed ENA would *not* be one of those schools. Instead, with its name changed to the School of Public Administration (EAP), it would provide year-long executive courses for those who had already begun civil service careers and for engineering graduates of other *Grandes Écoles*.

The Thiriez report was praised by iFrap's director, Samuel-Frédéric Servière, for putting an end to the 'lifelong annuity leading to revolving doors', until now entailed by the enrolment of top ENA graduates in the civil service Grands Corps (Servière 2020b). These elite bodies would be rationalised, including by mergers with related entities, according to their broad functional remit (e.g. financial controls). Other positive proposals would allow flexible recruitment of contract workers to senior civil service roles and increase the importance of technical roles relative to pure policy management.

The big uncertainty concerned the strength of the political will to implement this agenda with any seriousness at all. Philippe's initial reaction to the Thiriez report – saying that he wanted 'to draw inspiration from it' – sounded lukewarm (Lombard-Latune 2020). There was unsurprising pushback from vested interests, with whom decision makers such as Philippe – himself a career State Council official – clearly sympathised. A sure way to tone down such reforms is to advocate parallel reforms that will dilute the core agenda. For instance, enarchs started lobbying for easier access to PhD programmes. The new ENA or EAP might thus retain its status as the school for the 'best of the best' students, only now at the PhD level (incidentally removing from the ordinary universities one of their few existing competitive advantages – i.e. the ability to award PhD degrees). The technocrats had managed once more to smother a proposal offering a renewed vision of the public service based on serving the general interest.

As for the referendum (RIC) initiative, its proponents saw this as a way of addressing the aspiration for enhanced democratic accountability that had been highlighted by the yellow vests movement and which, in turn, reflected the broader waning public trust in elected representatives. Many participants in that movement were inspired by visions of a self-organised democracy, where people's opinions are expressed and then implemented by administrators; the latter will have been chosen by voters for that specific task based on relevant qualifications rather than allegiance to a political party.

The RIC proposals fell well short of such ideals – and even of the practice of several other countries, including notable European cases such as Switzerland and the Netherlands, where the law obliges the state to conduct referendums that are supported by a sufficient number of citizens. While purporting to respond to the strong public support for RICs as revealed in several opinion surveys (IFOP *en partenariat avec Valeurs* 2019), Macron's proposal would, in practice (and in line with the existing constitution), leave the final say on whether a referendum should be held with elected authorities. Referendum proposals attracting the defined minimum level of public support (together with the endorsement of 185 deputies or senators) would have to be considered by the national parliament. Macron did intervene to lower the threshold of public support required for a referendum initiative – from the level initially envisaged by the bureaucracy of one-tenth of the electorate (i.e. 4.5 million people) to just one million. Yet the reform proposal remained meaningless. For when a referendum proposal passing those tests appeared, instead of being automatically implemented as in other countries with such procedures, Macron's version would merely oblige the parliament to consider it. That *consideration* may take the form of the parliament simply deciding to discuss and vote on the matter itself – in this case, there would be no referendum. In other words, the governing majority could simply vote down a proposal that it disliked and avoid a referendum.

This watering down of the RIC initiative may well reflect concerns about the risk inherent in referendums: they can be used in situations where public opinion is particularly enflamed and therefore more easily manipulated, as is the case after terrorist attacks or other highly emotive events. Some critics pointed to the risk of such referendums resulting in the return of the death penalty or the prohibition of abortion. However, since democracy is evolutionary by definition, there is nothing to stop the creation of safeguards. In Switzerland, for instance, proposing a law to the population is never done in haste: the democratic process takes time, and voters receive material to help them come to an informed view on the questions that have been put to referendum.

Geoff Mulgan argues that the path to a better democracy does not lie in online petitions or digital referendums, as these tools risk magnifying the polarisation of a society rather than healing its fractures. Instead, it lies in how the opinions of millions of citizens, available online, are canvassed, processed, and synthesised in order to improve decision making. A strong democracy, capable of creating a more cooperative society, relies on independent media, trust, mutual respect, and empathy (Mulgan 2018). With those principles in mind, blockchain technology could be used to motivate citizens to participate more intensively in the political, economic, and social spheres (Galen *et al.* 2018).

Blockchain, or distributed ledgers, is a general purpose technology for securely validating and storing peer-to-peer information exchanges. While the first global impact of this technology has come with the emergence of cryptocurrencies, it can provide an equally sound foundation for digital voting systems. Its potential in this area has already been demonstrated in, for example, the US state of West Virginia, which used blockchain technology during the 2018 midterm elections to permit 144 members of the armed forces stationed abroad to vote on the mobile platform called Voatz. This system was originally developed to address the problem of low voter turnout among the military. Another example comes from the Swiss city of Zug, which ran a municipal voting test in 2018 where citizens voted via their mobile devices using the city's new electronic identification system. In France, the largest telecommunications operator Orange offers businesses and communities a service called *Le Vote*, which is based on the Ethereum platform, to allow local authorities and/or civic associations to consult their citizens or members on local themes (Richaud and Bloch 2018).

Most existing blockchain voting projects are financed by private investors, which can create conflicts of interest. They most often use open-source protocols assigned to other uses (such as cryptocurrencies or smart contracts). The best way to support the successful development of this trend would be to create a protocol running on an autonomous blockchain, built in open-source mode and exclusively dedicated to voting. There are many technical and functional issues to be addressed (e.g. identity authentication, confidentiality and isolation guarantees, validation solutions), and, to command the necessary confidence, any such project should be developed by public authorities rather than outsourced to private interests. Various initiatives in favour of this kind of technology-driven democratic renewal have sprung up in France, such as the Blockchain Commune Manifesto (*Manifeste de la Commune Blockchain*): this advocates a horizontal and collective cooperation financed by voluntary donations (Antiprince 2018). Donors would be motivated by their interest in promoting public consultation on certain topics, while the incentive for volunteers would be to gain access to a large and varied audience (Mulgan 2018). Wider initiatives in this area include the International Association of Trusted Blockchain Applications (INATBA), which was launched in April 2019 by the European Commission as a forum to promote cooperation and information exchange between regulators and policymakers working towards an agreed global regulation of blockchain technology applications (European Commission 2019b).

The introduction of this technology to France's political system offers a possibility of more horizontal social organisation and regulation, and a chance to get away from the French curse of centralised top-down rule by a bureaucratic oligarchy. The blockchain might thus help restore faith in democracy by enabling a more participatory form of politics centred on issues familiar and dear to people. This would be a form of democracy close to the heart of renowned Canadian political and social philosopher Charles Taylor (Rothman 2016).

2

The Great Present-Day Utopia:
The Euro

Europe's economic and monetary union (EMU) was instigated by the holders of state power in France – François Mitterrand and his entourage (notably Jacques Delors, at that time president of the European Commission). Their aim of protecting and, simultaneously, projecting French power was rationalised as the ineffable Manifest Destiny of France and Europe, or rather of France as Europe. Here, made reality, was the assumption of the French governing elite that their own gratification must represent the *General Will* according to Rousseau's formula for recovering primitive human virtue. Since inspiring the revolutionary terrorists of the 1790s, this has boiled down to an update, in the garb of the Enlightenment, of Louis XIV's dictum: *l'etat, c'est moi* (Barruel 2005). This metamorphosis of monarchy – from a royal to a republican casing – was laid bare by de Gaulle in a little discourse on the constitution of the Fifth Republic, which he came out with at a press conference in 1964: 'A constitution is a spirit, institutions and a practice …. But it must also be understood that the indivisible authority of the state is entrusted entirely to the president, by the people who elected him, that there exists no other authority, neither ministerial, civil, military, judicial, which is not conferred and maintained by him' (Jackson 2018, 562). This prompts the question, how is the 'indivisible authority of the state' going to be 'entrusted entirely to the president' when that very same state is a member not only of the EU but also of the EMU?

The genesis of the euro is a powerful demonstration of the toxic combination of utopian delusions and cynical realpolitik. Mitterrand wanted a shared currency with Germany to benefit from Germany's superior monetary stability under the stewardship of the

Bundesbank, while also gaining a decisive French handle on the Bundesbank. In response to the French proposal for a monetary union along the lines we see today, then German Chancellor Helmut Kohl quite rightly said (in 1990) that the euro would require a political union to work (this might be reckoned honest utopianism!). He was blocked by Mitterrand, who insisted on the current unworkable hybrid arrangement that has hampered positive domestic change, both in France and in the other unfortunate denizens of the eurozone. This episode exposes a pernicious underlying assumption of the French governing class – that economics can always be bent to political will. The political union counterproposed by Kohl was never on any French agenda, as it would have entailed the country's sovereignty being transferred to a supra state and therefore threatened the very essence of the Fifth Republic. This 'mutual incomprehension' of its founding members underlies the design faults of the EMU (Brunnermeier, James, and Landau 2016).

It is hard to have a calm discussion about the existence of the euro, given that this topic has become taboo in many 'polite' circles (Dedieu *et al.* 2014). Questioning the euro's viability or its costs is considered heresy, which is dismissed with the retort that any country daring to leave the EMU would face apocalyptic economic costs. The proponents of returning to a national currency are vilified as being nationalist or, worse still, populist. For Thomas Piketty, populism is a term used by elites to disqualify political movements over which they lack sufficient control (Piketty 2019). This is a view that Macron unwittingly endorsed when, in June 2018, he declared: 'You can see [populists] popping up a bit like leprosy all across Europe, in countries where we thought that it would be impossible to see them again, in neighbouring countries' (Rose and Jones 2018).

Defenders of the euro often present their case as a matter of upholding rational and technical pragmatism in the face of its 'populist' critics, whose recommendations would result in people losing all of their savings. In reality, the euro was always an inherently political project that fits the Parisian groupthink mind like a glove. This mind is educated to assume that theory and political will can and should take precedence over reality. So what if the euro meant putting the eurozone economy into a straitjacket at a time when the rest of the world was opting for more flexibility in its monetary, fiscal, and exchange rate arrangements? Groupthink is defined as having the following characteristics: a leader to champion a view;

external critics dismissed; internal critics silenced; and, therefore, a slide into undertakings of great – and unreasonable – risk (Béna-bou 2013). This boils down to a form of social psychosis among the inner circle of state policymakers and their entourage of boosters and conformist 'intellectuals' – the very same *clercs* whom French thinker Julian Benda accused of treason in his celebrated 1927 pamphlet (Benda 2003). The rhetoric of irrevocability is repeated in an infinite loop on all media supported by the euro clerisy. 'The euro is irreversible', declared then ECB president Mario Draghi in a 2012 speech, reflecting his strong attachment to the European single currency as a symbol of European unity (Draghi 2012). Commenting on this speech, British–American economist Willem Buiter wrote: 'I have a problem … with central bankers making public statements about policies or reforms that definitely go well beyond their mandate and quite likely also beyond their competence' (Buiter 2015).

American economist Barry Eichengreen, who is known for his work on the gold standard (Eichengreen 1992), arguing that it transformed what should have been a minor financial crisis into the Great Depression, surprisingly warned that dismantling the euro would give rise to 'the mother of all financial crises', adding that 'history does not reverse itself' (Eichengreen 2010). We would do well to recall in this context that when President Roosevelt wanted to leave the gold standard in 1933, he was warned that it would be the end of Western civilisation. Another counterexample to the thesis of 'historical irreversibility' is the decision of the Bank of France to raise its interest rate in 1935 to keep France on the gold standard while both the United States and Great Britain had already left. The economic consequences of that decision for French competitiveness and employment were dire. That historical perspective informed the grim foreboding of French economist Jean-Jacques Rosa in 2001 (i.e. just after the launch of the euro): 'Europe is making the worst mistake since the deflationary policies of the 1920s which turned the 1929 stock market crash into a decade of tragedy. The single currency is not a decisive advantage for the continent. It is a time bomb' (Rosa 2001). A similar verdict was delivered ahead of the euro's launch by American economist Martin Feldstein (Feldstein 1997). In 2015, I, along with my co-author Dominik Nagly, warned about the difficulty for governments of maintaining public support in the presence of persistently high unemployment and diverging living standards (based on the measure of per capita income) (Granville and Nagly 2015). We estimated that the long-term costs of staying in the monetary union may be higher than the short-term break-up costs.

At this point in the discussion, it is necessary to introduce the crucial economic concept of adjusting to changes in circumstances for the sake of maintaining the stable employment and healthy output that is so important for material welfare. In an open trading economy, an effective – if not *the* most effective – way of doing this is by altering the exchange rate to offset changes in one's own prices relative to those of one's trading partners. By devaluing its currency, a struggling country can reduce its relative prices and have more success in selling its goods and services. Since eurozone countries, the bulk of whose trade is with each other, are locked into irrevocably fixed exchange rates, their only remaining resort is 'internal devaluation' – that is, reducing relative wage costs (hence, living standards) in the hope that this will create the conditions for longer-term growth. The problem, however, is that the social and economic costs of internal devaluation are high, above all through the effect of increased unemployment (Weisbrot and Ray 2011) and the rising proportion of young people joining the ranks of the NEETS (not in education, employment, or training) (Ghoshray, Ordóñez, and Sala 2016).

For American economist Mark Blyth, the EMU exemplifies Einstein's much-quoted definition of madness as doing the same thing over and over again while expecting different results: 'Following the Exchange Rate Mechanism debacle, in a scene reminiscent of one in Monty Python's movie *The Holy Grail* in which the king tells his son that "they said you couldn't build a castle on a swamp, so I did it anyway and it fell down, so I did it again, and it fell down, so I did it again, and it fell down", the Europeans decided to go one step further than pegging to the deutsch mark – they would all become Germans by sharing the same currency and the same monetary policy' (Blyth 2013, 77). If the EMU is a form of madness, then refusing to discuss various scenarios for leaving the euro, as the French technocrats do, seems like culpable negligence.

POLITICS DISREGARDS ECONOMICS

De Gaulle's initial position in 1943 was: 'All that weakens Germany reinforces us' (Jackson 2018, 347). This attitude was duly reflected in the Monnet Plan (1946–50) for economic reconstruction, which aimed at securing leadership in European heavy industry for France, assigning to the Ruhr a minimal role (Milward 2006). It is clear that, at the time, Jean Monnet (1888–1976), the architect of French planning, was not the European federalist he would later become (Milward 1994). This transition was no doubt influenced by the United States through the Marshall Plan (1948–51), which was linked to the economic reconstruction of West Germany: this had become a priority in 1947 as the Cold War got underway (Berger and Ritschl 1995). Monnet eventually repackaged his initial plan into a supranational organisation, the European Coal and Steel Community (ECSC), to which France acceded in 1951 through the signature of its foreign minister Robert Schuman (Jackson 2018, 479). While its economic aim of regulating the industrial production of Belgium, France, Italy, Luxembourg, the Netherlands, and West Germany seemed rather benign, the plan's political aim was to set in motion a process of integration that resulted in our present-day EU. The process of integrating heavy industrial sectors into treaty-based 'communities' that began in 1951 led to the 1957 Treaty of Rome establishing a 'common market' and committing its six original signatory countries to the goal of an 'ever closer union'. The resulting European Economic Community (EEC) gradually enlarged, and by the 1980s it included the United Kingdom, Denmark, the Republic of Ireland, Spain, Portugal, and Greece. The Single European Act of 1985 laid the foundation for a frictionless internal ('single') market based on the free movement of goods, labour, and capital.

The idea of a European economic and monetary union was discussed extensively by the adepts of the European movement that emerged after World War II. As early as 1947, Maurice Allais, French economist and future winner of the Nobel Memorial Prize in Economics, envisaged the introduction of a single European currency as long as it was preceded by a political union (Union des fédéralistes européens 1947). Jacques Rueff, the economist and civil servant who advised de Gaulle, shared with de Gaulle a fear of inflation and a vision of France remaining the political leader of Europe with a single currency, which would eventually come to rival the US dollar (Rueff 1950). The quest was for exchange rate stability in the spirit of 'the discipline and certainty of the gold standard' to ensure the smooth functioning of the common market (Bordo and James

2014, 1). After some false starts towards this goal in the 1970s and a sometimes-troubled transitional experience of managed exchange rates in the 1980s, an agreement was reached in the 1992 Maastricht Treaty to launch the EMU on 1 January 1999. By that time, the EU comprised fifteen member states, and all but two – the United Kingdom and Denmark – joined the EMU.

In addition to establishing a reserve currency with the potential to rival the US dollar, the political motives for France were to achieve 'co-manager' status with Germany of the European project, to take a formal share in what had until then been the Bundesbank's de facto controlling influence over the monetary policy of France (Feldstein 1997, 28). In the decade preceding the agreement to launch the EMU, France had pursued integration with Germany through a policy mix that was then referred to as 'competitive devaluation' and had many of the same features as what we now call 'austerity'. The technocrats reckoned that by gaining an important share in the new single central bank (and France had a track record of exercising strong influence in European institutions), the need for such austerity would be reduced or, to the extent that it was unavoidable, could be attributed to the cause of European integration. This would reconcile public opinion to any necessary but unpopular economic policies (Kissinger 1994, 606). As for Germany, since it did not instigate the project, its agenda was more reactive – with the minimum goal of ensuring that its style of monetary policy would be preserved after the launch of the EMU. In other words, the German model would be projected onto the whole of Europe (Feldstein 1997, 29).

The French needed a theory to justify their political project. At first, the theory of optimal currency areas (OCA), which purports that a currency union boosts trade and economic growth by abolishing exchange rate transaction costs under conditions of unrestricted cross-border capital and labour flows, seemed to fit the bill (Mundell 1961). OCA proponents accordingly argued that the costs of losing monetary policy independence were outweighed by the benefits of the EMU. Such arguments were dismissed, however, by the European Commission in a concept report, which concluded that OCA was inadequate as a rationale for the proposed monetary union (Commission of the European Communities 1990, 46). The priority, therefore, was to develop a more obliging theory. This rested on two arguments. First, it was emphasised that in an open economy, exchange rate volatility has an impact on price stability. Second, it was emphasised that trade would intensify in the currency union, and, as a result, the benefits would exceed the costs (Micco *et al.* 2003).

The architecture of the euro, just like that of the gold standard, involves fixed exchange rates, price stability, and prudent fiscal policy. Convergence between the stronger (core) and weaker (periphery) eurozone economies was designed to be achieved through the smooth flow of capital from the surplus to the deficit countries, loosening the latter group's external constraint (that is, the limit on how far a country can import foreign savings to boost its domestic development without undermining its balance of payments) and thereby improving its output capacity and productivity (James 2012).

In the discussions leading to the establishment of the EMU, early critics highlighted the proposed currency union's lack of stabilisation mechanisms for dealing with recessions (Sala-i-Martin and Sachs 1991). This concern was underlined by two related themes: the no bailout rule and economic convergence.

Framed on the basis that the euro would be a common currency used by fiscally sovereign nation states, the no bailout rule was designed to avoid a situation where one or more participating countries would free ride on the backs of taxpayers in other countries (Chari and Kehoe 2008). This rule was enshrined in three articles of the EU's Maastricht Treaty, which prohibited monetary financing of budget deficits (Article 123), excluded direct bailouts in the form of cross-border transfers of public funds (Article 124) and precluded any liability of one member state for the liabilities of another (Article 125) (Beetsma and Giuliodori 2010, 607). The no bailout rule assumed that financial markets would exert a disciplinary effect on the conduct of macroeconomic policies because international capital flows adversely respond to imprudent macroeconomic policies (Stiglitz 2000). Yet research has found only mixed evidence of some such effect in monetary policy, and minimal impact on fiscal policy. This suggests that financial market pricing of government bonds (i.e. demanding a higher interest rate in response to perceived fiscal imprudence) is insufficient to ensure sovereign debt sustainability (Bordo and James 2014). The inadequate ability of financial markets to impose strong enough discipline on eurozone countries' independent fiscal policies made the introduction of fiscal rules – the Stability and Growth Pact (SGP) – a necessity for Germany: 'Without such a framework, government debt might eventually reach an unsustainable path, thus forcing the central bank to adopt an inflationary policy' (Brunnermeier, James, and Landau 2016, 135).

Fiscal rules, from the very start, did not seem to apply to France or Germany. In November 2003, both countries became the first to violate the SGP and used 'their political power to prevent sanctions against their own violation of the pact's fiscal rules' (Spolaore 2013, 13–14). That episode heralded what became a trend for France, which broke the SGP rule more than any other eurozone country. In November 2019, the EC, acting in its surveillance and enforcement capacity as regards the eurozone fiscal rules that have since evolved from the SGP, warned France that it was at risk of breaking the rules again (European Commission 2019a).

The second theme that casts light on the EMU's flaws (and its difficulty dealing with crises) is the importance of achieving prior economic convergence given the difficulties of correcting payment imbalances within the envisaged single currency area (Froot and Rogoff 1991). In the minds of the designers of the EMU, current account balances would cease to matter after the introduction of the single currency, and balance of payments crises were ruled out (Honkapohja 2014, 264). This doctrine continued to hold sway despite the publication of papers, both when the EMU was still in its planning stages and when it had just been introduced, warning that the balance of payments problems within the monetary union, far from disappearing, would steadily deepen in the event of economic divergence between eurozone member states, especially with regard to levels of competitiveness (which show up most clearly in varying unit labour costs) (Bagnai 2016). Here, the worst offender has been Germany, which, from 2004 onwards, ran an average current account surplus of about 6 per cent of GDP. The EU's Macroeconomic Imbalance Procedure (MIP) states that the European Commission should launch infringement proceedings against countries with average current account balances over three-year periods that exceed the 'indicative thresholds' of +6 per cent and –4 per cent of GDP (European Commission 2014). Under the MIP, an excessive imbalance procedure should have been launched whereby Germany could be ordered to present an 'action plan' to cut its external surplus. If that failed, Berlin could be forced to pay a deposit of up to

0.1 per cent of GDP into a special account while it remained on probation. Ultimately, that money can be seized if no effective remedial action is taken.

It goes without saying that, as in the case of France breaking the SGP, Germany was never sanctioned for running these huge and chronic current account surpluses as opposed to generating balancing domestic demand from which its trading partners could have benefited. The reality behind this inaction was stated in an arrestingly deadpan way in a 2018 European Court of Auditors report: '[T]he MIP is generally well-designed and based on good-quality analysis. But at some important stages, the process is political rather than technical' (EU Reporter correspondent 2018). Any such sanction would risk destroying German political consent for the euro. In other words, the rebalancing mechanism is jammed. Here we have a club whose initial rules were set according to the collective memory and economic structure of the club's core member, Germany, but whose rule book is not impartially enforced. In areas where the rules might be applied in a way that runs counter to the policy preferences of the German elite – as in the case of the MIP – those rules are simply not applied. The reason for this is that the paramount political priority is to hold the eurozone together: so, France, the EC, and the other eurozone members are reduced to working within the limits of the politically possible in Germany. To the extent that France has received a free pass regarding the eurozone's fiscal rules, this is a mirror image situation: the French elite's rule-breaking preference concerns not external imbalances, as in Germany, but higher-than-permitted budget deficits, and since there can be no eurozone without France, Germany will acquiesce to France's bending the fiscal rules. This political reality works to the detriment of the weaker members of the eurozone: those countries caught in a cycle of inferior competitiveness. The Greek crisis of the 2010s was the logical result of a process by which, on the basis of a 'patchy' theory, 'an incomplete monetary union, without the safeguards of labour mobility and a fiscal union, was forged' (Mody 2015).

CHRONICLE OF A CRISIS FORETOLD

Many economists warned the European politicians responsible for creating the monetary union about the folly of their actions, but those politicians maintained that the euro was for the best and disregarded these warnings (Bagnai, Granville, and Mongeau Ospina 2017). For Milton Friedman, 'Europe exemplifies a situation unfavourable to a common currency. It is composed of separate nations, speaking different languages, with different customs, and having citizens feeling far greater loyalty and attachment to their own country than to a common market or to the idea of "Europe"' (Friedman 1997).

The historical record of monetary unions shows that they have been formed with the best political intentions, but few survive. Many, such as the Austro-Hungarian Empire in 1918 (Garber and Spencer 1994) and the ruble zone in 1993 (Granville 2002), were dismantled. Three reasons have been advanced to explain why this is often the end result: nationalism; avoiding contagion from other members' monetary shocks; and ensuring control over the collection of seigniorage (that is, the revenue accruing to a government when the money it creates is worth more than it costs to produce) (Conway 1995, 1). A monetary union between sovereign states, as in the case of the EMU, locks in and deepens differences in competitiveness between participating countries. Those differences cause external surpluses or deficits in the countries that are, respectively, more or less competitive.

The euro lacks a 'safety valve', namely the possibility for a member to devalue in response to a shock. This would provide the oxygen for improved growth that would then correct the member's fiscal imbalances, the management of which could be facilitated by that member having its own central bank (Bordo and James 2014). Without the safety valve of external devaluation, divergent competitiveness can only be addressed in two ways. The first, which we have already noted, is internal devaluation – that is, 'a depreciation of the real exchange rate in the deficit countries via a cut in their unit labour costs, achieved either through higher productivity or lower nominal wages' (Belke and Dreger 2013, 14). The alternative approach is cross-border financial flows, which, in practice, means transfers from the stronger countries to the weaker countries in the monetary union. Given that exchange rates are irrevocably fixed, less competitive eurozone countries must rely on some mixture of these two remedies: internal devaluation and transfers. Both come at a price, with internal devaluation bearing down on unit labour costs and transfers being conditional on fiscal retrenchment.

The countries at the centre of the eurozone sovereign debt crisis in 2010–13 became dependent on official transfers; these, in accordance with the no bailout principle of the EMU, were strictly conditional on fiscal tightening designed to ensure compliance with the rules laid down in the relevant agreements, from the Maastricht Treaty to the Fiscal Compact that entered into force in January 2013. This medicine aggravated the disease: one of the negative effects of the fiscal tightening was to further damage labour productivity and thus deepen the competitiveness divergence among eurozone members. As foretold in 1996 by Rudiger Dornbusch, an outstanding economist who did not live to see the eurozone 'in action', uncompetitive economies that try to improve their position through wage compression experience low growth, at least until (in theory) their competitiveness has been restored (Dornbusch 1996, 113). The difficulty of driving wages low enough means that, in practice, this 'adjustment' produces rising unemployment and depresses the living standards of remaining wage earners, never reaching the point at which the hoped-for rewards materialise (O'Rourke and Taylor 2013).

Internal devaluation in countries such as France was driven by a starting position of inferior competitiveness, locked in by the level at which the franc–deutsche mark exchange rate was set when the euro was launched in 1999. The scale of the internal devaluation required became all the greater as France was busily decreasing its competitiveness with the introduction of the thirty-five-hour working week just as Germany was making itself more competitive thanks to a series of labour reforms decreasing its real wage growth (the Haartz IV reforms). In addition, following the GFC, Germany instituted a balanced budget policy as a constitutional requirement, a decision that reduced demand in Germany and throughout the eurozone.

The stagnation or decline in workers' living standards also resulted from the monetary policy response to the GFC engineered by then chairman of the US Federal Reserve (the Fed) Ben Bernanke. Drawing lessons from the Great Depression, Bernanke was convinced that intense monetary stimulus was the way to avoid repeating the policy mistakes that had aggravated this crisis of the 1930s. However, the direct beneficiaries of the stimulus – which involved protecting banks from insolvency risk by allowing them to make effortless profits as well as inflating asset prices – were the owners of assets (especially financial assets) as opposed to wage earners. This so-called quantitative easing (QE) thus had highly negative effects in distributional terms; it widened inequalities, all the more so because governments failed to match this unorthodox monetary policy with aggressive fiscal expansion aimed at benefiting lower-income households.

The combined effect of the decline in living standards of wage earners and, as noted in relation to QE, the enhanced rents enjoyed by asset holders led to a de-skilling of the working population. This led to a vicious cycle of slower productivity growth and, ultimately, to the erosion of the social and industrial fabric. In such an environment, the most qualified and talented workers emigrate, further impoverishing the aggregate human capital in their countries of origin.

These pernicious effects of divergent competitiveness inside monetary unions had been demonstrated a mere decade before the launch of the euro by the reunification of Germany. The irrevocable fixing of the East German ostmark against the deutsche mark at parity on 1 July 1990 resulted in the deindustrialisation of East Germany and the migration of around two million young and qualified East Germans (over 10 per cent of the total population of the German Democratic Republic) to West Germany. These effects occurred despite massive fiscal transfers from West to East to the tune of around €1.6 trillion between 1991 and 2015 (Dryancour 2019). A solution to the problems of high unemployment and declining productivity and living standards in the eurozone's less competitive periphery demands a high degree of labour mobility within the EMU – but, in reality, the opposite applies. The geographical mobility inside France is, on average, around 7 per cent, with equivalent figures for Italy and Spain of around 4 per cent; however, less than 0.5 points of these percentages represent people moving between eurozone countries (Amara *et al.* 2016). Some obstacles to mobility are language barriers and the difficulty of leaving behind established communities and social relations. In addition, European social safety nets further reduce the incentive for mobility. The reasons why the EMU has landed in this impasse predate the presidency of Emmanuel Macron. His rise to power outside the established party structure and his subsequent attempts to reform the eurozone should be seen as a symptom rather than a cause of the economic ill effects of the single currency.

TRANSFERS DID NOT HELP

In the period between the launch of the monetary union in 1999 and the GFC in 2007, transfers to less competitive eurozone countries took the form of private sector loans (except in Greece). Much of that was bank lending, offered at low interest rates close to German levels and collateralised by real estate (hence the Spanish and Irish mortgage and housing booms – and then busts). The eurozone's deficit countries lived under a 'soft budget constraint', borrowing money cheaply while delaying unpopular reforms (Fernández-Villaverde, Garicano, and Santos 2013, 151). This phenomenon of increased private borrowing to finance current account deficits was plainly visible as early on as 2002–3 (Honkapohja 2014, 263). All the while, the divergence of competitiveness measured by unit labour costs deepened, with Germany in particular becoming ever more competitive by, in effect, denying its own workers the just fruits of their productive toil (Chen, Milesi-Feretti, and Tressel 2012).

The private sector deleveraging after 2007 resulted in a counterpart expansion of state budget deficits that was aggravated by the need to bail out the liabilities of insolvent banks and by countercyclical fiscal stimulus measures designed to counter the GFC-induced recession (Coenen, Straub, and Trabandt 2012). The dramatic increase in the expansion of budget deficits and public debt levels unsettled financial markets, and the affected countries' bond yields increased sharply. Many EMU members faced a sovereign debt crisis and related systemic banking crises. As we have seen, the response to the eurozone sovereign debt crisis boiled down to emergency liquidity injections – and related relief for the worst-affected countries – conditional on sharp fiscal tightening. This policy was clearly designed to avoid (or limit) losses for the creditors of distressed countries' banks – and, increasingly, governments, as unsustainable post-crisis bank liabilities began to be transferred to sovereign balance sheets.

The political decision by Sarkozy and Merkel in 2010 to introduce private sector involvement (PSI), 'asking creditors, especially banks, to potentially take losses on government debt', vindicated Jean-Claude Trichet, then president of the ECB (2003–11) (Brunnermeier, James, and Landau 2016, 329). PSI meant the end of a single interest rate for sovereign debt. As soon as PSI became official, the cost of borrowing (for the most part, refinancing existing borrowing) for the countries with the worst deficit problems (Greece, Portugal, Ireland, and Spain) became prohibitive; investors lost interest in buying those countries' sovereign debt at interest rates that, however attractive on paper, were clearly unsustainable. Countries in this predicament were described as having 'lost access to the market' (Honkapohja 2014).

In contrast to the 'usual' currency crisis, eurozone members faced the double constraint of having both fixed exchange rates and capital mobility (Pisani-Ferry, Sapir, and Wolff 2013). This meant that it was legal for a Greek person, for instance, to open an account in euros in a German bank, which resulted in the Greek authorities becoming mere spectators of massive capital outflows from their country, unable to manage the interest rate to try to stop those outflows. In large part because balance of payments crises had been foolishly reckoned by the architects of the EMU to be impossible among eurozone members, the EU had no legal basis for intervening; nor did the International Monetary Fund (IMF), as the eurozone lacked a crisis resolution mechanism that would have allowed the restructuring of the sovereign debt of Portugal, Ireland, Greece, and Spain (PIGS) and insolvency procedures for dealing with their banks (Marzinotto, Pisani-Ferry, and Sapir 2010).

A month after the financial tensions surrounding Greece escalated with the coming to power in Athens of the radical Syriza government in January 2015, the ECB decided to stop accepting the paper of Greek banks as collateral against which it would provide liquidity. This step led at the peak of the crisis in July 2015 to the ECB bringing about a partial shutdown of the Greek banking system. This power of the ECB to control democratically elected governments stems from its refinancing facilities, through which eurozone members become dependent on central bank money. These ECB credits are extended without a clear technical evaluation of the collateral or of the implications for the capital of the ECB itself (Buiter, Rahbari, and Michels 2011). If Greece (and/or other troubled eurozone countries) were to leave the monetary union, the collateral it had provided for borrowing from the ECB would be depreciated upon conversion into reinstated local currencies. The European system of central banks would, therefore, see its own equity capital reduced, if not wiped out. If the ECB decided to correct a negative net worth position on its balance sheet by recapitalising itself, this could be inflationary.

Germany would thus be faced with the unappetising choice of tolerating a formally insolvent central bank or inflationary recapitalisation of the central bank (and probably also several commercial banks). This may be why Merkel rejected the possibility aired by her finance minister, Wolfgang Schäuble, in July 2015 to support Greece outside the monetary union. The strong support that she received on this point from her French counterpart, François Hollande, is significant. It may be that Schäuble's proposal was never serious in the first place, but instead designed to deter major eurozone members in economic difficulty, such as France and Italy, from pressuring Germany to accept a different kind of eurozone (i.e. a pooling of fiscal policy); it implied that Germany would be relaxed about the alternative of a eurozone break-up, when, in reality, Germany would be anything but. Imagine, for instance, that Italy decided to leave the eurozone during the 2011–12 crisis: in that case, the single currency would have broken down and, in the resulting losses to the European system of central banks, the share of the Bundesbank alone would have been around €700 billion (Minenna 2016, 89).

EURODOXY IN TROUBLE

The theory of economic integration by distinguished Hungarian economist Bela Balassa posits that monetary union does not work without political integration (Balassa 1961): 'political unity is the glue that holds a monetary union together. Once it dissolves, it is most likely that the monetary union will dissolve' (Bordo and Jonung 1999, 25).

The maintenance of a single currency depends on each member agreeing to enter a cooperative monetary union with all the economic and political constraints attached to such cooperation. The members of a functional monetary union should agree – in the words of John Stuart Mill (if we replace the word 'citizen' with 'government') – to 'be guided, in case of conflicting claims, by another rule than [their] private partialities; to apply at every turn, principles, and maxims which have for their reason of existence the common good' (Mill 1946, 150). Instead, each of the eurozone members follows its own strategy, and this uncooperative dynamic has had dramatic consequences: for instance, by 2020 the real per capita disposable incomes of Italian households were lower than they had been when the euro was launched two decades earlier. Former chief economist of HSBC

Stephen King described this economic setback as 'unprecedented in the developed world during the post-war era' (King 2017, 227). Political and financial market tensions surrounding Italy were rekindled in 2018 when, in an unsurpsing development, a more 'eurosceptic' government came to power. By way of comment on that Italian crisis in May 2018, Yanis Varoufakis posted on his blog an open letter sent to him in July 2015 (when he was still Greece's finance minister). The letter's authors were Professor Paolo Savona, whose euroscepticism had caused the Italian president to veto his appointment as finance minister, and Giulio Tremonti, a former Italian finance minister, and it detailed reforms to the EU that they considered necessary (Varoufakis 2015). The letter started with a quote from 'The future of Europe', a lecture given by French novelist Albert Camus at a conference in Athens in 1955 (Camus and Union Culturelle Gréco-Français 1956). Savona and Tremonti mentioned that, at this conference, participants agreed on there being essentially two structural characteristics of European civilisation: the dignity of the individual, and the critical spirit. They stressed that in 1955, with the horrors of World War II still a fresh memory, Europe's record on human dignity was blemished; but the European *esprit critique* seemed like a solid achievement. There were no doubts about the rationalist Enlightenment vision, which was the engine of continuous progress on the continent, as much in terms of technical and scientific advancements as of political, social, and economic preponderance in the world. According to the letter writers, more than half a century later, human dignity is highly valued, but the force of reason can no longer be relied on to underpin continued progress.

This same line of thought was taken up by Italian economist Roberto Perotti in a column for *La Voce* (12 May 2017), written in reaction to a letter signed by twenty-five Nobel Prize-winning economists published by the newspaper *Le Monde* (*Tribune* 2017). The signatories aimed their fire at Marine Le Pen, the nationalist opponent of Macron in the then imminent French presidential election run-off. They objected to Le Pen's citing some of their work in support of her eurosceptic platform, which included a commitment to leave the euro. Perotti stressed that the principle of authority – in this case, the signatories' status as Nobel laureates – is never a convincing argument to close a debate. In particular, he stated that 'economists like to boast of being hard-wired to debunk. So since when did the authority principle hold sway among them? This situation is starting to look like a small-scale version of the Protestant Reformation. For all the fire and fury of their pronouncements, anathemas, and excommunications, and for all their academic titles and ecclesiastical benefices, the scholastics found themselves swept away by Luther and Calvin' (Perotti 2017).

The dismissal of open discussion out of deference to authority causes the general public to react against being told what they should think by 'establishment' figures; this means they cast their votes in favour of politicians and causes (e.g. Trump and Brexit) precisely *because*, rather than *despite*, the warnings from the establishment of the dire consequences of such choices. Back in the mid-nineteenth century, Bastiat warned against the denial of dignity and agency to the general public that stems from this paternalist style, which he characterised in these terms: '[T]he government should know everything and foresee everything in order to manage the lives of the people, and the people need only let themselves be taken care of .... Nothing is more senseless than to base so many expectations on the state, that is, to assume the existence of collective wisdom and foresight after taking for granted the existence of individual imbecility and improvidence' (Bastiat 1845, II.15:58–9, quoted in McCloskey 2010, 428).

When politicians resort to political pledges that they cannot honour, reality catches up with them, at which point voters tend to retaliate against the 'lie'. The public opposition to 'reforms' deemed necessary to comply with EMU rules but perceived as painful by voters has given rise to widespread public protests and the electoral defeat of incumbent governments, as in France (May 2012), Portugal (March 2011), Spain (July 2011) and Italy (March 2018). In other words, these democratic elections revealed public discontent with the effects of the European political elite's pet project: the euro. By having economic effects that erode public confidence in the EU, the single currency has the potential to undermine the European project as a whole.

This risk shows up strongly in France. In 2019, Eurobarometer, which regularly surveys public opinion throughout the EU, found that, while in twenty member states a majority of respondents said they trusted the EU (up from seventeen the previous year), France had one of the lowest proportions of respondents trusting the EU (33 per cent); this compares with 29 per cent in the United Kingdom, 32 per cent in Greece, and 37 per cent in Italy. Altogether more concerning, given that France was one of the founders of the EU, was that only 50 per cent of French respondents were optimistic about the future. The other EU member states were more positive, with the exception of Greece, where 51 per cent were pessimistic (Standard Eurobarometer 2019).

From the start of the EMU project, a clear divide was visible in France between public support for the single currency and the political elite's determination to proceed with the project. The chief exhibit here is the September 1992 referendum on whether to ratify the Maastricht Treaty. The first two years of the Mitterrand presidency (1981–3), during which financial market pressures had forced to a halt an expansive economic reflation, had left a deep scar. That experience convinced the technocrats that sovereignty, for which they had been trained to do battle, no longer existed – at least in the monetary sphere. In turn, this helped to reinforce the idea of a European solution to France's tussle with financial market constraints. In practice, that meant seeking some leverage over the Bundesbank through a single currency. In the run-up to that 1992 referendum, therefore, the media and the political class launched a vigorous publicity campaign in favour of the proposed single currency. Their propaganda included such evocative slogans as: 'Maastricht is the Treaty of Versailles without war' (Dedieu *et al.* 2014, 90).

But the French are hard to persuade. They voted yes, but by such a narrow margin that many have wondered if the hand of the 'Florentine' Mitterrand rested lightly on the scales to tip the result in his favour: just over 51.04 per cent of voters approved the treaty, with 69 per cent of registered voters taking part in the referendum (Riding 1992). This episode suggests that France will never accept a full-blooded federal Europe transcending the nation states. It will tolerate closer integration only so long as fundamental French national interests remain unchallenged.

This was made even clearer when, in another referendum in 2005, French voters rejected the proposed new European constitution. With the eurozone sovereign debt crisis that broke out in 2010, several troubled countries – Greece, Ireland, Portugal, and Spain – found themselves 'welcoming' IMF staff (not seen in this mode in a rich country since 1977 in the United Kingdom) as part of a 'troika', which also included officials from the EC and the ECB. The public in the affected countries, despite staging various strikes and protests, did not have much of a voice and had to accept the terms of the agreement between their governments and the troika. Satisfaction with democracy in EU countries receded on average by seven percentage points between autumn 2007 and 2011, while trust in national parliaments decreased by eight percentage points (Armingeon and Guthman 2014).

The rise of challenger populist parties dates to that time, reflecting the disenchantment and frustration of millions of voters who just want their voices to be heard. This sense of hopelessness stems from the general blockage besetting both society and the economy. The origins and nature of that blockage might best be summed up by the old saying 'The road to hell is paved with good intentions', the relevant intention in this case being the launch of the EMU for the sake of prosperity.

From 2015 onwards, the damaging effects of internal devaluation started to be softened by the ECB's resorting to QE. This had the intended effect of weakening the euro relative to other major global currencies, but it failed to deliver a positive boost to demand on the required scale. A core problem with this tacit ECB strategy of targeting a weaker euro was that the competitiveness gap that matters is between Germany and its eurozone trading partners, not between the eurozone and the rest of the world. One effect of the ECB's QE was to make the French political class forgetful that 'government spending is no free lunch' (Barro 1974). The French government seized the opportunity to borrow more.

There has never been a shortage of authoritative and respected voices questioning the standard doctrines of the EMU. American–Canadian economist Andrew K. Rose compared sixty-nine cases in which countries have left currency unions with sixty-one cases in which countries have not left. After reviewing these experiences of monetary unions, Rose concluded that 'countries leaving currency unions tend to be larger, richer, and more democratic; they also tend to experience somewhat higher inflation'. He continued by saying that, 'most strikingly, there is remarkably little macroeconomic volatility around the time of currency union dissolutions, and only a poor linkage between monetary and political independence. Indeed, aggregate macroeconomic features of the economy do a poor job in predicting currency union exits' (Rose 2007, 127). Even Belgian economist and supporter of the EMU Paul de Grauwe noted that a single interest rate for all EMU members would be 'too low for the booming countries and too high for the countries in recession'. This suggests that the deficit and surplus countries would gain by having separate currencies (de Grauwe 2013, 6).

Leaving the eurozone in its present form is a fundamental precondition for France to generate the economic growth momentum it needs to address the wide-ranging structural problems discussed in this book. It would also be the best way to strengthen the European project. The trouble is that such views are rarely, if ever, heard, as public political debates are what terrify the eurozone establishment the most, lest their conclusions resemble that of Hans Christian Andersen's tale *The Emperor's New Clothes*. The narrow oligarchy that, as we saw in the previous chapter, wields decisive influence in today's France is always ready to stir up popular fears in order to defend their utopian dreams.

LEAVING THE EURO

To sum up the argument of this chapter: Europe has a 'fair weather' monetary union, i.e. it only works normally when economic conditions are good. It cracks as soon as economic difficulties arise, for lack of adequate mutual adjustment mechanisms between participating countries. Maintaining a single monetary policy in nineteen heterogeneous states is at best a challenge, at worst a folly. Without the ability to use monetary and exchange rate policy instruments, member states are forced, as we have seen, to resort to 'social' devaluations to improve their competitiveness. Such policies widen inequalities, curb domestic demand, delay economic recovery, and accentuate the rise in unemployment. These dire social and economic effects in turn threaten to poison relations within Europe. The myth that the gold standard brought stability and prosperity in the imaginary world of the technocrats was so strong that they had to design a replica: the euro. Just as with the gold standard in the interwar period, this euro, which claimed to banish the poisons of nationalism, became a threat to the health of European democracies (Kawalec, Pytlarczyk, and Kamiński 2020). French economist Jean-Pierre Vesperini does not hesitate to compare the introduction of the euro to the defeat of 1940: 'The common roots of the euro disaster and the defeat of June 1940 should ... be noted – namely, belief in outmoded concepts. The approach of the political leadership and General Staff was right at the end of the First World War but had ceased to be so twenty years after. Likewise, the approach of

Robert Schuman and Jean Monnet was no longer valid twenty years later' (Vesperini 2013, 211). The deindustrialisation and the loss of know-how in France and other deficit eurozone members are the bitter fruits of this error of judgment. The various drawbacks of the EMU exposed by the GFC and the ensuing eurozone sovereign crisis were aggravated by a core element of the eurozone policy response to those crises, that is, treaty-enshrined tightness of fiscal policy (the Fiscal Compact of 2011). An empirical study published in February 2019 analysed the winners and losers of the single currency over its twenty years of existence (Gasparotti and Kullas 2019). The model estimated the GDP of each eurozone member had the euro never existed. The findings are striking: as of 2017, output worth €3,591 billion in current prices had been foregone by France since the creation of the euro in 1999, which is €55,996 per person over the period 1999–2017. The equivalent numbers for Italy, a country that comes out of this study even worse than France, are €4,325 billion (€73,605 per Italian). For Germany, by contrast, these two numbers were positive: €1,893 billion in incremental GDP or €23,116 per inhabitant (the Netherlands boasted similar numbers). Two starkly contrasting ways ahead emerge from this analysis: either we continue with the euro, though the project would have to be completed with a political dimension being added to the single currency; or we return to the franc in order to regain competitiveness, which in the short-term would have destabilising effects on corporate debt and place severe constraints on economic policy.

To start with the first route, via fiscal and political union: based on recent experience since Macron came to power, the prognosis is bleak. In answer to his core proposal of giving the eurozone some fiscal capacity, his German counterpart Angela Merkel gave a polite *nein* – while, of course, taking care to dress up that rejection in the form of a pretended agreement (France Diplomacy 2018). Just as Macron had said *non!* when Merkel proposed a single European seat at the UN Security Council, now Germany and the other more competitive eurozone countries remained unmoved by Macron's call to advance – *En Marche!* The coronavirus pandemic changed this picture to the extent that, in May 2020, Germany agreed to what might prove to be an embryonic fiscal union. The mechanism would involve the EC, acting for this purpose like a real government of Europe, borrowing nearly 5 per cent of the eurozone's GDP – with the eurozone countries taking proportional responsibility for repaying that debt. The eurozone also agreed that the Commission could disburse this 'recovery fund' based on countries' relative need, rather than traditional conditionality. A long and politically fraught road lies between this one-off measure in response to a severe (pandemic) shock and a true fiscal union.

The difficulties do not only lie in the scale of the fiscal transfers that would be needed, assuming that such transfers ever become politically acceptable in Germany on a permanent basis (Sapir 2012). The more serious problem is that such massive fiscal transfers would not have the desired effect of building a European nation. To understand why, one need only recall the results of this very same political economy formula in Germany, Italy, and even the United States. The old East Germany remains depopulated and mired in weak productivity, despite massive fiscal transfers in the three decades since its monetary union with West Germany at an overvalued 1:1 exchange rate. In Italy, many more decades of a similar relationship between north and south have failed to lift the Mezzogiorno out of its 'poor cousin' predicament. In the United States, net federal transfers between rich and poor states have not rescued the latter from relative poverty (Kawalec, Pytlarczyk, and Kamiński 2020). The American example highlights how political union must come first, underpinning fiscal union, and not the other way around. In other words, even these unsatisfactory results of a full fiscal union remain theoretical until the formation of its corollary – namely, a political union (Mathieu and Sterdyniak 2019). The creation of any such European federal state would depend on meeting a crucial precondition: 'the prior full consent of its citizens' (Sinn 2014, 357). If consent is the essential prerequisite for a successful democracy, it is more like an impediment to be worked around for technocrats. Vesperini addresses this issue by calling on the principle of French historian Marc Bloch, that 'anachronism is the historian's mortal sin', contending that the time when a United States of Europe might have come about has long since long passed (Vesperini 2013, 211–12). The French want to remain what they are (Gauchet 2016); the Germans do not want a 'transfer Europe'; and most eurozone members want to retain their national discretion to set migration, education, and social policy preferences. The truth is that any solution to the euro crisis that does not allow exchange rates to correspond to countries' underlying competitiveness is ultimately unsustainable – as has been

shown by many financial crises caused by fixed exchange rate regimes that were maintained for too long (Granville 2013).

It is time, therefore, to envisage an exit scenario along the lines
suggested by, for instance, Stefan Kawalec, Ernest Pytlarczyk, and
Kamil Kamiński (Kawalec, Pytlarczyk, and Kamiński 2020). They
suggest that Germany and other surplus countries should be the
first to leave in order to minimise the risk of panic. Although this
would be anathema to the present German political class, the attractions for Germany of leaving the euro may grow as the ECB's
monetary policy continues to move away from the principles of the
Bundesbank, and as inflationary pressures rise in Germany. The
temporary loss of competitiveness from leaving the euro and returning to a revalued deutsche mark would be outweighed by the
avoidance of costly transfers to troubled eurozone countries. It is
likely that the strongest opposition to a return to national currencies would in any case come not from Germany but from France.
The whole generation of political decision makers who came to
power in the 1980s and 1990s has taken care to stifle any mention
of a return to the franc. Some statistics are quickly tabulated to give
credibility to their claims of the apocalyptic consequences of aban-
doning the euro and, with that, their honour is safe. It is easy to
silence dissident voices advocating a return to the franc – just accuse
them of nationalism and apply to them the stigma of the far right.

This is a strange mindset in a world where most advanced industrial countries have their own currencies yet are not xenophobic or
fascist, have open borders, and encourage international trade. In
fact, a complete dissolution of the euro would have both positive
macroeconomic and democratic consequences: France could decide on an interest rate adapted to its level of structural inflation,
its unemployment rate, and its preferred level of public expenditure, linked to its social model. This would suffice to empower the
Bank of France. By recovering its monetary sovereignty, the French
central bank could finance the budget deficit and thus provide
oxygen to the economy, allowing the state to reduce its massive debt
without needing to resort to new tax increases or to severe public
spending cuts. The financial markets would anticipate a currency
depreciation, but they would not anticipate a government default
or a crisis. In addition, uncomfortably high interest rates would not
be a foregone conclusion of a euro-exit, as confidence in a reinvig-
orated French economy would attract capital inflows. And, even in

the event of somewhat higher initial interest rates, the exchange rate depreciation would have an expansionary effect that could revive not only the French economy but also the spirit of French citizens, who might at last feel they are part of a national community that can make its own choices. A point-by-point retort to the 'project fear' arguments about leaving the euro has been supplied by French economist Jacques Sapir (Sapir 2017). I can only add a further question: Why would it be more difficult to exit the euro than to enter it, as if some infallible principle dictated that, like death itself, the euro is irreversible, final, universal, and inevitable?

3

The 'Nation State' Utopia:
The Village Is My Nation

Is a nation a community? The premise of this question, as posed by British economist Paul Collier, is that, for most people, the feeling of belonging to a community and sharing a common identity is essential for mental and material well-being (Collier 2014, 234–7). The word 'country' translates into French as *le pays*; yet, for my grandmother (1893–1988), *le pays* was not France, the nation state, with its internationally recognised borders, but the village where she lived, for this was her community. A stranger was therefore someone who was not from *le pays*, and this term was applied to any outsider: even one from the village just a few miles distant. In the absence of known reasons to the contrary, such a person was looked upon with a certain mistrust. The people in my grandmother's community spoke the same language – in the familiar sense of that phrase, meaning they understood every nuance of each other's speech. She knew every single member of the village and their families, and attendance at Sunday mass provided them all with a reliable opportunity to exchange news – mostly in French, but sometimes using words from the patois Côte d'Orien.

This type of particularist community spirit is inimical to the vision of the nation that was first aggressively articulated by the Jacobins, that most doctrinaire and uncompromising of the revolutionary factions. Their vision of the nation held that all citizens should share a unique cultural identity, implicitly favouring centralisation over regional diversity (Bachofen 2012). By dint of holding French nationality, an individual consents to the rule of law and the customary underpinnings of that law (including *laïcité*, the principle that the sacred (religious) sphere should not overlap with the public sphere), and they accept French culture, including the French language (Safran 1991).

Until the Revolution, a French individual was a subject of the king. When Louis XVI was executed on 21 January 1793, the Jacobins proclaimed: 'The king is dead, long live the nation!' The judicially murdered king was replaced by a new nation of people and its motto: liberty, equality, and fraternity. The revolutionary proclamation of the people's sovereignty created the nation state, where 'nation' meant a community of citizens wishing to live under the same laws. The Enlightenment thus associated the nation with a democratic basis for political legitimacy. There is a distinction between what makes an individual identify with a national community and their status as a citizen of the Republic, even if the two modes of belonging overlap, given that customs and laws support each other. The nation unites people through shared customs, inherited values, social practices, and language. Included under these headings are religious traditions and artistic, festive, and culinary practices, but not regulations and laws (Safran 1991). The Republic, based on law – starting with a basic law or constitution – frames this national way of life but is not synonymous with it. Yet in the revolutionary conception that gave birth to the republican government in France, the *General Will* unites all citizens in their adherence to the Republic's centralised political institutions. According to this vision, being French means, first and foremost, supporting those republican institutions.

But, contrary to the Jacobin myth, secularism did not begin in 1789, let alone on 9 December 1905, the date of a landmark law enshrining *laïcité*. The 1905 law may be seen as the modern product of experience built up over a millennium in which religion was subordinated to nation building. Theologian Jean-François Colosimo offers a vivid historical synthesis of French secularism, signifying in this context the assertion of temporal power in relation to organised religion (Colosimo 2019). Seeing this secularism as a constant distinguishing feature of French history and politics, Colosimo traces its origins back to the Capetians, the monarchical dynasty that founded the French state as a continuous political entity which exists to this day. It was then that the particular character of France's relations with the Church was born. Despite all the tumults and conflicts of the centuries from Philippe le Bel to de Gaulle, the central government of France has always sought to exert control over religion. As a result, there is a *French* Catholicism and Protestantism, a *French* Judaism, and Islam. Colosimo's present-day concern is that the French state has relaxed this millennial approach as regards Islam by allowing the Muslim community to be penetrated by hardline Salafism that is intrinsically hostile to the Republic. His conclusion is somber: while *laïcité* was once the crucible of the nation state, binding citizens together under a shared set of rights and obligations, the focus of *laïcité* has now shifted to the purely legal sphere in a way that erodes the nation state. The French state's practice of secularism used to define the permitted scope of religion, but now it guarantees immunity even for those beliefs that undermine the nation state.

All citizens are French either by inheritance or by choice, and all are subject to the rule of the Republic. The state thus becomes the guarantor of the national political identity, and state and nation merge in the sense that all citizens share the same set of political values. A core value is pluralism, which can tolerate all kinds of contradiction except challenges to the very existence of contradiction. This framework allows individual citizens to shape their own future with the support of a society ruled by law. Here, then, is the social contract of the modern republican version of the French state.

Since the Revolution, political authorities have sought to deepen national unity by promoting a common language and cultural model through compulsory and generalised education. Despite the millennial existence of a continuous French state, nation building has thus been a belated process. Until the end of the nineteenth century in France, a large fraction of the population did not speak the French language in its official standard form – codified and policed under state auspices – and sometimes did not even understand it.

The Jacobin view of the nation state has faced various challenges, leading to what American political scientist William Safran and other thinkers have called the 'crisis of the nation state' (Safran 1991, 219). A state that claims to be the expression of a unified national community will find its legitimacy in jeopardy if that community is riven with internal fractures for whatever reason (whether because of some deep historical tensions or because of very contemporary economic dislocations). Danish political scientist Ole Wæver summarises in telling terms the French version of this existential threat: 'If a state loses sovereignty, it has not survived as a state; if a society loses its identity, it has not survived as itself' (Wæver 1995, 405).

Until the 1980s, France was relatively self-contained as regards its political and cultural identity, thanks to protectionist measures that fuelled the illusion of economic and cultural grandeur. Cocooned by this confident self-assurance, the French were untroubled by anxieties related to identity: being French was enough. But the acceleration of globalisation, involving as it does intense economic and cultural exchanges and the standardisation of lifestyles, has called this certainty into question. After their 1940 humiliation, the technocrats decided to restore grandeur by means of a rapid modernisation designed to create a strong economy. This project eroded what had been the country's underlying social fabric of villages founded on agriculture and its associated family structures. The focus on productivity and competitiveness that was to enhance national pride led to growing disorientation in French society.

Protecting national identity, which always comes with some mythical components, already seems an ambitious enough project for a self-contained state; but since part of the functions of the French state have been delegated to the European level, the nation remains alone to defend its identity: 'For if Jacobinism has validity beyond France (as the revolutionaries claimed), then it must apply to Europe after 1992: if the state creates a nation, then a suprastate might lead to the creation of a European citizenship and, in consequence, the creation of a "supranation" that transcends Frenchness' (Safran 1991, 236). Indeed, the French revolutionary project inspired by the principle of natural law transcending origins and history might be reckoned the founding step of the European idea. In this, the technocrats are the true heirs of Jacobinism. Anyone inclined to dismiss such visions of the EU as too abstract or unrealistic to be taken seriously should recall that present-day nation states are equally artificial and relatively recent constructions.

The crisis of the nation state appears to hinge on a tension between the technocratic dream of economic prowess, achieved in part by deepening the European project and strengthening other external ties, and the general population of France, which remains attached to a specific French identity and feels increasingly unrepresented and unprotected by the contemporary regime. It may be time to proclaim that the nation state is dead. The goal of economic prowess may be viewed by its elite exponents as a patriotic project, since, in their view, only then will France have the global influence – projected in large part through an integrated European economic superpower – to defend and promote its interests in a superpower-dominated world. But this elite is also driven by a more selfish desire for gratifying global power status, and it has no patience – but rather contempt – for the obstacles and brakes created by the different priorities and attachments of ordinary French citizens. Emmanuel Macron is clearly a vessel of that elite mentality, though the harsh experiences of his presidency may end up providing him with the kind of humane education that, in general, a country's citizenry might hope its leaders received *before* they came to power.

Cross-disciplinary scholarship highlights from many angles the intuitive reality that people's well-being depends not only on their material sufficiency but also on relational and subjective circumstances. Economic policy often appears to be based on the assumption that *homo economicus* is a nomad who moves wherever employment and material opportunities are to be found. This assumption ignores that having a sense of belonging is as important to people's quality of life as material conditions (McGregor and Pouw 2017). The myth of *homo economicus* overlooks the broad springs of economic behaviour stemming from the interaction of personal and collective motivations reflected in social norms and formal institutions. Taking account of these realities seems all the more important for the proper cooperative functioning of a democratic society.

Such community spirit was much in evidence as the yellow vests movement unfolded. While local amenities in the 'peripheral France' of small towns and villages had withered for half a century, there was an uptick in the bureaucratic trend of constructing roundabouts – an approach to traffic management imported from the United Kingdom that became known in France during the 1970s as the 'English Roundabout' (Vermeren 2018). The yellow vests' frequent choice of these gyratory rings as protest sites was a statement about the impoverishment of community life. The following sections explore the various ways in which the fracturing of the national community, as visibly and dramatically expressed by the *gilets jaunes*, threatens the legitimacy of the French nation state.

THE NATION STATE FAILS THE TAXPAYER

The nineteenth-century economist Léon Walras was an early French articulator of the principles behind the rebellious American colonists' call for 'no taxation without representation'. In his *Elements of Pure Economics* (1874), Walras highlighted that, behind the state, there are the taxpayers, and public consent to taxation signifies acceptance of the duty to pay taxes as a social requirement for belonging to a community (Walras 1926).

American political scientist Vanessa Williamson found that Americans see paying their taxes as a source of dignity, but only if they feel that they benefit from their taxes – or, at least, that the government is spending the tax revenue it receives in the public interest (Williamson 2017). Williamson's conclusion is that fiscal policy should be transparent and that policymakers should be made more accountable. Paul Collier echoes this thinking by stressing the importance of the ethical rationale for tax compliance (Collier 2018). If the perception is that the tax is fair and transparent, then the citizen makes a civic gesture by paying willingly. Such perceptions will contribute to a broader level of trust in public authorities – trust that needs to be constantly maintained and renewed (Delalande 2011). In cases where those perceptions and underlying public trust are lacking, government instability beckons (Davies 1962; Gurr 1970).

The French Revolution was born in large part out of contestation of the state's financial opacity at the end of the eighteenth century as well as out of resentment caused by the perceived injustice of taxation (Colliard and Montialoux 2007). The interlinked fiscal and military administration of the royal government engendered a large officialdom that fuelled perceptions of the taxation system as opaque and unfair: 'What the royal subjects of every social class appear to have passionately hated – far more than tax rates, onerous or not – was an inconsistent, arbitrary, Byzantine system plagued with incompetence and abuse of both taxpayers and the system itself' (Chanel 2015, 65).

The Declaration of the Rights of Man and of the Citizen (26 August 1789) can be read as a charter for fair and rational taxation. Articles 13, 14, and 15 defined trust, consent, and accountability as the foundations of taxation. Another important principle articulated in those articles is that tax is a payment for services rendered (broadly defined as the state's capacity to provide public goods and defray the associated administrative costs). As for the declaration's assertion (Article 15) about the accountability of all public agents to society, this was transplanted into the preamble of the Fifth Republic's Constitution (4 October 1958), and the constitutional value of this principle was recognised by the Constitutional Council in

1971. Yet the realisation of this accountability principle never fails to disappoint.

The evolution of the modern French taxation system differs from its peer group quantitatively more than qualitatively. The use of tax revenues to provide public goods was expanded in the twentieth century into an extensive system of redistribution designed to correct market failures and their consequences, such as unemployment and poverty. The launch of this redistributive function in France was mainly the achievement of the Popular Front government that came to power in the wake of the Great Depression. The pursuit by these means of a fairer society raises questions about the appropriate limits of state intervention in the economic and social spheres, and about the dividing line between the public and private sectors (Piketty 2001). Concerns about the excessive cost and poor efficiency of this state-run redistribution resulted, from the 1970s onwards, in the accretion of yet more bureaucratic regulatory powers aimed at promoting economic efficiency. By the end of the century, another layer of fiscal policy appeared as a result of the Maastricht Treaty.

The last component of the Republic's motto encapsulates the key challenge for such systems of redistributive function as fairness or 'equity'. It is as if the revolutionary proclamation of *fraternité* betrayed an anxiety that it might be lacking in French society. Deep societal fraternity will always be required to cope with tension between citizens' dual status as taxpayers on the one hand and generally dissatisfied public services users and recipients of welfare payments on the other. Most French presidents start their term with promises to reduce taxes and public spending. Yet France remains the country with the heaviest tax burden. In 2018, the first full year of Macron's presidency, French tax revenues of 46.1 per cent of GDP were no lower than those of the previous year, and this against an average of 34.4 per cent of GDP in the whole group of OECD countries. The average marginal rates of several taxes are lower than the OECD average: for example, personal income tax yields 18.6 per cent of GDP compared with the OECD average of 23.9 per cent; VAT accounts for 15.3 per cent (versus 20.2 per cent); and corporate profit tax generates just 5.1 per cent of French GDP (versus 9.3 per cent). The French system imposes a uniquely high burden, however, on payrolls – employers' social security and related contributions amount to 36 per cent of GDP compared with an average of 26 per cent in the other OECD countries (see https://stats.oecd.org/).

This may be an effect of history, as the state budget has been in deficit since 1974. Even before then, France was among the countries with the highest tax burden. It was later overtaken by the Scandinavian countries until the 2010s, when it regained the lead (Granville 1998). Cuts in some taxes are almost always offset by increases in others: for instance, Macron reduced wealth and profit taxes but widened the tax base by introducing the taxation of personal income at source (i.e. on a withholding basis). Despite the traditional social consensus in favour of well-funded public services and generous welfare, the actual system of redistribution is held in low esteem. Large portions of the redistributed resources have become various kinds of rents captured by vested interests that, even as they suck the economy's lifeblood, foster what has proved to be insurmountable resistance to change.

The system of taxation is the subject of many criticisms: it is perceived as unfair and arbitrary, which, in turn, makes tax compliance burdensome. French economist Jean Tirole has observed a rare consensus among economists that the tax code should be simplified (Tirole 2016, 84). The opaque and complex tax system has been satirically labelled *millefeuille fiscal* (*millefeuille* being the name of a venerable multi-layered pastry). Running as they do through many subnational tiers – regions, counties (*départements*), communes, and intercommunal groupings – these layers reduce the effectiveness of many public policies and lead to excessive civil service employment. The extent of economic rents, privileges, official norms, and regulations acts as a brake on the economy (Lambert and Boulard 2013). As Georges Clémenceau said, 'France is an extremely fertile country: bureaucrats are planted in its soil, and taxes spring up.'

This 'millefeuille' problem has been starkly exposed by the director of iFrap, Agnès Verdier-Molinié, in her book *En marche vers l'immobilisme* (Verdier-Molinié 2018). She shows that the administrative burden on citizens and businesses resulting from the post-war process of stacking up administrative strata was willed and engineered by what she calls the 'technostructure' (meaning the enarchs – including, as we have seen, most of the top political leadership since Giscard) and the trade unions. The combined result spanning central government, local authorities, regional development agencies, and the social security administration has resulted in such a high degree of complexity and cost for businesses that simplification of the fiscal system is almost impossible. Swathes of well-intentioned public spending are funnelled into an engine of rent extraction, characterised by an explosion of public sector jobs in proliferating layers of state bureaucracy and agencies.

The tax administration is so badly organised and backward that tax fraud is vigorously combatted while misappropriation in public spending is virtually ignored. There is no reliable data on the embezzlement and culpable wastage of public funds. While identified 'social' fraud amounts to around €8.5 billion per year, it seems safe to double that number to account for the undetected portion. The laws and regulations governing the execution of public spending might be extremely strict, but their implementation is lax, and anti-fraud coordination – for example, between the databases of the tax and social security administrations – is non-existent. Tax and social fraud are often interdependent, as seen in such widespread phenomena as black-market moonlighting, social security contribution evasion, and VAT fraud. Tackling this problem will require a restructuring of public services. A more robust system might centre on issuing to citizens a single card, embedded with their biometric data, which would be their key to access health care and other public services. As things stand, entitlement to health care is attested by a more primitive version of such a card, known as the *carte vitale*; however, the number of valid *cartes vitales* in circulation greatly exceeds the country's overall population of around 67 million people. A report on this social fraud problem prepared in 2019 by two parliamentarians at the request of the prime minister left the big questions hanging (Grandjean and Goulet 2019). The presentation of the report's preliminary conclusions in September of that year produced so many controversies around the figures that the final published version omitted any such quantification, on the grounds that it had been made impossibly difficult to do so by uncooperative administrations. This episode reinforced the consensus that the true scale of this problem remains hidden and underestimated.

The exact number and scope of all taxes is not easily established either, since there is no published official count. Verdier-Molinié listed 380 different taxes: 150 directed at enterprises and 230 directed at households. These include 470 tax loopholes and exemptions, and 192 taxes yielding less than €150 million, many with obscure rationales and some costing more to collect than the revenue they provide to the budget (Verdier-Molinié 2015). A precise count of their number is difficult and remains questionable because it is often possible to consider that a contribution is only a variant of another existing tax, or conversely that the same tax covers several different contributions. The only certainty is that the list is so long that nobody can keep count. The resulting deterrent to economic activity is aggravated by the dense and often distorting web of state regulation and interference that affects all levels of the economy. One recent estimate of this burden has counted around 400,000 standards, 125,000 decrees, and 10,500 laws (Greef-Madelin and Paya 2020).

Successive governments have introduced numerous tax offsets, credits, and exemptions, often without a distributional or other clear rationale. It is a mystery, for instance, that foie gras should benefit from a reduced VAT rate – or, rather, it *would* be mysterious in a rational fiscal construction, as opposed to one where what Americans call the 'pork barrel' holds considerable sway. The more taxes are invented, the more numerous are the accompanying tax breaks: these cover a wide range of areas, from agriculture to public broadcasting, with cited rationales from territorial cohesion to environmental protection – not to mention the special needs of the overseas territories (*départements d'outre-mer*). Tax loopholes (*niches fiscales*) cost around €100 billion in foregone budget revenue in 2018 (or 4.4 per cent of that year's GDP) (Deharo 2018). This infernal tax complexity is incompatible with the core principles of sound taxation, such as neutrality and impartiality. It generates uncertainty through ceaseless tax code amendments, affecting investment and saving decisions.

Yet, even if we all agree that the tax system needs to be reformed and simplified, the question is, how? The task of ironing out this complexity seems to be one of paralyzing complexity itself.

I noted earlier a school of thought on the causes of the French Revolution that sees the old monarchy as having been pushed over the brink not so much due to the level of taxation as due to the system's inconsistency, opacity, and unfairness. While the public may tolerate taxation, their tolerance will not be limitless in the face of arbitrariness: once the limit is breached, the negative effects of increased taxes – distorted incentives, tax evasion, brain and wealth drains – will start to make themselves felt. In 2012, tax evasion was estimated to have resulted in assets worth €600 billion being hidden abroad (Peillon 2012). That same year, a Senate Commission of Enquiry gave a range of between €30 billion and €60 billion for the annual cost to public finances of tax evasion, even admitting that this estimate was probably 'on the low side' (Rabreau 2016). In early 2013, a body called *La finance solidaire*, by extrapolating the results of tax audits and consolidating existing studies, calculated that the total annual amount of 'various forms of illegal avoidance of tax' was between €60 billion and €80 billion – that is, about 20 per cent of the country's gross tax revenue.

A considerable economic literature has attempted to determine the limit of the tax burden: the line beyond which taxation becomes economically unbearable. The most famous answer to this question remains that of Arthur Laffer, whose reasoning provided the inspiration for President Reagan's economic programme. Laffer claimed that the best way to generate higher tax revenue would be to lower taxes, as that would stimulate economic growth and activity. In other words, tax cuts pay for themselves. His idea was a simple one: 'Too much tax kills tax' (Laffer and Moore 2011, 57). Once a country reaches the top of the so-called Laffer curve, higher taxes fail to raise more revenues and instead only manage to impede growth. Successful Scandinavian-style models avoid reaching the top of the curve because they have higher-quality public services financed by higher taxation: these generate productivity gains and, hence, incremental economic growth, which allows these good public services to be financed sustainably without further increases in tax rates. In short, an equilibrium is reached when high tax levels are matched by the enhanced provision of public goods and services.

Critics are prompt to emphasise that the optimal taxation rate is difficult to estimate and that Laffer overlooked the benefits of taxation to the community (Mankiw 2019). Some empirical studies have questioned the premise that higher taxation discourages people and thereby reduces the level of economic activity and hence the tax base. There is no reason to assume the relationship between tax revenue and tax rates is regular and predictable. The equilibrium point at which a government collects the most revenue possible without dragging down the economy is impossible to know and varies by country. Such controversies often ignore the key questions of whether certain kinds of tax reduction lead to faster economic growth, and to what degree higher growth will produce higher overall tax revenue.

Mathias Trabandt and Harald Uhlig calculated tax rates from 1995 to 2007 assuming fixed productivity growth and no labour mobility between the United States and the EU. They found that the United States could 'afford' to increase tax revenues by 30 per cent or 6 per cent by raising taxes on payroll or income and capital, respectively. The equivalent scope for hiking tax rates without losing revenue in the fourteen EU countries studied was 8 per cent and 1 per cent. The results of that study showed considerable variations between EU countries. For instance, the United Kingdom could raise labour taxes by 17 per cent, France by 5 per cent, Italy by 4 per cent, and Belgium by 3 per cent. The results for taxes on income and capital were that only one additional per cent could be raised in the group of EU countries considered, and zero in France, Italy, and Belgium. Interestingly, the model found that, for the United States, 32 per cent of a labour tax cut and 51 per cent of a capital tax cut would be self-financing; the equivalent figures for the EU countries were 54 per cent and 79 per cent, respectively. These rose to 62 per cent and 88 per cent in the case of France. The authors conclude that 'there rarely is a free lunch due to tax cuts. However, a substantial fraction of the lunch will be paid for by the efficiency gains in the economy due to tax cuts' (Trabandt and Uhlig 2009, 27). Note that for the purpose of this study, the authors had to assume constant labour mobility. In practice, however, where mobility is relatively easy for the WEIRD not only in a legal sense but also in geographical, linguistic, and cultural terms, the top of the Laffer curve will be reached more quickly. To put it another way, once the limit of tolerance for higher taxation is reached, people will leave.

Emmanuel Macron seemed aware of this threat when he implemented a partial abolition of the wealth tax (*impôt de solidarité sur la fortune* – ISF) that, as noted in chapter 1, helped end his political honeymoon. First introduced by Mitterrand in 1982, and since repeatedly modified, this ISF exemplifies the flaws of the tax system – in particular, its complexity and low yields (iFrap 2005). Wealthy taxpayers can afford the most sophisticated professional advice on how to structure their assets in a way that minimises or altogether eliminates ISF liabilities, and the official ISF regulations themselves offer multiple complex channels to avoid having to pay the tax. (The list of exemptions and allowable deductions is a long one, including business assets, art collections, and 75 per cent of the value of forest lands.) In 2015, only 400,000 households paid any ISF tax sums, which amounted to just 1.8 per cent of that year's net tax revenue.

A core feature of the ISF is that it targets stocks rather than flows. It imposes a cash levy expressed as a percentage of asset values, regardless of whether the assets in question have yielded a cash return; this is unlike the taxation of inheritance or capital gains, for example, which targets wealth but in such a way that tax liabilities arise only in connection with transactions or transfers. The most obvious damage caused by the ISF is that it created an incentive for business owners to leave the country (in the sense of ensuring that they were no longer tax residents in France) and a disincentive for international companies to locate their European headquarters in France. Their executives, paying income tax on their salaries, had no desire to pay additional levies on their assets. Reforms by centre–right governments in the first decade of this century attempted to address this problem by capping wealthy taxpayers' ISF liability to a percentage of their actual cash income in the relevant tax year, but Socialist president Hollande then reinstated the wealth tax in its 'full glory' in 2012. Macron's reform of the ISF was an attempt to encourage wealthy French taxpayers to invest in business by limiting the scope of the tax to real estate assets (in other words, by exempting all financial assets). The tax burden on investment income was reduced with a view to attract investors into the country. No other president before Macron attempted such a thorough and rational reform of this tax, which, however ineffective in practice, remains a symbol of the egalitarian ideal.

Many studies of the negative effects of taxation move from the general problem of tax constraining economic activity to the specific issue of tax afflicting business payrolls and adversely affecting employment (Romer and Romer 2010). This most damaging form of taxation is a speciality of the French system. French public spending is funded by a mixture of ballooning government debt and a skewing of the burden of a complex plethora of taxes and quasi-taxes (also known as 'social contributions') onto firms as opposed to households (Paya and Greef-Madelin 2020). The tax burden on businesses – targeting their salary base even more than their actual profits – damages competitiveness and stifles economic growth and job creation. This heavy taxation of payrolls results in lower wages being paid to employees before they in turn are taxed on those same wages. The yellow vests movement highlighted the social and political sensitivity of the resulting erosion of purchasing power. While the number of households paying personal income tax has been decreasing since 2014 (in 2019, only about 44 per cent of the population paid any income tax), the share of the yield of this tax in total budget revenue is on the rise (Servière 2020a). This means that the average tax paid per taxable household has increased.

Globalisation since the 1970s has made the tax system of the twentieth century obsolete, since that was based on closed national economies with customs barriers and restrictions on cash payments and capital outflows. We now have capital that is more mobile and therefore more difficult to tax. The result has been increasing inequality, especially within advanced industrial countries such as France. One of the causes of net incomes becoming increasingly unequal has been the decrease in the relative amounts of tax paid by mobile top-income earners, leaving the rest of rich countries' resident taxpayers to finance a larger share of the cost of desired public services and welfare. 'Governments must, can, and do increasingly rely on fewer and relatively immobile tax bases, which are essentially three: property and wealth, sales and consumption, and the labor income of relatively immobile workers' (Egger, Nigai, and Strecker 2019, 354). In these circumstances, taxes tend to be imposed not on the basis of broad social and political priorities, but on the basis of what can be taxed. The result, in an ironic variation on Ronald Reagan's famous critique of the 'big government' attitude ('if it moves, tax it'), is instead closer to 'tax whatever cannot move'. In terms of income, this means the salaries of middle-class employees, who will be less likely to pursue international careers. In terms of capital, this means, above all, the wealth caught up in housing stock.

A good example of what seems an increasingly desperate and futile resort to property tax expedients is the so-called pre-emptive archaeology tax (*redevance d'archéologie preventive*). This tax is imposed on anyone planning any kind of construction on their property, such as a garden shed or, in the case of wealthier households, a swimming pool. Its stated purpose is to raise a pot of money to protect the archaeological heritage that may be unearthed by the proposed construction works. The government has charged two separate agencies with the task of collecting this tax: the Ministry of Culture, which must carry out impact studies, and the Ministry of Urbanism, which grants the actual planning permission.

There is also a long list of real estate taxes. Depending on the location of the residential property or operational premises, individual taxpayers and companies are liable to pay special *équipement* taxes relating to publicly owned land in the hands of subregional and central government (not to be confused with the special *équipement* tax of the newly created public institution called the Société du Grand Paris); a property tax surcharge on undeveloped land; a special tax for the benefit of the Île-de-France region (again, not to be confused with the above taxes); a tax for garbage collection; stamp duty for the benefit of chambers of commerce, industry, trade, crafts, and agriculture; and a tax on commercial wasteland. This is not to mention the flat tax levied by municipalities on companies operating all kinds of infrastructure networks (IFER), from wind turbines to railways and power distribution.

Researchers from the Observatoire Français des Conjonctures Économiques (OFCE) published a study, included in the National Institute of Statistics and Economic Studies (INSEE) report 'France Portrait Social 2018' (INSEE 2018), that showed a 1.2 per cent decline in real household income in the decade following the GFC. This contrasts with increases in household revenue per unit of consumption by 13.8 per cent in 1984–92, 11 per cent in 1992–2000 and 11.3 per cent in 2000–2008 (Madec *et al.* 2018). Although these headline figures hide some distributional nuances, there is no disguising the brutality of the impact of the GFC on the mature economies. In France, the tax pressure on households has been an integral component of that impact. The average French taxpayer spends the equivalent of the first seven months of the year working for the state treasury (de Guigné 2018).

The French version of the welfare state (*Sécurité sociale*) – generally and self-admiringly referred to as the country's 'social model' – was developed during the 1950s and 1960s against a backdrop of strong economic growth. It covers four major risks, or events, of income loss: ill health, retirement, job loss, and the financial burden of dependants (young children or the old and infirm). While the social model performs relatively well by cross-country comparisons of poverty and inequality measures, it is costly in terms of purchasing power and employment.

The social security system is funded for the most part by compulsory levies on employers that are assessed as a proportion of payroll costs (i.e. the wage bill). In the EU, France is the country that extracts the highest relative amounts in such contributions from its companies. These complex and onerous charges are levied in all circumstances, including in the absence of profits. They vary by industry sector, company size, job type and status, and remuneration level. This emphasis on taxing employment has been, in political terms, the path of least resistance, since it perpetuates the political and social perception that welfare is cost-free because it is financed by companies (read 'rich bosses') as opposed to ordinary people. The combination of relentless government borrowing and these high payroll taxes has allowed the political class – sometimes unwittingly, sometimes cynically – to foster the illusion among citizens that they are getting something for nothing, while entrenching successive governments' misconception that taxing business payrolls is a painless way of financing welfare and public services. This illusion of a free lunch is also fuelled by the way pensions are financed. The pension system essentially consists of pay-as-you-go (PAYG) schemes, whereby contributions levied on present-day workers' wages fund the current pension entitlements of retirees. Such mandatory occupational pension arrangements account for 70–80 per cent of retiree incomes.

The system thus depends for its solvency on there being full employment. Since there has been anything but full employment in France for the past half a century, part of the funding burden has therefore been shifted to savers and to pensioners themselves. Employers will pass on at least part of the burden by setting lower wages for their workers, who must also make some direct contributions out of their own pay packets. The system thus impoverishes low-income workers and further widens inequalities. This helps to explain the yellow vests protests about workers' weak purchasing power and why the *gilets jaunes* marched in the streets to defend their pension arrangements from losses threatened by enlightened technocratic reforms (also known as tax rises).

At the same time, this social model has guaranteed some public sector workers' featherbedded early retirements. A couple of standout examples are the state railway (SNCF) and Paris mass transit system (RATP), whose workers can retire as early as age fifty-five. They benefit from pension perks justified on the basis of their having 'hard and tedious working conditions' (*penibilité*); yet no such advantages are given to many others who would seem to be eligible on that basis, such as trash collectors or small farmers. In the name of equality, an inegalitarian system has emerged.

In the face of this fiscal pressure on purchasing power and the broader stagnation of real incomes to which it contributes, the total household saving rate has fallen sharply since 2003 as people have drawn down savings to maintain their consumption growth. IN-SEE's detailed statistics quantify the transfer of inherited wealth by distinguishing between disposable income with and without 'private transfers' (INSEE 2018). For the most part, these transfers represent bequests from parents to their children. On average, about half of the savings of lower-income households are funded by private transfers: in other words, by bequests from relatives. This phenomenon is more marked in the case of people below the age of thirty. It would appear that people are becoming increasingly unable to put aside adequate savings from their earned incomes.

While real estate is the preferred savings instrument, property acquisitions increase households' indebtedness in the form of mortgage loans, which are taking ever longer to repay. With most mortgages carrying fixed interest rates, borrowers have not benefited from the ever-lower interest rates seen during the decade post GFC. The risk comes from the share of income devoted to housing: in March 2020, the stock of household debt amounted to 62 per cent of GDP. This rising share of debt service in family budgets poses risks to financial, and ultimately social, stability (Banque de France 2020).

The tax policy towards entrepreneurs in some sense recalls Louis XIV's revocation of the Edict of Nantes (1685): this drove the Huguenots (Protestants) out of France, depriving the country of many talented and industrious people. Religious intolerance in the seventeenth century and ill-designed tax policies in the twenty-first century have had the same effect of draining France's entrepreneurial lifeblood. One damaging feature of the French tax system regarding corporate competitiveness is that the mere fact of setting up a company makes it liable to pay taxes on transport, VAT, and payrolls. An American entrepreneur reportedly quipped: 'In the US, taxes are levied on eggs that have been laid. In France, the hen must pay tax to get the right to lay her eggs.'

This heavy burden of taxation on businesses is one of the main causes of chronic unemployment in France. It is also the main drag on the competitiveness of French industry – which, in a vicious cycle, contributes further to high unemployment. Many firms export jobs and manufacturing capacity to countries with lower wages and, importantly, lower state-imposed payroll levies. French households are left to pick up the tab as citizens face higher taxes, cuts to public services, and declining living standards.

At the start of his term in office, François Hollande landed a heavy blow on the country's economic recovery from the GFC and ensuing eurozone sovereign debt crisis by raising taxes. This produced a crisis of confidence among entrepreneurs and investors, who slowed hiring pending a change of course by Hollande's government. This duly came with the introduction of the Competitiveness and Employment Tax Credit (CICE) in 2013, followed by the 'Responsibility Pact' in 2014: two measures that offered a degree of tax relief to businesses on the condition that they hired and invested in France. These measures had started to bear fruit by the time Macron became president in 2017, a year in which the global economy also reflated. As a result, Macron's first year in office was flattered by a rare improvement in unemployment data. However, the problem of French industry's poor competitiveness remained unaddressed.

Defenders of the French system quibble over labour-cost statistics in their efforts to prove that France is not so different from its European peer group. But the facts of the last decade – including a significant loss of global export market share and a deteriorating current-account balance – paint a different picture. This poor export performance has been accompanied by low-profit margins of enterprises, constraining their capacity to invest, innovate, and create jobs. The damaging effects of this method of financing welfare and public services have been aggravated by the closely related phenomena of excessive state regulation of the labour market and distorting state interference in product and service markets.

Successive governments have attempted to lighten the burden on payrolls, especially as felt by small businesses. These reliefs include a lower level of payroll tax for workers earning the minimum wage, tax breaks to encourage the hiring of young employees or apprentices, and support for employers in areas defined as economically disadvantaged. However, the complexity of such measures makes it difficult for firms to take advantage of them and requires additional civil servants to administer them. In this respect, the French model is riddled with exceptions that provide work for the ever-expanding state bureaucracy, which, in turn, comes up with ever more complex distortions impeding wealth creation.

Firms' 'self-financing' capacity – that is, their ability to fund their operations from cash flow, without recourse to debt – started to recover from the crisis after 2013. But lacklustre economic growth combined with high taxation forced companies into excessive borrowing to finance investment and inventory expenditures. By March 2020, outstanding debt owed by all 'non-financial' French companies (i.e. not counting banks and other financial intermediaries) had ballooned to 140 per cent of GDP (Banque de France 2020).

The lion's share of this risky expansion of corporate debt resulted from borrowing by large companies, with much of it shifting from bank loans to the issue of bonds on the capital markets. Companies' expanding capacity to borrow has been supported by low interest rates, strong investor demand for any securities that yield more than government bonds, and purchases of corporate bonds by the ECB (as part of its QE programmes). Another key trend is that the proceeds of this borrowing have been used not only to provide working capital and cover the cost of business investment, but also increasingly to fund dividend payments and share buybacks. These distributions enhancing shareholder returns have doubled since 1997, and their share in value added has tripled since 1986. Another increasingly common form of debt-funded financial operation is acquisitions, often directed abroad (i.e. equity investments in foreign companies).

This corporate debt mountain creates risks in times of financial market downturn and economic recession, such as that produced by the outbreak of the coronavirus pandemic. While debt-funded investment has been typical of large companies, given their size and international activity, small and medium-sized enterprises (SMEs) have reduced their borrowing since the GFC. One reason may be that they do not have easy access to the capital market, while bank lending is clogged by increased regulation on banks, such as stricter (Basel) rules forcing banks to increase the ratio of their own capital base relative to their assets. This is negative for the economy in a way different from the failure of large companies to direct the proceeds of their large-scale borrowing mainly towards investment. That is because SMEs play a key role in economic growth, job creation, regional and local development, and social cohesion. In 2019, French SMEs accounted for 48 per cent of total employment (aggregating all part-time SME jobs to their full-time equivalent), generating 43 per cent of value added and 15 per cent of export turnover. Access to finance is a prerequisite for their growth.

Returning to the core problem of public finances, the state's dependence on borrowing barely changes in line with economic cycles: even in good times, it continues to have to borrow more. But what is called public debt in France is less than half of what would be listed under that heading in countries such as the United States. As officially defined, public debt does not include the future cost of paying pensions due to retired civil servants, the deficit of the public health care system, or various private debts taken over by the state. Therefore, the public debt recalculated to make the data internationally comparable would be much higher than the 100 per cent of GDP advertised by the French authorities for 2019. Even that official public debt ratio represents a fivefold increase since 1980. Four-fifths of this debt is owed by the central government, with local public administrations and social security organisations accounting for the remainder in roughly equal shares. As for public spending, which depends on such state borrowing if it is to be financed, the single most important item is education, which absorbs almost 22 per cent of all state expenditure, followed by defence (13.1 per cent). In fourth place comes debt service – i.e. interest payments on previous borrowing (€42 billion in 2018). The expansion of public debt has been fuelled by the policy response to successive crises in the form of tax breaks and recovery plans. The fiscal consequences of the GFC and eurozone sovereign debt crises may now be dwarfed by the coronavirus pandemic.

The bulk of this state borrowing currently takes place on the capital markets, with a substantial portion of the various kinds of security issued – Treasury bills and bonds – merely refinancing previous issues that have reached maturity. Most of this paper is acquired by non-resident buyers (54 per cent of the total in mid 2018, according to the figures published by Agence France Trésor (AFT)). These foreign creditors are mainly institutional investors (pension funds and insurance funds in particular), but sovereign investment funds, banks, and hedge funds are also included. The resident buyers – holding a quarter of the outstanding public debt – are mainly banks and insurance companies, which invest the life insurance premiums received from their customers in government bonds. The upshot is that individual French citizens are indirect holders of a significant part of the public debt.

To sum up the importance of chronic public deficits to our theme of the fracturing of the national community, it is not as if the nation state has benefited from this fiscal 'generosity' and ballooning indebtedness. On the contrary, ever more public debt has coincided with deteriorating overall economic performance. In the twenty years since the launch of the euro in 1999, real per capita output and household disposable incomes per adult family member have grown barely half as fast as in the preceding two decades (OECD 2019).

If the nation as a whole feels short-changed by the state's fiscal operations, rural and small-town France have a particular cause for grievance: after all, public expenditure is perceived to benefit better-off city dwellers at the expense of citizens in peripheral areas. This is the subject of the next section of this chapter.

THE NATION STATE FAILS RURAL FRANCE

France is typical of advanced as well as emerging countries in prioritising the development of metropolitan areas (especially large ones) over small localities. But there are several features of this phenomenon in France that are distinctly *French*.

About half of the variance in incomes globally is linked to where a person lives. In other words, for a person born in a poor country to have as good a life as a person born in a rich country, factors other than the country of origin would have to weigh twice as heavily in the case of the poor-country person for them to live as well as their rich-country counterpart. The same factor – i.e. place of origin and/or residence – also determines one's relative living standard (Milanovic 2015). The life chances of anyone growing up in the centre of Paris (or any of the country's other big cities) will be materially superior on average to those of someone from rural France or the disadvantaged urban periphery, for which the bureaucracy has dreamt up the label 'sensitive urban area' (*zone urbaine sensible* – ZUS). The changes in the world economy that have unfolded since the 1980s can be summed up in two words: knowledge and globalisation. The costs and benefits of these profound shifts are well understood. On the positive side, the number of people living in poverty around the world has dropped. On the negative side, the counterpart costs of those gains have fallen disproportionately on lower-skilled workers in high-income countries, which, as a result, have seen a reversal in the post-World War II trend of declining inequality.

The jobs of many such workers have moved to poorer countries with cheaper labour. The losses are transmitted by the labour market and are concentrated geographically. Successful companies are located in largely metropolitan areas, to the benefit of the incomes and services enjoyed by the urban population, while the periphery and rural areas are marginalised (Longhi and Musolesi 2007). In short, your chances of having the minimum 'human capital' required to have a good life will be greatly enhancd if you have been lucky enough to be born in the right place.

Another key element of luck is the more familiar question of parentage. American economist Alan Krueger's so-called Great Gatsby Curve demonstrates the (intuitively unsurprising) reality that those born to the 'right' parents (where 'right' means those with after-tax inflation-adjusted incomes that put them in the top 1 per cent) have a better chance of ending up at the top of the ladder, or at least not at the bottom (Krueger 2012). The Great Gatsby Curve signals that more inequality is associated with less intergenerational mobility (Corak 2013, 98). In a vicious cycle, the globalised mobility of higher-paid knowledge workers erodes the tax base (under existing tax systems) for funding education and health programmes key to improving the economic standing of people on low and middling incomes. (Milanovic 2016). Growing inequalities provoke anger among those who feel aggrieved by a system from which they are excluded.

Before the French version of this anger became visible to the world in the form of the yellow vests, it was already clear from the previous year's national election results that the country had become starkly polarised between the relatively well-off in the big cities and the marginalised low-income and economically redundant periphery of France's middle- and small-sized towns and rural areas. This great fracture was reflected in the first-round vote result of the 2017 presidential election, where Emmanuel Macron's vote share was 23.75 per cent (in absolute terms, 8.53 million votes), placing him ahead of National Front leader Marine Le Pen with 21.53 per cent (7.66 million votes) (Gee 2017). Most of Macron's voters were located in the western half of France and in the Île-de-France region around Paris, while Le Pen's voters were concentrated in both the northeast and the southeast. Macron won in the big cities while Le Pen was the favourite in less densely populated regions. This geographical divide in voting patterns reflects an economic divide, with Macron's voters being higher-educated and higher-earning people, on average. France's rural areas are characterised by lower rates of enrolment in high school, training, and higher education for fifteen- to twenty-four-year-olds, as well as literacy problems. For instance, 18 per cent of the population in the Aisne and Somme *départements* in the Hauts-de-France region of northern France is affected by poor literacy attainment, compared with a national average of 11 per cent. Even in the poorest of the Parisian suburbs, Seine-Saint-Denis, this negative indicator is no higher than 11.7 per cent. These citizens' disenchantment and sense of alienation is also reflected in their political apathy, which resulted in a 24.5 per cent abstention rate in the second round run-off of the 2017 presidential election: this is much higher than the 16.2 per cent and 20.5 per cent recorded for the 2007 and 2012 elections, respectively (Service infographie and Beyer 2017).

At the dawn of the 'Republic of the Technocrats' in the 1960s, several protests erupted in rural areas against the modernisation reforms introduced by the government (in 1962, rural residents still accounted for about 30 per cent of the population). De Gaulle's stand against the protesters led to the accusation that 'Gaullism had been hijacked by inhuman technocracy' (Jackson 2018, 642). Geographer Jean-François Gravier (1915–2005), who published *Paris et le désert français* in 1947, inspired the planners of the Fourth and Fifth Republics while working for the Ministry of Urban Planning and Reconstruction. Gravier focused on the gulf between Paris and the provinces (*la province*). His dislike of Paris echoes that of Jean-Jacques Rousseau and, seventy years later, the yellow vest protests: 'In all areas, the Paris agglomeration has behaved since 1850 not as a metropolis giving life to its hinterland, but as a monopolist group devouring the substance of the nation. Its action has multiplied the effects of the first industrial revolution and sterilized most provincial economies by depriving them of their dynamic elements. Centres of decision making, new thinking and scarce services: Paris has appropriated for itself all these leading activities and has left only subordinate ones to the rest of France' (Gravier 1972, 60, quoted in Marchand and Salomon-Cavin 2007, 31).

Under the influence of the territorial planners inspired by the ideas of Gravier, regions were created and then regrouped, political decentralisation was reinforced, regional cities were developed more dynamically, and high-speed railway lines were constructed. Regional newspapers and cultural festivals emerged. The big cities became smaller versions of Paris regarding their role in the nation's overall economy. Proliferating urban sprawl distanced residents from amenities and jobs. No economic concept informed these policies, and there was no room at all for empirical observations, let alone consultations with people 'on the ground' or even representatives of local businesses, trade unions, or elected local councillors.

Instead, this 'territorial reorganisation' was a Parisian bureaucratic exercise in top-down authoritarian spatial planning based on abstract notions about land use, the optimal size of cities, and components of the built environment (Marchand and Salomon-Cavin 2007, 47–8).

Between 1958 and 1968, a major exodus of the rural population to the cities took place under the guiding framework of what was considered a necessary 'regional balance' of industrialisation avoiding excessive geographic concentration (Marchand and Salomon-Cavin 2007). What those planners failed to foresee was less the contrast between Paris and the 'French desert' (i.e. the provinces as a whole) than the gulf between, on the one hand, the large cities with their hinterlands (smaller than Paris, but similar in kind) and, on the other hand, the small towns and the countryside that became a neglected and depressed periphery (Davezies 2012).

The challenge for policymakers in this area of spatial political economy is to design policies that promote both regional diversity in its natural breadth and a coherent nation state (Linz, Stepan, and Yadav 2004). In the 1980s, the Socialist government recognised the case for allowing subnational authorities a greater say in policy and administration. On this basis, that first left-wing government of the Mitterrand presidency proceeded with decentralisation reforms between 1981 and 1983. This immediately highlighted the tension between such decentralisation and the traditional identification of the nation state with centralised power: 'In relocating substantial decision-making and revenue-gathering powers to subnational units, these policies in effect reestablished the legitimacy of subnational identities, thereby reducing the absolutist claims of the "nation" and its government' (Safran 1991, 223).

More than two decades later, decentralisation policies came back into fashion, but the goal had shifted from enacting a broad vision of governance to, more pragmatically, controlling public spending. A core focus was trimming the public service headcount, especially at the regional and local levels of administration. In 2007, Nicolas Sarkozy launched a general review of public policies (RGPP). This advocated replacing no more than one in two retiring civil servants and merging the provision of public services for which responsibility had become divided between various levels of subnational government. In 2012, François Hollande replaced this policy with a new agenda: 'modernisation of public action' (MAP). Ostensibly, this approach aimed to correct certain shortcomings of the RGPP – in particular, by promoting more extensive consultation with local communities. In reality, the new agenda was the old agenda in different garb – one of reducing the number of civil servants and saving money by replacing physical delivery points for local services with online provisions. The trouble was that these policies primarily targeted rural communities, who already felt abandoned because of past cuts to public services, and that closures were in practice decided on without consultation with elected local officials. The online transition was difficult for the predominantly elderly population to make, and the rollout of broadband access infrastructure in peripheral France was patchy.

Years of such top-down decision making by technocrats have resulted in wasteful policies with dramatic consequences. For the purposes of this analysis, it matters little whether 'city' voters will continue to prevail numerically over 'periphery' voters in elections (as happened in the presidential and parliamentary elections of 2017). The crucial point is the already gaping polarisation between the regions and the metropolis, and between those with and without skills that are valued in the new knowledge economy (Guilluy 2019).

Instead of acknowledging the contribution that the countryside could make to the nation's welfare, the establishment is striving to write rural France out of the script. The once highly respected office for national statistics (INSEE) is now being used to support the government doctrine that France is urban. Local and regional administrations were reorganised in 2016 into fourteen metropolises and thirteen mega-regions. This reform has allowed INSEE to conclude that there are 241 large metropolitan areas accounting jointly for 83 per cent of the population. Eurostat data runs counter to these results, showing that the actual rate of urbanisation stands at 42 per cent. INSEE methodology allows the government to argue that poverty is mainly urban (Guilluy 2019, 83–93).

The long-standing divergence between the metropolis and small to medium-sized towns is rooted in the shift of economic value creation from industrial production to services. This divergence 'has fuelled stress, a growing sense of insecurity, and an "existential" quest for a new identity among the French,' according to Jean-Pierre Dormois, who goes on to say that French people 'have become the world's largest consumers of tranquilizers – as well they might: a Frenchman (Laborit) patented the first brand' (Dormois 2004, 10).

The public sector became the only significant source of employment for people living in peripheral France; but since the turn of the century, more and more public services have been discontinued in rural areas, with consequent job losses. Thousands of depopulated French villages have been reduced to rural deserts. Part of the French population feels increasingly excluded and forgotten. Their aspiration is to be able to live in their towns and villages, to work there, and to send their children to the village school. In 2012, nearly 53 per cent of French people lived in the *département* where they were born. This proportion reaches nearly 60 per cent for the whole of peripheral France and falls to less than 40 per cent in metropolitan France (Guilluy 2017, 231–2). A survey carried out by the Society and Consumption Observatory for the Mobile Lives Forum, which questioned 2,227 people aged eighteen to sixty-nine years, found that seven out of ten inhabitants of Île-de-France (the region around Paris) would like to move to another region of France with a better climate, less stress and pollution, and a lower overall cost of living (Razemon 2019).

The various failures of vertical state governance have resulted in an increased demand for a more horizontal system more geared to the well-being of citizens. The yellow vests movement arose from an online petition published in May 2018 that attracted nearly a million signatures. At the end of November that year (after the start of their public protests), the yellow vests boiled down their list of grievances to forty-two items organised under seven broad headings: purchasing power, social policy, taxation, democracy, the economy, immigration, and public services. Upon hearing these grievances, the government was surprised to discover that people in rural France cannot always use their bicycles to commute, as the average commute is 40 kilometres. It also learned that tax measures adopted since 2017 under the budgetary constraint imposed by France's eurozone membership have weighed heavily on family budgets. The share of non-discretionary expenses (such as rent, groceries, energy and utility bills, taxes, and insurance) is constantly increasing. In 2017, it represented 30 per cent of the total average household budget and consumed all the available resources of poorer households. Even for the somewhat better-off, the disposable remainder is reduced to a minimum. No wonder a growing number of French people have been giving up hope (Bas 2019, 134). The yellow vests are the working poor, and their purchasing power has suffered from heavy taxation, but they are not benefitting from France's generous welfare state because they are often employed, not poor enough and mostly live in areas of France in which public services have been cut back over the past few decades. The closure of hospitals, public services centres, schools, and post offices has been the norm in rural areas since the start of the century.

A team of French researchers has attempted to quantify the factors explaining the yellow vests social crisis by developing an index of malaise for each commune where a mobilisation of *gilets jaunes* occurred in November and December 2018 (Algan, Malgouyres, and Senik 2020). The researchers explored whether there is a link between five key factors explaining the current state of mind of a population: employment, local taxation, the disappearance of local shops and public services, real estate market conditions, and the 'thickness' of local civic society (such as voluntary associations fostering community spirit). Their study concluded that while unemployment plays an important role in such unrest, the main cause in this case stemmed less from the absolute level of joblessness and more from its relentlessly negative trend. An important factor was the disappearance of public services, such as those linked to health or education, and private ones, like small grocery shops, which often play a socialising role. The study recommended ending national policies such as rural regeneration zones (ZRRs – launched in 1996, no doubt under the direction of yet another of Gravier's disciples) and instead giving local mayors more discretionary powers regarding the allocation of such resources. These same researchers also warned against the project, viewed as tempting by the Macron government, of completely digitalising local public services, which are currently provided in brick-and-mortar centres known as *maisons France Services*. These centres were established to help people living in rural areas to handle administrative procedures related to social services, job searches, public transport, child benefits, energy, preventative health care, postal services, and so on. In addition to all that, these service centres can also be an all-too-rare venue for socialising. One problem, however, is that they are quite widely scattered, so many people must travel a long distance before finding one. There were 1,340 such offices listed in June 2019 throughout the country. After the *Grand Débat* in 2019, when President Macron toured France listening to mayors and citizens, he promised to increase their number to 2,000 by 2022.

A further problem with this trend towards digitalisation, also highlighted in that study on the causes of the yellow vests uprising, is that the help it offers is self-defeating because it is online. The population includes many 'offline' elderly people who are unable to collect their pensions or to pay their taxes when these are processed online. In addition, some areas have no access to the internet. According to the relevant regulator (ARCEP), 541 small municipalities were euphemistically classified as 'white spots' (*zones blanches*) in 2017. The reason these *zones blanches* exist is that regulators failed to build adequate conditions into telecom providers' bandwidth licenses. As a result, these firms have reaped handsome commercial gains from network buildouts while avoiding any erosion of their profit margins from the €150,000 cost of each new wireless communication tower necessary for a low-density population to benefit from the new technology. Only in January 2018, after six months of negotiations with the government, did France's four major mobile operators (Bouygues Telecom, Orange, SFR, and Free) agree to invest €3 billion to ensure full coverage by 2020 (Connexion journalist 2020).

Small farmers are acutely affected by the social and economic blight of rural France. More than a tenth of France's 400,000 farmers are characterised as poor, with half of all farmers earning less than the median monthly minimum subsistence income: this was estimated at €846 (the national poverty threshold) in 2016 (INSEE 2020b; the latest available data on poverty is for 2016). This problem is not new, as decades of research shows the persistence of poverty among farmers and in rural populations more generally (Behaghel 2008). Their situation has not been materially improved by relevant national or European public policies. The EU's Common Agricultural Policy (CAP), while benefitting mainly high-income farmers, does help small farmers to survive; yet the CAP was not designed as an instrument of rural poverty relief. National poverty reduction policies are likewise not specifically tailored to rural areas. While poverty and exclusion are generally related to unemployment or underemployment, 25 per cent of farmers could be described as the working poor with full-time jobs. This is despite there being some government welfare and minimum income policies directed at rural areas: for instance, the so-called *Revenu minimum d'insertion* (RMI) was extended in 1992 to the working poor in rural areas and was replaced by the *Revenu de solidarité active* (RSA) in 2009.

Poor farmers do not seem to be claiming the RSA: a fact that calls into question the efficacy of basic public policies. One aim of the RSA is to provide low-wage workers with complementary income so they do not suffer the perverse effects of earning less through employment than they would through various state benefits if they were unemployed. Estimates of the number of farmers eligible for the RSA established by the Caisse Centrale de la Mutualité Sociale Agricole (CCMSA) in 2010 amounted to 20,120 farmers, while only 9,818 benefitted from the RSA that same year (Deville 2015).

For Christophe Guilluy, official talk on interconnectedness, mobility, exchange, and social diversity is intended to conceal the effects of unequal economic development – an approach to territorial organisation that, he argues powerfully, results in the 'ghettoisation' of disadvantaged social groups. The prosperous big cities integrated into the global economy contrast with 'peripheral France', which consists of suburbs (often with heavy concentrations of immigrants), smaller towns, and rural areas. In the eyes of the metropolitan sophisticates, these 'peripherals' are regarded as the French equivalent of Trump-voting 'deplorables' in the United States (Guilluy 2019).

A report published in 2019 by the public accounts watchdog (Cour des comptes) found that the Île-de-France is the richest economic region of the country, accounting for 30 per cent of national GDP. For all its relative aggregate wealth, however, this region also has the highest internal economic and social disparities. For example, the median disposable income in the Hauts de Seine *département* is more than 50 per cent higher than that in Seine Saint Denis (Cour des comptes 2019).

The big metropolitan centres account for an ever-greater share of economic activity at the expense of entire regions of France that have become depopulated and relatively depressed. Such 'desertification' affects small towns or cities of less than 100,000 inhabitants. This economic and social weakening of many territories shrinks their tax base, leading to a vicious cycle from which these localities struggle to escape. While showing how this deep societal fracture has fuelled the growing vote share of Marine Le Pen's party, Guilluy explains that this phenomenon extends well beyond party political sympathies and voting intentions. He depicts a large section of society that has turned in on itself – and away from a threatening and alien wider world. This alienation has resulted in attitudes of detachment and disenchantment towards politics intensifying into disgust and a desire to break the system completely (Guilluy 2017, 107). Public authorities explain away the problem of these depressed localities as stemming from their labour force profile: companies that need to hire have difficulty finding suitable workers in such regions. It follows that these regions become 'low density', leading in turn to their being singled out for public services closures.

The allocation of public funds earmarked for supporting rural areas is opaque. Incentives in the form of tax breaks provided to companies setting up businesses in ZRRS seem promising in principle, but they have made no demonstrable impact on the most disadvantaged areas. It is not easy for firms to shift their operations away from big cities and to attract workers tempted by lower house prices: poor rural infrastructure deters urban dwellers from migrating to rural areas to take advantage of the lower costs of living, the better quality of life, and, in the post-Covid world, the attractions of remote working. The scarcity of public facilities, high-speed broadband, and insufficient transportation systems creates spatial segregation, disconnecting people from job opportunities. The rural population already has difficulty getting access to essential services within a reasonable distance with reliable public transport; meanwhile, banks, post offices, schools, hospitals, police stations, and railway stations are closing, forcing more and more people from these communities to use their cars. The decline in the number of rural primary schools is linked to a strategy of grouping schools over two to six municipalities. The localities where health care facilities are further than twenty minutes' drive away are all in rural areas (Guilluy 2019, 85). The number of maternity units in these regions has declined steadily over the past forty years. Unsurprisingly, it has been found that the greater the distance to a community's closest maternity unit, the higher the incidence of riskier out-of-hospital births. There is no policy regarding prenatal care for women living far from a maternity unit. The lack of child-minding services combined with the aforementioned transportation problems accentuates the difficulties for women living in rural areas to find and hold down jobs, contributing to rural household financial difficulties (Behaghel 2008). In Burgundy, increased travel times between 2000 and 2009 and adverse prenatal outcomes were positively associated (Pilkington *et al.* 2014). Service access times are highly dependent on the population density of municipalities, with Corsica and Burgundy being the worst affected (Barbier, Toutin, and Levy 2016). A law enacted in 2015 envisages consolidating local public services in a smaller number of population centres that supposedly serve a hinterland of rural towns and villages. Such 'intercommunity grouping' favours those who move to better-served areas and widens the gap between them and those who cannot make such a move.

Geographer Pierre Pistre shows that the depopulation of rural France, which began with the mechanisation of agriculture a century ago and reached a fever pitch of city-bound migration in the post-war period, has gone into mild reverse since the 1970s and 1980s. He attributes this change to a mixture of the increasing attractiveness of the rural way of life and tourism (Pistre 2013). This development suggests that the future may hinge on recognising and taking advantage of the value of the country's vast rural endowment. The current model, which aims to cram most people into crowded metropolises, runs counter to what many people would regard as 'the good life'. In his book *Decolonize the Provinces*, French philosopher Michel Onfray echoes the 1966 manifesto of independent-minded Socialist and politician Michel Rocard, who proclaimed that 'the rebirth of regional dynamism presupposes the disappearance of the tutelage of the State and the prefect'. For Onfray, if the nation is an idea, the locality is a reality. To move from the pious lip service paid to increased citizen involvement in politics to the reality of such a change, real power should be given to town halls and regional administrations, while regions should be better represented in the national parliament. The transfer of greater power and decision making to local country areas would encourage increasing numbers of people, especially the young, to move their lives and businesses to rural France (Onfray 2017).

A rural revival would also be consistent with the goals of the Paris Agreement (COP-21) to the extent that it would promote local consumption and production. The greenhouse gas reduction goals in the COP-21 framework require more systematic policies along the lines of prioritising sustainable development and making it easier for more people to live in small-town and rural environments with a human dimension. In 2020, traffic jams in big cities and the Île-de-France region were estimated to cost €539 per second (more than €17 billion per year), representing €1,943 for each car-using household and eight wasted days per year for Parisians. This overall cost has been estimated as the sum of direct incremental costs (fuel and wasted time) and indirect costs (impact on the prices of goods and services sold by companies) as of September 2020 (see ConsoGlobe's homepage for more details). If such realities still fail to prompt policy changes, the Covid-19 pandemic may yet serve as a decisive wake-up call for the technocrats.

While the 'death of distance' effect described from a global perspective by British economist Frances Cairncross has yet to be fully realised, thanks to the abovementioned slow rollout of high-speed broadband connections to many rural areas, a demographic renewal in rural areas – and with it the emergence of rural knowledge-based service firms and entrepreneurs – seems to have begun (Cairncross 2002). The death of distance in this context will be driven by IT, making the permanent physical presence of work teams in the same office increasingly unnecessary (Haskel and Westlake 2017, 157).

Despite years of systematic degradation caused by excessive centralisation, the countryside shows great economic and social diversity. In his study of poverty and social exclusion in France, economist Luc Behaghel confirms that the rural depopulation trend bottomed out in the 1970s (Behaghel 2008). The social and professional profile of new rural dwellers is quite diverse. These are no retirees retreating to the countryside: the so-called neo-rurals have proven to have more economic, social, and/or cultural resources than the local population and are, on average, more highly qualified than the existing rural population. Their relatively higher professional qualifications and greater skills are contributing to the revival of local economies. These recent arrivals on the rural scene are most often associated with heritage-related and landscaping projects, such as the renovation of churches, bread ovens, and dry stone walls, the creation of footpaths, and ecological projects such as forest biodiversity preservation. The newcomers also contribute indirectly to maintaining local agriculture, which is diversifying both in terms of what is being produced and how it is being made, with production methods moving towards the best environmental practices (Richard, Dellier, and Tommasi 2014).

Much research has documented the role that IT has played and continues to play in the demographic recovery and development of rural areas throughout Europe and the United States. Scholars often identify the combination of IT and amenities as a major factor of this 'rural rebound' that is attracting working people and entrepreneurs from the 'creative class' to the countryside. For example, to address school closures in rural areas, digital education could lead to a more equitable distribution of educational resources (Goldfarb and Tucker 2019). The United States has seen a rapid increase in 'telecommuting', where employees of small companies as well as self-employed persons engage in a wide array of activities that can be undertaken remotely. These include the production of digital content and a wide range of digitally deliverable professional services (Moriset *et al.* 2012). Regional policies could boost this rural repopulation and revival as the first 'connected' (i.e. born with internet access) generation arrives on the labour market. Such a policy mix could combine public funding for knowledge infrastructure – such as IT-based education and scientific research – with facilitating transport links and access to all services in rural areas. While measuring the productivity gains brought about by digital technology is a source of debate among economists, few contest the many economic benefits of digitalisation, which tend to be amplified in rural areas.

The twentieth century saw a shift from decentralised (mainly agricultural and artisanal) to centralised (industrial and urban) production. Now, the rise of digital tools is reducing that centralising pressure by allowing more work to be done remotely and nomadically in a flexible organisational framework. In the countryside and other more sparsely populated areas, independence and versatility are far more needed than in cities. A person can work at least part of their time at a distance and collaborate remotely. People can enjoy the benefits of rural life, setting up a workspace at home and participating in reducing climate change by cultivating their gardens and eating more of their own produce. Developing rural areas by exploiting the potential of technological progress should also benefit mental health, as people would be living in more pleasant surroundings instead of commuting to a bland office every day.

This is not, however, to deny that remote employment, even in pleasant surroundings, involves drawbacks and challenges, such as working long hours and struggling to draw a line between professional and private lives (Méda 2016). Other hazards of this model include feelings of isolation due to a lack of interactions both personal and professional. Digital tools and social networks can help people stay in touch with family and friends, who can visit and be visited if transport structures are in place. Another way to cope with the seclusion of working alone all day, every day has been developed by self-employed professionals, who organise physical meeting places so that they can get together at regular intervals. Working in the countryside but having a hot desk in a shared office fills employees' need for a sense of community and inclusion while still allowing them to escape their daily commute into the city. This helps to develop networks while simultaneously boosting the rural economy.

These co-working hubs are a potential driver of the revival of rural economies, and the Macron administration proved keen to support their development in the countryside and urban peripheries. About €110 million was committed to creating 300 such hubs by 2021, especially in neglected regions (Caillaud 2018). Almost half of the hubs currently in existence are located outside the big cities, and they are likely to attract neo-rurals, provided the government also delivers on its promise to ensure broadband access throughout the country by 2020 (upgraded to very high speed by 2022). These hubs also have a positive financial impact: in 2018, it was estimated that they generate on average about €57,000 of incremental value added and €37,000 in tax revenues per year for each municipality (*Fondation travailler autrement* 2018).

Yet seclusion is not the only obstacle to new settlement in rural areas. For instance, existing rural communities may not welcome newcomers owing to prejudices, negative experiences in the past, or poor knowledge of these 'outsiders'. There are also economic, financial, and administrative obstacles, such as low local job market visibility, the high cost of moving, and difficulties in getting access to credit and land. Other problems relate to the lived environment, such as there being a lack of community services and recreational facilities available to the neo-rurals.

It seems that innovation and technological change, especially in advanced technology sectors such as the 'internet of things', life sciences, and clean tech, are concentrated in clusters, typically comprising universities and companies. The literature on 'the end of geography' and these clusters claims that digitalisation has so far done little to lessen the concentration of the knowledge-based economy in well-connected cities (Moriset *et al.* 2012). However, in the past decade, changes in France seem to be accelerating: examples include the Hauts-de-France, a depressed former industrial region in the northeast that is transitioning to a waste-free, clean-tech-fuelled circular economy, and the Nouvelle-Aquitaine region in the south-west, which is leading agricultural tech innovation in Europe. To encourage economic development, and to send a clear signal to peripheral France, Guilluy suggests emulating the US example of relocating universities outside big cities. For instance, although the decision was taken in 1991 to move the ENA to Strasbourg, a better choice of new location would have been a smaller provincial city, such as – to pick somewhere along the line on the map between Paris and Strasbourg – Troyes. Similarly, the headquarters of public administrations could be moved from metropolitan areas to small and medium-sized towns in peripheral France. Such relocations would also create a favourable context for economic development (Guilluy 2017, 239). In addition, to promote a more horizontal and less centralised top-down model of governance and society (which would play to the strengths of France's diversified geography), regional infrastructure and transport links could be upgraded. For instance, railway lines across the country could be reopened to improve public transport links within and between regions, and to reduce overcrowding on trains.

NATION BUILDING AND THE RIGHT TO BE DIFFERENT

Nation building has been an inherent function of the French system of universal education since its origins under the Third Republic (1871–1945). This function has returned to centre stage during the Fifth Republic, although by no means in a wholly favourable way. For, in the modern period, the education system no longer carries out its nation-building mission in core respects such as promoting mobility between social classes or mixing children from different social backgrounds during their school years. The whole construction – from primary schools to tertiary education – would require a fundamental overhaul to fulfil the Republican contractual promise of mobility and a 'level playing field' regarding access to the labour market. As things stand, French schools have increasingly become nurseries of inequality.

France's universally accessible education system was supposed to bring about a society-wide assimilation of the Republican value set, with secularism (*laïcité*) at its core. These values are enunciated on the first page of the Fifth Republic's constitution (Constitutional

Law, Article 2, June 1958; Constitute 2020). To be a French citizen entails first and foremost loyalty to the state and the assimilation of French culture (Hoffmann 1993). This idealist conception of the nation state leaves no room for multiculturalism reflecting diverse origins and identities (Holm 2002, 2).

France has never been ethnically homogeneous. Long before the post-colonial immigration of modern times, what would nowadays be described as ethnic minorities populated regions such as Corsica and Alsace. Continuous waves of immigration from all over Europe were the norm from the nineteenth century onwards, with post-war immigration from former colonies in Indochina and the Mahgreb having since been supplemented by migrant flows from many other parts of Asia and Sub-Saharan Africa (Escafré-Dublet 2014). In France, the proportion of the population with an immigrant background is the second highest in the EU (25 per cent compared with the EU average of 16 per cent) (OECD 2015).

While anyone arriving at Parisian tourist gateways such as the Gare du Nord railway station or Roissy ('Charles de Gaulle') airport will observe that France is culturally, ethnically, and racially diverse, the official line is that France is a homogeneous society where everyone has the same rights: a myth that persists, since the authorities ensure that the data required to measure the discrimination that occurs remains unavailable. To quote American author Alexander Stille, 'France has developed its own euphemistic language: neighborhoods with a high percentage of descendants of immigrants are often referred to as *quartiers sensibles*, or sensitive neighborhoods, and their school districts are called *zones d'éducation prioritaire*. Every country has its own tangled history with race. The French deal with theirs by using the old Republican ideas of "one France, indivisible" to cover over very deep differences. The question is whether they can also heal them' (Stille 2014).

Paul Collier offers a powerful account of politicians' reluctance to discuss, let alone tackle in a credible way, the mixture of economic discontents and anxieties about immigration. Public opinion on immigration is driven by issues that go well beyond gains and losses in the labour market or the welfare state. Many worry that non-European immigrants represent a cultural threat to their way of life and reduce social cohesion (Collier 2014).

Ethnic classifications have been excluded from national statistics since 1872 (Holm 2002, 13). The official shibboleth of 'one indivisible France' results in rules that prevent researchers from collecting or discussing ethnicity statistics. These legal barriers to the collection of data about citizens' racial origins complicate the task of measuring France's level of diversity, as the only information permitted to be recorded in the census is nationality (i.e. whether a person is legally a citizen of France and/or of some other country) (Escafré-Dublet 2014). The recording of racial profiles is deemed to run counter to Republican values. The danger of refusing to address the reality of diversity on the specious grounds of equality damages one's sense of belonging to the nation state and therefore alienates (migrant) 'nationals'. Meanwhile, (indigenous) 'nationals' are left feeling that migrants are not respecting the social contract and that the welfare state prioritises immigrants. Michèle Tribalat, a demographer, and Christophe Guilluy, a geographer, have both produced detailed accounts of the death of the Republican assimilationist ideal since the 1990s (Tribalat 2013; Guilluy 2019, 67–8). The blockade on data about the racial make-up of the population renders it virtually impossible to design appropriate policies addressing the problems that immigrant communities face, such as income inequalities and below-average educational attainment (Milanovic 2016). Scholars such as Guilluy and Tribalat have been vehemently criticised for their work on peripheral France and on immigration (Bastié 2018). According to Guilluy, demographer Hervé Le Bras, who is director of studies at the National Institute of Demographic Studies (Ined), seems to have used his position to stop any serious research on diversity, whether regional or international. Guilluy describes Le Bras and his supporters' activities as ostracising anyone who dares to voice a dissident opinion: 'Opposing voices are silenced. Yesterday the defenders of small business were accused of fascism. Today the defenders of small towns and cities, and more generally of the French countryside, are accused of Pétainism' (Guilluy 2019, 93).

Such struggles over data about ethnicity have been going on for decades. An early opponent of Le Bras, back in the 1970s, was Michèle Tribalat. She pointed out statistical errors and erroneous methods in his work. Rather than engaging with this criticism at an academic level, Le Bras compared her attempt to measure immigration and its racial components to the protocol of the Wannsee conference at which senior officials of the Nazi regime planned the Final Solution (Morvan 2017). For some, collecting data on 'ethnicity' is seen as a bitter remembrance of dark periods associated with the Vichy regime. While Tribalat's research was stymied, Le Bras and other members of his camp have been able to opine on immigration questions in the columns of *Le Monde*, a pulpit that gives off an aura of infallibility in the French public arena.

Regular surveys are undertaken by INSEE, collecting statistics on a person's country of birth, their nationality at birth, and their current nationality. The argument is that the information on country of birth together with nationality at birth will reveal whether a person is an immigrant (a foreigner born abroad and resident in France) or not. In reality, this method fails to measure the naturally expanding cohort of offspring of immigrant families. Occasional official surveys of subjective data such as feelings about identity and belonging, discrimination, and religion are also carried out. On the basis of these surveys, 2.7 per cent of the French population were registered as foreign in 1881, 7.5 per cent in 1975, and 11.6 per cent in 2013 (Escafré-Duble 2014, 2).

Thanks to various EU directives and the creation in 2004 of the 'diversity label' (awarded to employers who comply with equal treatment criteria when hiring), some progress seems to have been made and observed among the label's 1,600 corporate signatories (Escafré-Dublet 2014, 12). Yet migrants from North Africa and their descendants face numerous obstacles in the French labour market. INSEE surveys have shown that people with Arabic-sounding names are less likely to be invited for job interviews or accepted as tenants for rented housing, but more likely to be checked by the police (Senik and Verdier 2011). Here, survey data is once again no substitute for the proper statistics that cannot legally be collected, making it difficult to measure trends on racial discrimination (Musterd 2005). As this data is unavailable, tracing changes in the situation of second-generation immigrants is impossible, a problem that has been made more serious by the substantial increase in non-European immigration in recent decades (Verdugo 2011).

Michel Houellebecq's novel *Submission* (*Soumission* – the title is the literal translation of 'Islam') was published on 7 January 2015 (Houellebecq 2015). At 8.20 a.m. that day, Houellebecq was on breakfast radio giving his first interview about the book, which even before publication had drawn criticism as an Islamophobic provocation. When asked about his 2002 acquittal over inciting racial hatred after saying Islam was 'the stupidest religion', Houellebecq said that, upon reading the Qur'an, he had changed his mind and now felt Islam could be negotiated with.

At about 11.30 that morning, two French brothers named Saïd and Chérif Kouachi forced their way into the offices of the satirical weekly magazine *Charlie Hebdo*, which had published caricatures of the prophet Mohammed in 2011 and 2012, and shot dead twelve people. Among them were director of *Charlie Hebdo* and cartoonist Stéphane 'Charb' Charbonnier and French economist Bernard Maris, a friend of Houellebecq who had never once mentioned Islam in any of his opinion columns about economics.

The next day, Socialist prime minister Manuel Valls, seeking to unite the nation against what he deemed hateful finger-pointing at ordinary Muslims, said: 'France is not Michel Houellebecq ... it is not intolerance, hatred and fear' (Tronche 2015). He was echoing François Hollande's reaction to the publication of *Submission* two days earlier, when Hollande had invited the French 'not to let ourselves be devoured by fear'. The following day, 9 January, Amedy Coulibaly, a close friend of the Kouachi brothers, killed four hostages in the Hypercacher kosher supermarket siege.

Houellebecq's novel portrays with powerful effect the intellectual, media, and political classes as cowardly and unprincipled. Echoing Hannah Arendt's work, he portrays these elites as displaying the same passivity that made it possible for Hitler to come to power in 1933. Many of the attitudes he describes are accurate reflections of the real state of affairs in France: the media omitting to mention violent street clashes, and the political anti-racism of the left overriding its feminism, in the sense of making it wary of criticising patriarchal structures within immigrant communities. Houellebecq's scenario imagines the open destruction of the nation state, where politicians, for want of resilience, give up on secularism – the very essence of the Republic – and submit to a religious government. Houellebecq's unflinching treatment of taboos to do with immigration, the nation state, multiculturalism, ethnicity, and religion resulted in the prime minister of France denouncing him as a sinister opponent of the Republic's values. He seems to have unnerved the Republic's leadership by showing how small compromises made on secularism over time might lead to a big upheaval: in this case, the triumph of Islamism in France. The outrage expressed at the novel's depiction of an Islamist party taking power amid dark violence suggests Houellebecq may have struck a chord.

At any rate, great novelists have often held a mirror up to contemporary society. Norwegian author Karl Ove Knausgård, in his brilliant review of *Submission* for the *New York Times*, wondered how Houellebecq must have felt about being on the receiving end of such a vehement political reaction to his novel, and about being made a symbol of baseness and evil at a time when he was grieving the murder of one of his closest friends: 'I wondered what exactly had taken place in France in the years since 1968, when Sartre was arrested during the May riots and President de Gaulle pardoned him with the declaration that "you don't arrest Voltaire." Conceptions of the writer's, the artist's, the intellectual's role in society, and of the value and function of free speech, must have altered radically during those 47 years' (Knausgård 2015).

The extent of the denial embedded in state policies was revealed by a political row in March 2016: this was sparked by a radio interview with Minister for Urban Areas Patrick Kanner on the subject of the 2015 terrorist attacks by Salafists in France. He started the interview by repeating the party line that Islamist terrorism is rooted in poverty and unemployment. Next, the conversation turned to the by then established fact that several of the perpetrators had prepared the attacks while staying with their friends or kinsfolk in the Brussels district of Molenbeek. This neighbourhood is heavily populated by people of North African origin (a point that in Belgium, unlike France, can be recorded in official statistics) and is under Salafist control. Replying to the question 'How many Molenbeeks are there in France?', Kanner found the courage to tell the truth: 'There are today, we know, a hundred neighbourhoods in France that present potential similarities with what's happened in Molenbeek' (Vinocur 2016). Kanner had broken a taboo and was savaged for his pains by much of the media and many of his Socialist Party comrades. He was accused of blaspheming against the values of the French Republic and of stigmatising the population of those neighbourhoods. The first secretary of the Socialist Party, Jean-Christophe Cambadélis, accused Kanner of 'dissolving national harmony', while Socialist deputy Julien Dray said he deplored 'stigmatising people' in that way. Unintimidated by this smear campaign, Kanner reoffended the next day by detailing the French origins of the murderous terrorists: 'Amedy Coulibaly [the killer in the Hypercacher attack] was from the town Grande-Borne à Grigny, Mehdi Nemmouche [the Brussels Jewish Museum killer] … was in Burgundy [i.e. in France] before moving to Tourcoing [a town in northeast France close to the Belgian border], and Mohamed Merah [a serial killer in southwest France] was from the Mirail neighbourhood in Toulouse' (Vinocur 2016).

One who did not align himself against Kanner was Malek Boutih, another Socialist lawmaker, who had this to say: 'It is the first time that a minister of the suburbs [has said] even a little bit of the truth, namely that the ghettos have turned, little by little, into zones that we cannot control very well ... Neighbourhoods that are incubators for terrorists' (Floux 2016). For Boutih, author of a report on the radicalisation of youth, some territories where there is constant social disorder have been left on the margins of the Republic. There is an urgent need to reconnect these territories with the tradition of a Republic that guarantees the equal treatment of all citizens and ensures their safety.

The numerous publications on such territories, dating back two decades, leave no excuse for ignorance or denial of these problems, especially as they manifest themselves in the education system. As far back as 2002, for instance, a book titled *The Republic's Lost Territories*, written by an anonymous group of teachers, denounced the spread of anti-semitism, racism, and sexism in schools located in catchment areas with dense immigrant populations (Bensoussan 2002, republished in 2015 after that year's Islamist terrorist outrages).

Paul Collier claims that having a high proportion of migrants in a community is associated with a lack of trust: 'indigenous people living in a high immigrant community retreat into themselves, trusting less and taking less part in social activities, having fewer friends, and watching more television. Immigration reduces the social capital of the indigenous population' (Collier 2014, 74). People are becoming increasingly doubtful that public authorities have the will or the ability to ensure the safety and future of their children (Laffont 2018). British historian Andrew Hussey goes so far as to describe the situation of violence in the public housing projects of suburban France as an *Intifada*, animated by a vein of hatred among the Muslim population for the former colonial power (Hussey 2014).

To return to the acute vulnerability of schools in such environments, the penetration of radical Islamic values into the education system was documented as long ago as 2004, in a report on the subject by then Chief Inspector of Schools Jean-Pierre Obin that was first covered up, then vilified as Islamophobic. Obin updated his findings in a book published in September 2020 with the aim of sounding the alarm about, as he put it, 'the ravages caused by Islamism among young people and the damage it does to public schools'. His warning was still hot off the press when, in October 2020, it was atrociously vindicated by the horror of a Muslim youth beheading a schoolteacher, Samuel Paty, in a suburban Parisian street. The teaching materials used by Paty for a civics class on tolerance had sparked social media campaigns against him. An outraged teaching profession has long denounced the way that colleagues like Paty are 'rewarded' for doing their job – instructing pupils in national values – with complaints from families of offended pupils (Paty himself had gone out of his way to shelter sensitive pupils from possible offence) and criticism from cowardly educational bureaucrats for having 'rocked the boat'. With their studies thus degraded and sometimes undermined by violence, children whose parents can afford it are being sent in increasing numbers to private schools, further worsening the lot of the disadvantaged children left behind (Obin 2020).

The suburbs (*banlieues*) described in the stilted language of French bureaucracy as sensitive urban zones contain around a quarter of all Algerian immigrants and their descendants. Of the 751 urban areas thus designated, 64 are listed by law enforcement agencies as dangerous 'ghettos' where immigrants can account for up to half of the population and the unemployment rate is 23 per cent (45 per cent among young people) (JDD 2017). These suburbs are the result of a surge in the construction of social housing (*habitations à loyer modéré* – HLM) designed to deal with the massive housing shortage after World War II and the ensuing colonial wars. Shanty towns sprung up from the 1950s to the 1970s, populated mostly by a foreign workforce composed of Algerian, Italian, Moroccan, and Portuguese people. They highlighted the extreme poverty of a growing population of immigrants living in hazardous and unhygienic (often rat-infested) conditions, lacking access to water, sanitation, drainage, and electricity. The housing shortage stemmed not only from the bombs and shells that rained on cities such as Rouen and Amiens during World War II, but also from the post-war 'baby boom' and large-scale migration into cities from the countryside. Government regulations and rent-control policies also played a part, as these discouraged private home-building investment.

The way this social housing (*grands ensembles*) was conceived in the 1970s and 1980s was strongly influenced by the modernist architectural movement shot through with utopian visions (Mallonee 2015). However, it was not long before the gigantic towering structures designed to shelter people from the dirt and noise of the city were in need of urgent repair or demolition, while their inhabitants descended into a nightmarish existence where poverty and crime prevailed. Subsequent developments produced suburban new towns, where the buildings were not so gigantic. Instead, these towns consisted of architecturally characterless housing with no natural focus of community life. Such housing projects emptied the centre of Paris and other large cities of their small businesses and working class, contributing to the social exclusion faced by low-income families and immigrants (Paskins 2009).

Since the 1990s, there have been so many scandals about social housing being allocated to the elite that public opinion seems inured to them. For instance, there has been much corruption in the awarding of construction and maintenance contracts for public housing projects in Paris and its surrounding districts. But the potential criminal liability for such an abuse of public assets does not appear to be a sufficient deterrent. Perhaps this is because eventual convictions tend to result in nothing worse than a suspended prison sentence, as finally occurred in the case of former prime minister Alain Juppé in 2004. The equivalents of such scandals have occurred all over the country. For example, Philippe Pujol, in his book *La Fabrique du monstre* (*The Monster Factory*), relates the story of Marseille, France's third largest metropolitan area, where desperation induced by high unemployment and little hope of finding a job feeds the illegal economy in the lowest strata of French society. Activities such as supplying weapons and drugs, fuelling the real estate corruption that stems from electoral clientelism, wasting public money in fraudulent housing associations, and invoicing for fake social housing repair works are rife (Pujol 2016). In Annabelle Demais's *Rose sang* (*Pink Blood*), the northern suburbs of Marseille are synonymous with economic stagnation, political patronage, and drug trafficking (Demais 2014). Both authors show how corruption ran deep in Marseille under long-time mayor Jean-Claude Gaudin. In a 2013 OECD study, the city's poor municipal administration was criticised, but its underlying realities of high unemployment, inequality, crime, and despair were merely hinted at (OECD 2013).

This study also painted Marseille as one of the most unequal French cities, whether in terms of income or access to education. It showed that, at time of publication, the youth unemployment rate exceeded 50 per cent in the north of the city (and some other deprived districts), where more than a third of the population had no formal educational qualifications.

Pujol concludes by saying that Marseille is nothing other than the visible illustration of the malfunctioning of the Republic. Jean Tirole has pointed out that while various French policies are supposedly egalitarian, they tend either to turn against their intended beneficiaries or to bring them only minor benefits at disproportionate cost (Tirole 2016, 85). Many policies aimed at creating a fairer world end up discriminating against the very people they are supposed to support. For instance, tenants are protected from eviction should they find themselves unable to pay for their housing, but this policy leads owners to choose their tenants based strictly on whether they have a safe and regular way of generating monthly income. That excludes all tenants without permanent employment unless they can put up ample collateral. In the same vein, a rent-control policy always ends up producing housing shortages, with the poorest people being the worst affected. These policy failings have aggravated homelessness: almost half of the homeless population is aged between thirty and forty-nine; 38 per cent are women, 26 per cent are under eighteen, and 25 per cent are over fifty years old (Yaouancq *et al.* 2013: this is the latest available survey, with data from 2012). Since the GFC, real wage increases have lagged rental prices, signifying that simply having a job is increasingly less likely to allow one to find affordable accommodation. These problems also affect the educated: 14 per cent of French homeless people have a university degree, and a further 10 per cent have a high school diploma (Cordazzo and Sembel 2016). French housing policy illustrates the contradictions of government policies ostensibly designed to favour the disadvantaged. The French state spent almost 2 per cent of GDP on subsidising tenants' and landlords' costs of improving the quality of dwellings (Grislain-Letremy and Trevien 2014). The irony of this subsidy is that it has inflated rents (Cordazzo and Sembel 2016).

Spatial segregation is evident. Guilluy mentions that, in 2011, the average share of young people with an immigrant background at the national level was 20 per cent, but the concentrations observed in Parisian suburbs such as Aubervilliers and La Courneuve were as high as 77 per cent (Guilluy 2017, 70). A total of 2,500 neighbourhoods are classified as 'priority neighbourhoods', a euphemism for extremely poor areas where most inhabitants are either immigrants or second or third generation descendants of immigrants (Escafré-Dublet 2014, 6). For the many politicians, academics, and others who focus on the problems of these neighbourhoods, the goal is not to stigmatise the people who live in them; on the contrary, it is to highlight the extent to which these people have been abandoned by the state. Far from being 'prioritised', the inhabitants of these zones are among the most frequent victims of lawlessness, delinquency, and violence – and they cannot leave, as they cannot afford to move elsewhere. They have no choice but to be ruled by gangs, drug dealers, and extremists. Given the periodic violence seen in these suburbs, such as the disorders in Trappes in 2013 and the nationwide riots in 2005, acting as if these 'sensitive' neighbourhoods do not exist means leaving an entire population to its own devices. The realities of everyday life in these sensitive zones were well represented in a popular TV crime series called *Spiral* (*Engrenages* in the French original).

French officials (and others) have a taste for abstract rationalisation; but such reasoning all too often camouflages irrational emotion, which can be a vehicle for intolerance and violence. Gilles Kepel, a French scholar on Islamism, documents how the problem of terrorism and other violent crime in France stems in part from the monopolisation of policymaking by high-level civil servants, steeped in their hermetic self-regarding corporate culture. They are impervious to inputs from scholars with deep knowledge and expertise in this field and are resistant to any advice from such quarters. Keppel contrasts this arrogance unfavourably with what he sees as the more open political systems of Britain and Germany, where policymakers do not shy away from co-opting relevant expertise – such as, in this case, academic specialists on Islamism (Kepel 2015, 303). He also criticises local politicians for acquiescing to the opening of many mosques under Salafist control. A total of forty-one mosques in the regions of the country's three largest cities (Paris, Lyon, and Marseille) have been identified as being targets for extremist infiltration, where respected imams have been replaced by Salafists.

In 1989, the headscarf worn by Muslim women became a symbol of defiance against Republican values when three schoolgirls insisted on wearing this veil-like garment at school. This should not have been such a surprise in a society with a cultural tradition of rebellion against any symbol of authority. These girls may have felt like wearing headscarves not purely for religious reasons but as a symbol of revolt against authority – a gesture that in most other contexts would have been regarded as innocuous teenage rebelliousness. The girls' defiance became the source of a heated debate, which the outside world observed with near total incomprehension. The headscarf became a threat to the nation state not only because it affronted Jacobin ideals, but also because it called into question the status of women in French society. A law passed in 2004 by a huge majority in the parliamentary vote (494–36) prohibited the wearing of all 'ostensible religious insignia' in state schools to promote the values of the French Republic.

Two researchers from Stanford University, Aala Abdelgadir and Vasiliki Fouka, have evaluated the effects of the 2004 French headscarf ban on the socio-economic integration of French Muslim women. Their findings are that the law has reduced the secondary educational attainment of Muslim girls and has hampered both their prospects in the labour market and their family composition. These researchers argue that the introduction of this law has coincided with increased discrimination as well as a reduction in assimilation by casting religious and national identities (national in the sense of the French nation state) as incompatible (Abdelgadir and Fouka 2020).

However, the findings of another team of researchers point in the opposite direction. They have found that the disadvantages faced by Muslim women do not seem fundamentally different from those affecting the children of all underprivileged families. These authors looked at various indicators, such as fertility, marriage and divorce rates, inter-ethnic marriage, spousal age gaps, the gender gap in education, employment rates, national identity, religiosity, and language use, to assess cultural integration in France. They found that there is a strong feeling of French identity among second-generation immigrants with family origins in the countries of the Maghreb (Algan, Landais, and Senik 2012).

The headscarf controversy might have been avoided if school uniforms were still required. These were abandoned in 1968 to promote equality. Ironically, this move has had the opposite effect, as discretionary dress codes more easily reveal differences in wealth and social capital. Another rule change that caused disquiet was the 2015 law exempting turban-wearing Sikhs from the legal requirement to wear a safety helmet. Such an exception was regarded in some quarters as a threat to the values of the Republic and an open door to sectarianism (*communautarisme*) as an organising principle of social and political life. While the Latin roots of the word *communautarisme* signify 'jointly facing common problems', this term has become widely used since the 1990s in the pejorative sense of communities, mostly Muslim ones, jeopardising Republican values.

A reinvigoration of schools and the army as vehicles of civic training has become an increasingly popular cause taken up by the political class. However, little is said about how this might be done. During his presidential campaign, Macron promised to restore a mandatory universal national service (UNS); its preliminary launch was announced in June 2018, but the timeline for implementation kept slipping. Its aims as stated by Édouard Philippe are 'to encourage the participation and commitment of every young person in the life of the Nation, to value French citizenship and the feeling of belonging to a community gathered around its values, to strengthen social cohesion and boost the Republican melting pot'. The planned duration is one mandatory month, followed by a voluntary period of a minimum of three months, consisting of activities related to defense and security, social care, and the preservation of heritage and the environment. In June 2019, a pilot phase brought together some 2,000 young volunteers. This first phase was to be followed by two weeks of general interest attachment to a civil society association, a community, or an organisation while in uniform. The most recently announced plan envisages UNS becoming compulsory for all young people aged sixteen by 2022–3. Doubts about the project have to do with its potential cost and compulsory nature, and the puzzle posed by the need to accommodate and supervise annual batches of hundreds of thousands of young people.

EDUCATION: EQUALITY OF OPPORTUNITY

The French Republic with its monarchical style has created a confined elite, isolated from the day-to-day lives of the electorate. This class governs France with inert complacency. Starting with their children's schooling, they do not share the difficulties of their compatriots: a simple phone call to the right contact suffices to smooth access for this upper crust to the best of the public goods – especially in education and health care – that the country has to offer. The concept of risk is alien to them, as taxpayers provide for them throughout their lives, including via generous pension entitlements. In recent decades, the Republican tradition of equality of opportunity, enshrined first and foremost in state education, and legitimising the governing elites produced through the pinnacle of that system, has been looking increasingly threadbare.

The education system was built on the principle of meritocracy: many of the best students are chosen through highly competitive and selective examinations that determine lifetime career paths, ranging from ordinary schoolteacher to high-flying civil servant. Even spies are recruited only by competitive examination (*concours*). Thereafter, competition and selection cease, and salary scales are determined strictly on seniority rather than performance.

From 1997 until his untimely death in 2012, Richard Descoings was the director of Sciences Po, a prestigious higher education institution that, as we saw in chapter 1, is the main 'feeder' of students into the ENA. Sciences Po numbers among its alumni several French presidents and prime ministers, and half of the current CEOs of France's 200 largest companies. Descoings remarked that French high schools are 'training generations of anxious youths, who worry about their future, feel treated like numbers [and] distrust one another and the system'. In 2009, he visited eighty high schools, organising debates that brought together teachers, pupils, mentoring teams, and students' parents. In total, nearly 10,000 people participated in these roundtables (including 7,000 pupils) as part of a government review of *lycées* (high schools). The feedback from pupils was that their experience of school veered 'between boredom and dread' (Descoings 2009). Researchers Hugues Poissonnier and Pierre-Yves Sanséau later noted that 'for young French schoolchildren, the discovery of the value of work seems to take place in suffering' (Poissonnier and Sanséau 2017).

Some foreign analysts looking at French schools have concluded that these institutes crush the spirit of pupils (Boniwell 2017). School is the beginning of learning about life in the community, of discovering knowledge; it is where the initiation of know-how and a deepening of self-discovery take place. Yet French schoolchildren come out of successive cycles (kindergarten, primary, secondary) anxious and lacking in self-confidence (Poissonnier and Sanséau

2017). School children are graded on a scale of 0 to 10 or 0 to 20. A cultural tradition rules out giving pupils the top mark (i.e. a 10 or a 20, depending on the scale being used). The message this conveys to children is that, however hard you work, you will never quite make it. Instead of nurturing children through positive and confidence-building feedback, they are constantly discouraged, often in a humiliating way. The typical result for many children is a lack of confidence and reticence when it comes to expressing themselves orally because they are afraid of being accused of stupidity. The direction your life will take is also decided early on. Teachers decide if you are the 'right material' for the *Grandes Écoles* or for the lower-status university system (an alternative easily perceived as presaging lifetime achievement or failure). Nothing is done in the education system to make a child feel confident and positive about life. All this has led researcher Claudia Senik to the conclusion that the primary school system plays a role in a range of individual and social pathologies prevalent in France (Burrows-Taylor 2017).

French education has tipped into a severe decline: the country's numeracy and literacy levels are among the worst in the EU, especially among children from immigrant families. The educational inequalities linked to socio-economic status have been constantly widening during this century, and significant regional disparities remain (European Commission 2015). Jean Tirole has synthesised academic studies to demonstrate how the pursuit of the education system's declared egalitarian goals (by ensuring uniformity of the syllabus and the pupil mix) actually generates large inequalities, to the detriment of the least privileged and to the advantage of students from families living in higher-income neighbourhoods (Tirole 2016, 86). A cross-country survey by the OECD in 2015 had this to say: 'A child's academic performance is more dependent than elsewhere on parents' social and occupational status, contrary to the principle of equal opportunities' (OECD 2015, 23). National education, as France's centralised state-run school system is known, has become a national failure, where underpaid teachers in overcrowded classrooms are left exposed to shocking levels of violence that administrators and officials are impeded by various taboos from addressing.

An irresponsible expedient against youth unemployment has been to herd all young people with a basic high school qualification, known as the *Baccalauréat*, into universities (since obtaining that qualification virtually grants you the automatic right to embark upon tertiary education without any process of selection or other entry requirements). According to the Ministry of Education, the *Baccalauréat* success rate reached 88.1 per cent in July 2019: in other words, the level of that examination has fallen so low that almost everybody passes. But only students with the highest grades will be admitted into the so-called preparatory classes – a programme that leads towards the competitive entrance examinations to the *Grandes Écoles*. The not-so-lucky remainder will head towards the over-crowded lecture halls in France's universities.

The first day of the school year on 4 September 2017 was centred on music: this initiative marked the launch of new Minister of National Education Jean Michel Blanquer's ambitious reform drive. These reforms were aimed at improving overall educational attainment and were concentrated on schools (primary and secondary) and vocational training rather than higher education. In the past, vocational training was stigmatised as the failure track (Culpepper 2008), with the consequence that many young people lacked the skills required to find a job by the end of their training (OECD 2015, 28). The participation of senior high school students in vocational education and training remains below the EU average (OECD 2017c). France also ranks low in basic adult competencies and entrepreneurial skills (European Commission 2015). One major defect of the education system, however, has not been addressed by the Blanquer reforms – namely, the split of the higher education system into two tracks: the selective *Grandes Écoles* and the non-selective, and increasingly degraded, universities. This divide reflects, in many ways, a broader cleavage in society as a whole – all in the name of *égalité*.

Equality is symbolised by the refusal to make university entrance selective (Tirole 2016). University tuition is virtually free of charge, and any student who passes their *Baccalauréat* with an average score of at least 50 per cent theoretically has the right to enter the university programme of their choice. Faced with an influx of 30,000 additional students a year, universities are struggling with financial difficulties: students are packed into overfull lecture halls of 1,500 students. Selection occurs by means of students failing their exams at the end of their first or second year of university. This results in the least well-prepared students not only losing the opportunity to gain qualifications but also being discouraged, even stigmatised, after having squandered up to three years of their lives. An average of around 60 per cent of students fail during their first year, and another 60 per cent or so fail to gain a bachelor's degree after their first three years of study. Universities have almost no financial autonomy, with lecturers depending on the National Ministry of Education and most academic research being conducted at national research institutes. Tirole suggests including reasonable and progressive tuition fees, to be paid by the families who can afford them, with some of the proceeds being recycled to fund scholarships for students from poorer backgrounds. These scholarships would be conditional on the recipient students proving successful in their studies (AFP 2018). However, any such reform would be received with extreme hostility, as it would openly break with the myth that the system offers cost-free access for all to equal educational opportunities.

In contrast, only a small minority of students are admitted to the *Grandes Écoles* after spending at least a year in a preparatory class to take the entrance exam. Among those admitted to one of these elite institutions, the pass rate at graduation is nearly 100 per cent, and their fortunate graduates then have an assured career path and secure employment prospects. Most of the *Grandes Écoles* offer professionally oriented, specialised training, ranging from engineering to business.

We saw in chapter 1 how students' cultural and financial capital is decisive in having the necessary confidence to succeed in those highly competitive entrance exams. As a result, some reforms have been undertaken to render the *Grandes Écoles* more accessible to the least privileged parts of French society. The first attempt at such positive discrimination was launched in 1981 with the election of Mitterrand. The ZEPs (*zones d'éducation prioritaires*) programme within the national education system was launched in 1982 by the Socialist government and expanded to more 'zones' in the following two decades. The aim was to address social inequalities at schools in immigrant suburbs and rural areas by allocating extra funding to allow more teaching hours and smaller class sizes. However, an evaluation of the performance of the programme during the first phase (1982–92) observed that no specific line item for 'priority education' appeared in the National Ministry of Education's budget. Furthermore, neither the amount nor the nature of this extra funding was ever specified, nor the actual procedure by which priority status was to be determined. The authors of this evaluation mentioned that they had to carry out 'detective work' to discover the grounds 'for a school to become a ZEP'. The results of their investigations were not overly positive, revealing a large degree of arbitrary and untransparent decision making (Bénabou, Kramarz, and Prost 2009, 346). They found that when material resources for ZEPs were allocated on a scale comparable to those of analogous positive discrimination programmes in the United Kingdom and the United States, these resources were badly targeted. Only half were being used to fund additional teaching hours or to reduce class sizes, areas where the researchers found little improvement: on average, there were only two fewer pupils in a ZEP class than in an ordinary class. They also found that teachers tended to feel stigmatised by their ZEP status. As a result, the proportion of experienced teachers working in ZEPs decreased in favour of less experienced and younger teachers, despite the financial and career incentives these zones offered. ZEP student numbers also decreased during the period examined in this study. Finally, and perhaps most concerning of all, the authors did not find any major improvement in academic achievement. They warned of the risks experienced by programmes targeted at the poor when the source of the financing is not clear and when vested interests are at play. The evaluation cited Lionel Jospin, minister of education from 1988 to 1992 (later prime minister from 1992 to 2002) and a schoolteacher by profession, as saying the 'attribution of the ZEP status was linked to political considerations' (Bénabou, Kramarz, and Prost 2009, 353).

Another attempt at positive discrimination followed in 2001. This programme, known as the *Conventions d'éducation prioritaire* (CEP) and initiated by Descoings, sought to favour high school students from the ZEPs at the competitive entry stage to Sciences Po by introducing performance-based interviewing (PBI). This would replace the two-day written examination taken by other applicants. Because of the difficulty of that entrance examination, many students enrol in courses to prepare for it, and these courses can be quite expensive – a considerable burden on middle-class parents, and unaffordable for low-income families. By 2015, Sciences Po Paris had cooperation agreements in the framework of this positive discrimination programme with 106 ZEP high schools. These agreements helped overcome the reputation and perception of the *lycées* in question as sinks of violence and failure. While the CEP met with opposition, as some viewed such positive discrimination as a violation of the French constitutional guarantee of equal opportunity, the programme has generally been regarded as an important step towards inclusion and reducing educational inequalities (Sabbagh 2002). The positive difference made by the ZEP Sciences Po programme was highlighted by journalist Isabelle Rey-Lefebvre, who wrote about the experience of the *lycée* Aristide-Maillol, located in the disadvantaged area of Vernet in the southwest region of Perpignan. Before the agreement was signed with Sciences Po in 2005, Aristide-Maillol was in crisis, at the centre of which was violence between its neighbouring North African and Gypsy communities. Joining the CEP programme altered this picture and blunted the ghetto effect. While most of Aristide-Maillol's pupils still come from relatively poor families, the scheme has attracted students from better-off families to this *lycée*, contributing to its change of image. Since 2005, forty graduates of this high school have been admitted to Sciences Po, and the number of its students enrolling in preparatory classes for the Sciences Po entrance examination has increased from eleven to thirty-seven (Rey-Lefebvre 2014).

However, it was only in June 2014 that Minister of Higher Education Benoît Hamon signed off on a measure, implementing a law enacted the previous year, stipulating that, as of September 2014, 10 per cent of the best high school students (as defined by their *Baccalauréat* results) in every *lycée* would have a 'right of access' to the preparatory classes for the *Grandes Écoles*. The idea is to offer opportunities to bright students who, through lack of information or resources, would never have imagined trying for the *Grandes Écoles*. This reform is particularly important for preparatory classes where half of the students come from privileged backgrounds.

Regardless of the results of the CEP or other positive discrimination programmes, their very existence reflects the failure to realise republican values in practice. Journalist Robert Graham highlighted how unusual Nicolas Sarközy was among leading French politicians in supporting positive discrimination ('affirmative action'), which, in the 'egalitarian' Republic, runs counter to the official position that every citizen has equal rights (Graham 2003).

In France, general government expenditure on education as a proportion of GDP is above the eurozone average. Yet the OECD has pointed out that major flaws are present in the allocation of that expenditure: 'overcoming the early-childhood handicaps besetting pupils from disadvantaged social groups will require a better allocation of resources over the school cycle. Today, spending per pupil in primary school relative to upper secondary is among the OECD's lowest' (OECD 2015, 23). Although higher education spending is stable in real terms, spending per student has declined, owing to rising student numbers in universities, while funding for the *Grandes Écoles* has increased (European Commission 2015). *Le Canard enchaîné* revealed in February 2016 that the École Polytechnique had just been granted a €60 million five-year financing facility to maintain its level of excellence. A portion of those funds was used to build a golf course, and the sum in question was equivalent to the annual cost of the 1,000 new jobs created in 2016 across all universities in the country. *Le Canard* added that this golf course was essential to complete the range of sporting facilities necessary to the welfare of the students. This list included two swimming pools, two volleyball courts, two tennis courts, eleven fencing strips, numerous workout rooms, a climbing wall, four football fields, two rugby pitches, an artificial lake for rowing and canoeing, and a stud of thirty horses. On top of this, sixty sports teachers dedicate their time to ensure the fitness of a student body of just 400.

A 2014 report on École Polytechnique highlighted the striking contrast between the school's international ambitions and its anachronistic management (Cornut-Gentille 2014). This report also stressed the financially untransparent involvement in the school of leading industrial companies setting themselves up as the 'polytechnique community'. Despite this ample financial support, the school is virtually invisible in the Academic Ranking of World Universities (ARWU), also known as the Shanghai Ranking. Its position in the 2020 ranking between 301 and 400 out of 1,000 selected establishments compares poorly with that of Paris Saclay University, placed fourteenth, and Paris Sciences et Lettres (PSL) University, placed thirty-sixth.

THE OLD WORLD STRIKES BACK

This chapter started out with the question of whether France has been passing through a crisis of the nation state. The symptoms of that crisis stem from the following combination. On the one hand, the French state traditionally aspires not merely, as may be the case in other nation states, to provide a secure vessel for a thriving national community, but also to be the supreme expression of a unified community. On the other hand, the nation is riven with internal tensions and fractures: such pathologies would erode the legitimacy of any state. There is a still more serious conclusion to be drawn from the above survey of those fractures associated with taxation, immigration, localism, and educational access. The picture is made worse by the fact that it is the state itself causing, or at least aggravating, these fractures by its actions and omissions, which are always garnished, as if to add insult to injury, by the trademark arrogant complacency of the bureaucratic oligarchy. In reaction, people have been rediscovering sentiments of a deep identity of which they may have been barely aware, and which often run counter to the state's agenda.

While reflecting on these matters, I came across *In the First Person* (*A la première personne*) (Finkielkraut 2019, 61–79), a pamphlet by Alain Finkielkraut. He is a veteran Parisian 'man of letters', whose account does better justice to this change than my economist's pen could ever manage. Finkielkraut depicts a nation so deeply shaken by jihadi attacks that a 'nation within the nation' has emerged. Society can no longer be reduced to economic projects; it finds energy not only in the pursuit of material interest but also in a strongly felt sense of belonging, oriented around customs and religious traditions. Since the 2000s, the violent anger seen in the 'sensitive neighbourhoods' has ended up in a kind of secession. Faced with this internal separatism, many citizens have felt like internal exiles. They grew up in a culture of secularism (*laïcité*) that was taken for granted but was then, suddenly, challenged – and even mocked (notably by Anglo-Saxon commentators). After long years of barely giving a thought to *laïcité*, they now find themselves defending the laws that underpin secularism for the sake of their own freedom.

Continuing in this vein, Finkielkraut evokes a citizenry not only reawakening to the importance of their core values but also rediscovering their attachment to a more abstract sense of a way of life forged by history. They had previously gone along with what were presented as the progressive projects of Europe. They accepted the corollary – that France was a backwater, and attachment to Frenchness was some kind of quaint fiction. But that has been overtaken by recent events. People are now aware that such an attachment is precious and sense that they are responsible for preserving it. The tears set off by the spectacle of the cathedral of Notre Dame de Paris being engulfed in flames in May 2019 reminded them that their history was vulnerable to being annihilated. Long-disparaged words such as 'nation' and 'heritage' have made a comeback. Far from becoming fixated on a national identity, people are becoming more drawn to a sense of historical continuity. This is the same outlook that was evoked by Antoine de Saint-Exupéry, the author of *The Little Prince* (*Le Petit Prince*) and *Wind, Sand and Stars* (*Terre des hommes*): 'Of all that I have loved, what will remain ... I am thinking not only or mainly about people, but rather ways of life, unique shades of being, a certain spiritual light' (Saint-Exupéry 1994, 282, quoted in Finkielkraut 2019, 68).

This kind of elegiac and poetical thought will always stand apart from the mentality of the social scientist, straining for evidence. But when such finely expressed intuition captures the accumulated evidence, like a great portrait painter renders the inner being of his subject, the reader or viewer snaps to attention. Whatever the style of such thinking, its substance is furiously denounced. Finkielkraut, a resolutely secular Jewish intellectual, is routinely criticised as a reactionary or even a racist. In my own professional niche, similar criticism is meted out in response to critical analysis of monetary unions in general and the sacred cow of the euro in particular. This is the point where people tell me, 'You never liked France'.

Sympathy for the cause of the yellow vests is a red rag to the phalanx of the ruling technocrats and the comment journalists who play the role of courtiers. Their scorn finds another target in an area that is the subject of the next chapter – the project to 'democratise the school system'. The target in question is those who resist this agenda by defending 'elitist' educational values of solid grounding in literacy and numeracy. Drawing on what I view as a wider sense of the nation state, my retort to those 'courtiers' would be: 'It is you, rather, who ride roughshod over your own Republic as if you feel it is beneath you.' In the form of the coronavirus, history has turned the tables on this oligarchy, presided over by its brittle and verbally incontinent young leader, Emmanuel Macron. The people from beneath, who make daily life liveable, have become visible. These are the trash collectors, the nurses, the teachers, the supermarket cashiers, and the many others who have previously been overlooked.

A successful national community must be one whose members are all visible to each other – and hence to themselves. A former master of the worldwide Dominican order (as it happens, an Englishman) had this to say about the yellow vests: 'To wear them is to say "Look at me". They [the yellow vest protesters] have become symbolic of the feeling of millions of people that they have become invisible. No one notices they exist' (Radcliffe 2019, 316–7). The fracture of the French nation state has resulted in a previously lost nation demanding attention from those who control and condition the state.

4

Dignity for French Workers

The Great Recession triggered by the GFC worsened the country's economic and social predicament in ways that extended well beyond the obvious. The visible blows were already bad enough, as the chronic problems of high unemployment and stagnating living standards deteriorated further because of that shock. A deeper problem, however, emerged ironically from the authorities' very efforts to improve the economy. The goal of higher economic growth seems self-evidently justified, for how else was the lot of the poor to be improved in a sustainable way? A striving to recover the lost economic prowess of the post-war decades would allow more redistribution by the state, whose paternalist beneficence would reflect well on the bureaucratic oligarchy, which would meanwhile enhance its status and prestige thanks to the country's stronger economy. Yet for large sections of French society, there would be no such rewards of recognition and status, since economic 'revival' strategies had no role for these people in the drive for superior economic efficiency – except the passive role of receiving, in the best case, a marginally improved dole, a few more crumbs from the table of the globalisation feast. These were the invisible people who, at the end of the lost decade of the 2010s, donned high-visibility vests in a bid to be seen and a drive for recognition.

Back at the beginning of that decade, the grounds for this social reaction were lucidly described by Etienne Grieu, a French Jesuit theologian, in these terms: 'A world dominated by competition engages in a formidable process of classification, not only of performances but also of people. Right at the bottom of the chart are those who are not efficient enough. They thus become invisible to others, as they are unable to demonstrate their usefulness in any of the various exchanges we take part in ... they also feel humiliated because they scarcely have the means to say who they are or to make people notice the unique treasure they bear' (Grieu SJ 2011, 118).

The importance of social recognition was revealed a few years earlier by the precise definitions of German philosopher Axel Honneth (Honneth 2006). He distinguishes three spheres of recognition necessary for self-realisation. The first is the sphere of love, which relates to the emotional bonds uniting a person to a small group. Honneth emphasises the importance of these emotional bonds in building self-confidence, which is essential for participation in social life. The second sphere is juridico-political: it is because an individual is recognised as a subject of rights and duties that they can understand their actions as a manifestation, respected by all, of their own autonomy. In this sphere, legal recognition is essential to the acquisition of self-respect. Finally, the third sphere is social recognition, which allows individuals to relate positively to their particular qualities, to their concrete capacities. Social esteem, specific to this sphere, is essential for the acquisition of self-esteem.

Social recognition is in short supply, and hence widely craved, in France – especially by the working poor. The failure to consult and to rally the economic and social actors behind the rationale for reforms – namely, the necessary sequence of sustainable increases in wealth creation preceding increased redistribution – has created distrust towards the political class. Governing democracies is never easy, but it becomes 'mission impossible' in the absence of respect, cooperation, and some minimal consensus in the sense of widely shared understanding. This lack of social consultation and dialogue leads to a standstill. The government then does what it has always done: instead of piloting difficult transformations and cushioning the accompanying painful dislocations, it uses public funds to maintain zombie firms and to create artificial jobs (a policy labelled 'protecting jobs').

In its search for a way out of these quandaries, the French political class has developed a long-standing attachment to the Scandinavian model. In an authoritative survey of this phenomenon, researchers Kjerstin Aukrust and Cecilie Weiss-Andersen traced its origins back to the 1960s. They characterise this French fascination with the Nordic – specifically Swedish – model as a utopian striving for an ideal society: 'Scandinavia represents the opposite of France, the positive reflection of France's shortcomings at a given time' (Aukrust and

Weiss-Andersen 2019, 157). For many French enthusiasts of the Nordic world, Scandinavia represents an egalitarian system combining a high degree of income redistribution with a high standard of living. This model is characterised by a high level of political participation and organisation among citizens, political deliberations aimed at neutralising conflicts and reaching compromise, and a relative absence of social division. The high level of trust in Swedish society is attributed by Aukrust and Weiss-Andersen to eighteenth-century legislation authorising people to have access to a wide range of information on their fellow citizens, such as tax and income data. That transparency fosters trust in the integrity of fellow residents and politicians. Utopian perceptions of the Scandinavian model are based on these countries' superior competitiveness, higher ranking in happiness indices, more harmonious social relations and lower levels of corruption than in other industrialised countries.

Belgian anthropologist and historian Olivier Servais has highlighted the danger of an over-simplistic perception of a Scandinavian standard, given the differences and occasional contradictions between Nordic countries (Servais 2006, 23). He also points out those countries' distinctive features – low-density populations, abundant natural resources, and a certain environmental homogeneity – that make emulation problematic. The top-performing Scandinavian model is rooted in a particular history and geography, marked by constrained isolation and a harsh climate, proximity to nature, and also the ethics of Lutheranism – giving rise to a taste for innovation, action, simplicity, and a firm attachment to equality. It is by focusing on training, innovating, and researching that these small countries have found their place in the global economy. Scandinavian societies are among the most social-democratic or, as it would be labelled in the United States, *liberal*, in the world. Their approach to women's rights in particular serves as a model throughout Europe. In addition, social rights, in matters of unemployment or retirement, are suited to the high level of competitiveness required of their companies. The Scandinavian countries thus succeed in reconciling flexibility, job security, high productivity, and a high rate of compulsory contributions (Le Foulon 2006).

Despite these Scandinavian conditions being remote from the French experience, since the mid 1980s, most societal and economic reforms undertaken in France have been described by their proponents as drawing on some elements of the Scandinavian model. This goes for new laws aimed at achieving more transparency and integrity in public life as well as for economic reforms designed to narrow the competitiveness gap – in particular, as we saw in chapter 2, with Germany. Here, we see the constant appeal to an imagined Nordic utopia reconciling economic competitiveness and strong social protection. During the 2017 presidential election campaign, Emmanuel Macron often mentioned the Nordic countries (Aukrust and Weiss-Andersen 2019, 165). Scandinavian models were invoked in several reforms that Macron implemented upon becoming president, including his changes to the Labour Code and unemployment insurance, and his party's move towards a points-based system for pension entitlements. Macron's proclaimed political priority of improving ethical standards in public life also drew inspiration from the traditional Scandinavian values of transparency and openness.

Aukrust and Weiss-Andersen have a sceptical view, however, of Macron's Nordic credentials (Aukrust and Weiss-Andersen 2019, 166). They point to his handling of the yellow vests movement, where social dialogue took second place to violent clashes between demonstrators and police, and to his many scornful remarks about people who lag behind – a far cry from the Scandinavian spirit. His use of the *premier de cordée* metaphor (concerning the leader of a group of mountain climbers, who pulls up those who follow him) to describe the society to which he aspires is neither respectful nor egalitarian. Despite Macron's frequent contemptuous references to French workers as *shirkers*, this characterisation is not borne out by data on hours worked or from values surveys. On the contrary, survey evidence shows French people placing a high value on work and being distressed by fears of losing their jobs.

In a country where the central state bureaucracy controls all decisions that matter for social and economic development, reforms have often been introduced almost surreptitiously in the name of Europe or have been inspired by some utopian model. It is rare that reforms are the result of a parliamentary agreement or have public opinion rallying behind them. Most often the government has resorted to its powers of legislation by decree (under Article 49-3 of the constitution) to ram through such measures, or else it has simply abandoned them. Remarkably, in the case of Macron's pension reforms (reviewed in more detail later in this chapter), the government did both of those things.

The state's low confidence in its own citizens is reflected in the fact that trade unions are subsidised. Social dialogue is mandatory at the national level, with multi-employer bargaining agreements that barely account for participating companies' varying sizes, financial conditions, and geographical specificities. Ironically, Macron's most problematic personal qualities – his lack of empathy; his inexperience in politics and French cultural traditions – may have better equipped him to undertake reforms in this area of the labour market. While not exactly Scandinavian, such reforms did make the political class more accountable while putting industrial relations and wage bargaining into a more horizontal, less centralised framework. Although Macron's personal qualities proved no obstacle in this area, a headwind came from another source. Austerity policies, prescribed by the eurozone's fiscal rules and adopted after the GFC, have hampered France's structural reform efforts by denying sufficient oxygen to the economy, which instead suffocates under the weight of the technocrats' beloved regulation and palliative measures.

This chapter reviews a half-century of incompetence: of technocrats producing an unwieldy and ineffective state financed by heavy compulsory levies that discourage hiring, foment chronic unemployment, and create a general sense of hopelessness. It also describes how the French have begun taking into their own hands the task of creating a fairer and more dynamic society. France is in the middle of a cultural change.

FRENCH WORKERS ARE NOT SHIRKERS

Perhaps the most politically fatal trait in a head of state or government is to have a clearly ingrained dislike for ordinary people – or, at least, an inability to disguise that fact. Macron is not the first French leader to display this failing. When Valérie Trierweiler – the disenchanted former girlfriend of François Hollande – revealed in her book *Thanks for the Moment (Merci pour ce moment)* that Hollande called the poor the *sans dents* (toothless) (Trierweiler 2014), the public were disconcerted, as it seemed that a Socialist president had been making fun of people's suffering. But that reported gaffe by Hollande seems trifling compared with the series of tactless, and even offensive, comments by Macron: calling the female workers of a slaughterhouse 'illiterate'; contrasting 'the Gauls who are resistant to change' with the (industrious) 'Lutheran people'; and, in a speech in Athens in September 2017, labelling the opponents of his labour law reform as 'shirkers'. Still, it is worth examining on what evidence Macron might base such apparently disdainful assertions.

To begin, let us look at the nation's work ethic. When gathering statistics on working time, the first hurdle is deciding which measure to use: 'normal working hours', 'legal working time', 'actual hours of work', 'number of hours worked per inhabitant', and so on. For 2009, the annual average number of hours worked in France was 1,444 hours according to INSEE, 1,554 hours according to the OECD, and 1,601 hours according to Eurostat (Delhommais 2013). Such definitional questions continue with the distinction between full- and part-time workers. Comparative indicators for the EU in 2018 provided by Eurostat show that, on average, UK workers spent the highest number of hours per week at their main job (42.3 hours). France is well down the list at 39 hours, but above Italy (at 38.8 hours), while Denmark, with a working week of 37.8 hours, is the only country in which the average number of working hours is below 38 (Eurostat 2018).

Is there some inherent feature in French 'beliefs' that explains why France is burdened by so much unemployment? Might, for example, leisure be valued more highly than work by her people? Both the World Value Survey (WVS) and the European Value Survey (EVS) show that work is considered as quite important or very important by the French. The data series used in both those surveys begin in 1981. Both surveys include the following question: 'Indicate how important work is in your life.' Respondents can choose from four responses: very important, quite important, not important, and not at all important (Inglehart et al. 2014).

The result of the WVS for 2006 was that 62.2 per cent of French respondents (1,001 observations) said that work was very important. This compares with 49.6 per cent for Germany (2,064 observations). The EVS survey for 2008, analysed by French sociologist and philosopher Dominique Méda, showed that nearly two-thirds of full-time workers and three-quarters of part-time workers, unemployed, and retired people in France thought work was very important, while in the United Kingdom and Germany this opinion was mainly held by full-time workers and the self-employed. Méda highlights that in more recent international surveys, French respondents are among those who most frequently rate work as being very important – 67 per cent compared with 45 per cent on average in the United Kingdom and Germany.

Méda contends that the high level of unemployment in France is not the only explanation for work being more highly esteemed. It is the intrinsic interest of work that is valued as well as the relationships established with others through it (Méda 2016). Cultural factors are also important. France is a society where work is particularly valued as a source of dignity. People are who they are thanks to the kind of diploma and the work they have obtained. A job in France can therefore often be a more powerful social marker than in peer group countries. One's career generates an expectation not only of receiving a salary, but also of enjoying a consistently recognised *place* in society.

This evidence on French attitudes towards work finds strong support in a study by researchers at the Fondation Jean Jaurès (Fourquet, Mergier, and Morin 2018). They observed that 88 per cent of the workers surveyed for the study considered their work 'useful for their business', but that only 44 per cent said they felt their work is recognised for its fair value: that is 20 points less than in the United Kingdom and more than 30 points below the equivalent indicators for Germany and the United States. This gap in the French workplace between employees' perceptions of usefulness and the recognition they actually receive causes stress that is reflected in absenteeism, sick leave, and burnout. Summing up these findings, Chloé Morin, the director of international projects at Ipsos, had this to say: 'The France Télécom scandal could not have happened in a society of slackers, whose paramount goal was leisure. No one would take their own life for professional reasons if work did not have a core social function' (Morin 2020). Morin was referring here to the infamous case of harassment and bullying by the top management of France Télécom that had fatal consequences. A silver lining to this grim episode came in December 2019, when, for the first time in French history, the Paris criminal court convicted that company (in addition to the individuals concerned) of the crime of 'institutional harassment'. By that stage, France Télécom had changed its name to Orange (although the state remained the dominant shareholder). Its former CEO Didier Lombard and two other former executives were given prison sentences and fines for their role in creating a culture of routine workplace bullying that led to several suicides in the company. Four other executives were convicted as accomplices and given four-month suspended sentences and €5,000 fines.

This judgment has been seen in France as a landmark case in the area of industrial relations and well-being at work. Sébastien Fosse, a researcher on management issues, observed that if most social movements reflect various types of suffering experienced in a society, being able to describe and name that suffering is an essential step towards rebuilding (Fosse 2020). This articulation of the meaning given to work was one of the achievements of the France Télécom trial, in which more than a hundred civil parties participated, including the families of the employees who had committed suicide.

This story begins in February 2005, when Didier Lombard became the company's CEO. He arrived in the job with impeccable credentials: a graduate of both the École Polytechnique and the École des Mines (an elite engineering school), he also held a doctorate in economics. Lombard was tasked with carrying out the group restructuring initiated by his predecessor, Thierry Breton, who had left the job upon being appointed minister of the economy in the government of Dominique de Villepin. (A typically unsinkable French elite technocrat, Breton was sent by the French government to Brussels in December 2019 to take up one of the top jobs – responsible for the EU's single market – in the new European Commission led by Ursula von der Leyen.) This 'internal reorganisation' at France Télécom was designed and imposed by senior management without consultation with the trade unions. Lombard's strategy included eliminating 22,000 jobs and retraining another 10,000 workers over three years (2006–8). In most cases, that retraining meant a demotion to working in the company's call centres or high street stores. Some employees were transferred away from their families or left behind when offices moved – and then assigned demeaning jobs. The court examined thirty-nine cases of employees, nineteen of whom had taken their own lives and twelve of whom had attempted to do so. Some of them left messages blaming France Télécom and its managers. The others had lived with depression or had been otherwise unable to find other work.

Perhaps the most basic measure of despair is the suicide rate of a society, reflecting as it does mental and physical suffering. While individual causes will always play a role, social trends also contribute to the malaise that results from economic insecurity and exclusion from the labour market and, hence, from a dignified life. American economist Anne Case remarked in April 2019 at a lecture at Purdue University that 'it's not inequality in general that is causing rising death rates [among working-class white Americans], but the way the economy works today, which is unfair to many. It's holding down real wages in the US, especially for those less educated and who do not have bachelor's degrees.' In France, it is not only structural economic factors that cause despair, but the way firms are managed. Economist Thomas Philippon has pointed out that, regardless of firms' ownership (most are controlled either by the state or by families or collective investment structures), corporate leaders tend to be appointed on the basis of inheritance (family) or parachuting (former civil servants with similar educational and social backgrounds) rather than internal promotion. These organisations tend to limit their employees' scope for initiative, hampering the prospect of talent rising to the top. Such factors contribute to workforce dissatisfaction (Philippon 2007).

Mutual mistrust between managers and employees explains why so many in the active workforce are impatient for retirement or pre-retirement. The value placed by French people on retirement must reflect their experience of lack of recognition at work. Feelings of frustration in active life lead to retirement being invested with ever-greater attractions, real or imagined: a new life without a boss and managerial constraints, offering social recognition and freedom – including from suffering, whether psychological or physical. It is little wonder, then, that the Macron administration's proposed pension reforms (affecting the pensionable age and retirement incomes) proved so socially sensitive. Perhaps the most fundamental strategic error here was the failure to address these problems of relations in the workplace (Morin 2020).

An important determinant of well-being is the quality of social relations. Researchers Yann Algan, Pierre Cahuc, and André Zylberberg observe that the post-war rise in material living standards in industrialised countries was not accompanied by commensurate increases in many standard indicators of well-being. They contend that a decisive factor in the French case was, and is, an engrained distrust, which undermines the social fabric. They describe a society in which distrust feeds on itself in a vicious cycle of mutual indifference. They attribute this characteristically French problem first and foremost to the prevailing culture in the country's schools. These same authors deplore the absence of group work among school pupils and demonstrate how the cost of this dysfunction manifests itself in poor results and inequalities. Schoolteachers' training and resulting teaching methods lay the foundations for a professional world that is hierarchical in the extreme, causing anxiety and distrust that handicap the economy. In such an environment, it is not surprising that so many large French companies have a relatively poor record as regards career development and internal promotions. According to Algan, Cahuc, and Zylberberg, 66 per cent and 51 per cent of senior management in large companies in Germany and the United Kingdom, respectively, have had an internal career, whereas this is only the case for 21 per cent of executives in France. This vicious cycle comprises weak social dialogue and a culture of conflict, fostered by low levels of unionisation in workforces. State intervention inhibits social dialogue, yet it is the absence of adequate social dialogue that prompts the state to interfere in the first place (Algan, Cahuc, and Zylberberg 2012).

Eurofund's European Working Conditions Survey (EWCS) measures the quality of working life by assessing the physical, emotional, and social pressures on workers in thirty-five countries. The 2015 survey, for which nearly 44,000 workers were interviewed, revealed increasing emotional pressures leading to mental health issues, fatigue, and burnout (Eurofund 2016). A high level of adverse social behaviours such as bullying, harassment, and violence in the workplace was reported in the Netherlands and France, with both countries showing the worst scores in these areas. A startling 46 per cent of all workers in France reported hiding their feelings compared with 31 per cent in the EU28 and only 18 per cent in Denmark (the country with the best score in this area). On physical stress (physical hazards) at work, improvements had been made in most European countries since 2005 except for France and the United Kingdom. That same EWCS survey noted that the transformation of the nature of work in a high unemployment environment (a French hallmark) has contributed to the deterioration of social relations at work since 2010. A multiskilled and autonomous workforce is becoming increasingly necessary, and while this should mean a more horizontal way of functioning at the firm level, the reality is that supervision and control have been reinforced (for instance, by computerised employee appraisal systems).

These surveys draw attention to the need for a change in corporate culture. The time of the omnipotent French CEO (*président directeur general*), presiding with little consideration for social dialogue, may be over (O'Sullivan 2007). Economic historian Deidre

McCloskey says that successful enterprises need to adopt 'the soccer playing, ice hockey view of the world', combining a 'we're out there to compete' attitude with 'immense amounts of cooperation' (BBC HARDtalk 2014).

Philippon points out how the stakes involved in social relations have been raised by the evolution of economic structures (Philippon 2007). The Fordist method of firm organisation, based on mass production generating economies of scale that still prevailed during the economically successful post-war decades, could foster but also cope with a certain mistrust between employers and workers. The new growth model, in place since the mid 1980s and grounded in innovation and the development of services, entails an increase in levels of human interaction. Through it, complex human and organisational networks driven by IT have emerged, leading to the automation of repetitive manual and mental labour. The increasing importance of the human factor has increased firms' need for effective cooperation, which, in turn, depends on respect and trust. For this, flexibility rather than standardisation is required; but this is being hampered by the absence of in-firm negotiation between management and organised labour, which was historically driven by the dominant role of the state in industrial relations in France (Culpepper 2008).

One commonplace is that Europeans believe less than Americans in the idea that effort pays – in other words, that exertion is closely linked to income. Europeans therefore support a larger public sector. Americans, in contrast, are more likely to believe that people, by and large, get what they deserve, so they advocate a smaller government. Survey evidence consistent over long time periods shows that 60 per cent of Americans believe that the poor are lazy as opposed to unlucky; only 26 per cent of Europeans hold this belief (Alesina, Glaeser, and Sacerdote 2001). While reality belies such perceptions on both sides of the Atlantic, the pessimism of the French public at least finds support in data: regarding social mobility, for example, the number of years required to move from middle income to upper middle income has increased, on average, from twelve years in the 1960s to thirty-five years in the 2010s (Guilluy 2019, 75). A study carried out in 2006 revealed that of the top 100 managers in France, 77 per cent are from upper- or upper-middle-income backgrounds compared with 64 per cent in the United Kingdom; and whereas in the United Kingdom 25 per cent of those on a lower middle income and 11 per cent of those on a lower income make it to the ranks of the top 100 corporate leaders, in France the equivalent proportions are only 19 per cent and 4 per cent, respectively (Maclean, Harvey, and Press 2006). This picture of relatively lower levels of social mobility in France stems also from the social requirements of elite membership. Firms' promotion policies tend to be biased in favour of educational background and governmental connections rather than expertise or performance (Bloom *et al.* 2012). The notion of 'empowerment' is poorly assimilated by French management (Garicano, Lelarge, and Van Reenen 2013). The technocrats – leading engineers, captains of industry, and top politicians – are an increasingly hereditary elite, the sons (and sometimes daughters) of those who themselves had advantageous family backgrounds.

BLAMING THE UNEMPLOYED FOR UNEMPLOYMENT

The GFC caused the unemployment rate to spike in France, as it did in all developed countries. In the French case, however, this increase came off a high base. Even before that crisis, unemployment had frequently risen above 10 per cent of the active population for long periods. This indicates structural causes, which are reflected in the large share of long-term unemployed among the total number of jobseekers. A related problem is the low level of employment: a testament to the large number of people who are of working age but are not looking for jobs. This phenomenon of weak labour market participation is particularly pronounced at the lower and higher ends of the working-age spectrum (i.e. among school leavers and those approaching retirement age).

When challenged about this problem in September 2018 by a young unemployed man with a qualification in horticulture, Macron had this to say: 'If you are ready and motivated, in hotels, cafés and construction, everywhere I go people say to me that they are looking for staff. I can find you a job just by crossing the road!' (Europe 1 2019). The young gardener appeared unpersuaded, explaining that he had sent many CVs and personal statements to potential employers, none of whom had even replied. This was one of Macron's several combative public comments that reflected poorly on him, for at least two reasons. First, he displayed his typical lack of empathy by implying that the young man was a layabout (or, at least, had been insufficiently diligent – or too picky – about his

Table 4.1   Unemployment as a percentage of the active labour force.

	Total unemployment					Aged 20–24	
1969	1980	1993	1997	2008	2018	1975	2018
2.0	6.3	12.2	12.5	7.4	9.1	5.3	20.8

Source: INSEE/Observatoire des inégalités, Eurostat 2019.

job search). Even after hearing about all of those ignored job applications, Macron could not bring himself to utter a gracious word of encouragement; instead, he pursued his point, insisting that he was *sure* that some of the cafés in the Paris Montparnasse area needed staff (Berdah 2018). Second, he revealed a poor grasp of the realities of the French labour market – including, as shown by his urging this young person with vocational training as a gardener to find a job in the construction or hospitality sectors, the disjuncture between the skills supplied by the education system and those needed by the economy.

Sociologist Gilles Moreau got to the bottom of the error implied by Macron's little dialogue with the budding gardener: the president's position was apparently substantiated by an official Labour Exchange (*Pôle emploi*) figure of 300,000 job vacancies in December 2017; in reality, applications had already been submitted for all but 19,500, or 0.6 per cent of that total (Moreau 2019, 43).

High unemployment has scarred the French economic landscape for more than half a century. During Giscard's presidency (1974–81), unemployment rose every year (table 4.1). The policies of that administration aggravated the negative effects of the oil shocks and global stagflation. It was in this period that the total burden of taxation and mandatory levies on businesses exceeded 40 per cent of GDP, and the public sector was expanded (iFrap 2005). The performance of the economy in the 1970s contradicted the promises of rapid growth and reduced unemployment that helped bring François Mitterrand to power on a left-wing platform in 1981. By September 1997, two years into the term of President Jacques Chirac, the unemployment rate had reached 12.5 per cent – and this despite a much improved global economic backdrop compared with the 1970s.

The next occupant of the Elysée Palace, Nicolas Sarkozy, resembled his predecessors by prioritising job creation. He made better initial progress on this front, with the unemployment rate trending down to 7 per cent during his first year in office (2007–8). However, this progress was reversed by the recession caused by the GFC and the eurozone sovereign debt crisis, which saw unemployment climb back up to 10.5 per cent (Barbier and Knuth 2010, 34). A leitmotif of François Hollande's rhetoric during his five-year presidential term (2012–17) was claiming the unemployment rate was about to peak and start declining. It never happened: during the last full year of his term (2016), Hollande presided over an unemployment rate of almost 11 per cent of the active population (compared with only 5 per cent in Germany). But life is unfair. When Hollande gave up re-election ambitions and passed the baton to his successor, Emmanuel Macron, unemployment had the cheek to decline – albeit for a short period. The main reason was that Macron came to power in a good year for the global economy, and by 2019 unemployment had fallen to 8.1 per cent. In line with the definitions of the International Labour Office (ILO), these unemployment figures all refer to the ratio of jobseekers to the active population. Yet many people of working age are not counted in these figures, as they have dropped out of the labour market. Such people exist in a halo of unemployment. They span a wide range of career paths and profiles: some are relatively highly qualified, remaining in the halo only temporarily, while others, usually less qualified, are informal part-time workers, the discouraged unemployed, the older unemployed (who are exempt from job searches) and people whose personal circumstances are incompatible with taking on a job (Ducoudré 2019, 55).

The human cost of unemployment, which has ground down the actual and potential living standards of the stranded part of the population, has increased due to the wasteful use of public money to protect jobs. Another aggravating factor has been the policy of pushing as many young people as possible towards university education, as this has had the perverse result of diverting many among the massed ranks of students entering higher education from other forms of potentially more beneficial training (in the sense of making them more employable). The main losers in this situation are clearly visible: they are young people under the age of twenty-four (table 4.1). The employment rate – that is, the proportion of employed people in the working-age population – was 65.7 per cent in January 2018. This is below the European average of 72.2 per cent and far behind the employment rates of the Netherlands, Germany, and the United Kingdom (which are all around 76 per cent).

Thomas Philippon notes that this difference of almost 7 percentage points in the labour participation rate between France and Europe as a whole represents millions of underutilised workers; it entails not only a significant human cost for the people affected but also a material loss of income for the overall economy (Philippon 2007).

Now, moving from the theme of unemployment to the other problem highlighted by Macron's exchange with the young, unemployed gardener – namely, the failings of the education system (especially from a labour market perspective) – let us start with a brief survey of the secondary school tier. This is a hierarchical structure that distinguishes between general and vocational education. France being a country where family background is a particularly strong predictor of educational outcomes, the children of working-class parents are more likely to be directed to the vocational pathway (Schleicher 2019). At the same time, most of the unemployed come from underprivileged backgrounds (Gendron 2009). This points to problems with vocational training that can be traced back to a division within the vocational pathway introduced in the 1960s. A reform launched at that time in effect downgraded the pre-existing vocational training after basic (primary) education that led to the certificate of vocational aptitude (*Certificat d'aptitude professionnelle* – CAP). This reform introduced a technical or vocational stream into France's secondary schools themselves. After their first two years of secondary education, pupils are divided between their school's general and vocational streams, the latter of which leads after two further years to a vocational studies certificate (*Brevet d'études professionelles* – BEP). Having been thus integrated into the education system of the 1960s, vocational training began to take precedence over the apprenticeship training associated with the CAP, which was now reserved for pupils with academic difficulties. The general stream leads after five years to the *Baccalauréat* (high school diploma), based on either a broad curriculum (the *Bac Gen* introduced by Napoleon in 1808) or a curriculum weighted more towards science and technology (the *Bac Tec* introduced in 1968). Since 1985, the pupils outside this general stream, instead of leaving school after the CAP or BEP, have proceeded to the vocational *Baccalauréat* (*Bac Pro*): this was designed to open access to higher education – and therefore social and professional advancement – to all pupils.

Movement between those three *Baccalauréat* tracks is possible in principle but rare in practice. Children born into advantaged backgrounds are rarely oriented to the *Bac Pro*, and few holders of this qualification move on to higher education. Of these few, only a tiny percentage manage to obtain a university degree (Gendron 2009), and none qualifies to enter the *Grandes Écoles*.

The lengthening of vocational and technical education pathways in the 1980s was a response to rising unemployment (Moreau 2019, 45–7). These reforms changed the established track followed by typical working-class families and posed a difficult choice for them: which diploma – the CAP or Brevet/*Bac Pro* – would lead to the best employment opportunities for their children? Moreau argues that vocational education has been devalued by the introduction of the *Bac Pro*. He observes that the curriculum in vocational *lycées* has become reorganised around the *Bac Pro*, with the BEP becoming the minimum reference diploma and the CAP being relegated to a 'sub-BEP' diploma. Shorter periods of vocational education have fallen out of favour. Increasingly, the standard has become the higher technical certificate (*Brevet de technicien supérieur* – BTS), established in 1959, which requires two further years of study after the *Bac Pro*.

The *Bac Pro* was introduced in response to changes in the labour market, with a view to equip worker-technicians with improved and more versatile (transferable) skills. The result would be a more adaptable workforce, with a greater sense of initiative and autonomy, thereby enhancing the population's overall life chances as measured by social status and living standards. Moreau shows that practical experience has fallen disappointingly short of those goals. One problem is the difficulty of getting access to vocational education, whether on the CAP or *Bac Pro* tracks: places depend on final labour demand on the part of employers. Young people want to work but all too often find that companies do not want them.

If the education system is segmented between a pathway for the *elect* and the *also-rans*, the divisions in the labour market between outsiders and insiders have become as entrenched as the public–private employment division. Researchers have showed that in France, a country with a preference for state-directed solutions, and where the civil service enjoys high levels of protection and trust, labour flexibility was introduced in the form of temporary contracts to appease well-organised and protected insiders (Granville and Martorell-Cruz 2016). Employees with permanent and fixed-term (i.e. temporary) contracts are, respectively, the insiders and outsiders of the French workforce. The percentage of outsiders in the total is relatively low, but growing (Mercier 2017), and workers employed on such temporary contracts are predominantly young and/or female. Among the fifteen- to twenty-four-year-old age group in employment, 50 per cent are hired on fixed-term contracts: compare this with 12 per cent for the rest of the workforce, on average, and 24 per cent in the OECD area as a whole (INSEE 2018). That comparison with the wider OECD peer group is particularly striking, as it shows that while young new entrants to the labour market face tougher conditions in all countries, the phenomenon is much more pronounced in France. One reason for this is that a deterioration in labour market conditions led successive French governments from the 1970s onwards to skew labour regulation in favour of hiring young people. Their employment conditions differ significantly from those of insiders: they face job insecurity and substantial wage gaps, which widen further in proportion to (young) age, immigrant status, or short job tenure (Kahn 2015).

All this spells a higher risk of falling into poverty and results in an effective bar on young workers getting access to rental accommodation or credit, both of which typically require one to have a permanent job contract. French economist Hervé Charmettant links the dualisation of the labour market to increasing precariousness (Charmettant 2017). He shows that temporary contracts constitute a 'trap', as the risk of becoming unemployed within a year is six times higher for people with a fixed-term contract than for people with a permanent contract. This ratio shifts to ten times higher for the most marginal temporary workers, as the duration of temporary employment is also decisive: fixed-term contracts lasting less than one month are two times more likely to lead to unemployment than contracts with terms lasting more than one year. Charmettant also highlights the social divide between the permanent and temporary segments of the labour market, with the latter containing more relatively disadvantaged people such as non-graduates, immigrants, and those at either end of the working-age spectrum.

In the private sector, the sheltered insiders (i.e. with permanent contracts) are well protected by OECD standards, while the opposite goes for the outsiders with temporary contracts. As for civil servants, their jobs are outside the scope of the Labour Code, and they are subject instead to the *Statut général de la Fonction Publique* (the employment conditions of the judiciary and military personnel are governed by other specific regulations). At the same time, the public sector has its own 'outsider' employees, who work on either fixed-term or open-ended contracts. To circumvent the 2005 EU directive stipulating that after six years of uninterrupted service in the same employment a worker's contract should become permanent, outsider schoolteachers (an occupation categorised as part of the civil service in France) are dismissed before the summer holidays and reappointed at the beginning of the school year (Audier *et al.* 2012).

These divides are rooted in the social stratification and flaws of the education system, including as regards continuous professional training. Crossing the street is clearly not always a reliable way of finding a job!

SISYPHEAN PURSUIT OF THE GERMANO-NORDIC DREAM

French societal and economic reform programmes are laced with words such as 'transparency', 'confidence', 'trust', 'decentralisation of collective bargaining', and 'flexicurity'. For French politicians of all ideological stripes in the 2000s, Denmark became a fashionable exemplar of that flexicurity: it was seen as having the best of all worlds, where workers were not in a precarious position despite the country's flexible labour markets. Denmark's approach was based on a cooperative spirit in industrial relations and on judicious spending of the proceeds of its heavy taxation on personal incomes. This idea became fashionable in France due to the observation that its export performance was deteriorating, owing to a structural decline in competitiveness relative to Germany in the years following the launch of the EMU (OECD 2017a).

Belgian economist André Sapir noted this divergence in competitiveness as a threat to the euro. In a report prepared for an informal meeting of the EU's finance and economy ministers in 2005, Sapir identified four distinct approaches in Europe to pursuing the goals of efficiency and justice. His verdict on the Nordic countries (i.e. Denmark, Finland, and Sweden, and he added the Netherlands to this group) was that they were both 'fair and efficient'. The next two groups each fell short on one of those two counts: the countries in what he called the 'continental' group (Austria, Belgium, France, Germany, and Luxembourg) were fair but inefficient, while the Anglo-Saxon countries (Ireland and the United Kingdom) had it the other way around. As for the final – 'Mediterranean' – group of countries (Greece, Italy, Portugal, and Spain), these were held to fail on both counts – i.e. they were both unfair and inefficient. Sapir described the Nordic countries as having a high level of social spending and strong unions, with wage restraint and ease of dismissal compensated for by generous unemployment benefits (Sapir 2005, 5–6).

By the end of the twentieth century, France's highly centralised system of collective bargaining had entrenched rigidities and a confrontational culture. The reasons for the state's dominant role in industrial relations and the government's direct involvement in collective bargaining lie in the historically large number of state-controlled firms. As a large employer, the state influenced negotiations in the private sector (Culpepper 2008). Faced with a dirigiste state, trade unions concentrated on organising protests and strikes rather than developing a system of mutually binding collective bargaining. Disproportionate power is concentrated in the French state's reach in collective wage bargaining: despite the unionisation of the workforce falling from 21.7 per cent in 1970 to 7.9 per cent in 2008, the coverage of wage bargaining, engineered by the state, increased over that same period from 70 per cent to 92 per cent (Visser 2013). The path to successful labour market reform accordingly came to be seen as lying through decentralisation in the sense of allowing firms more margin to negotiate wages and conditions with their own workforce.

Successive drives to address such problems had little to do with the actual practice of Scandinavian countries that French reformers cited as their model. Besides reversing that excessive centralisation of industrial relations, the wider labour market reforms boiled down to redressing in favour of 'flexibility' a balance that was seen to have swung too far in the direction of 'security' (in the sense of over-rigid pay and conditions, especially job protections); this was thought to underlie the country's chronically high unemployment. Yet, as French entrepreneur and author Alain Lefebvre explains, the 'flexicurity' that evolved in Denmark over the preceding two decades was just that: a system maintaining an equilibrium between worker protections and practices that promote efficiency (Lefebvre 2018). Danish flexicurity does not, therefore, mean 'easy to fire staff'; and in Sweden, it is more difficult to lay off people than it is in France. Swedish unemployment insurance is not as generous as the

French suppose – although it is better targeted, since jobless bene-fits in Sweden are higher than in France for low-paid workers.

The flexibility side of the Scandinavian equilibrium comes much less from reducing the protections enjoyed by workers than from enhancing their performance. Thanks to the limited hierarchy in-side Swedish firms, well-trained staff have considerable autonomy and scope for team-level initiative, and this helps them to adapt quickly to customer demand. The main problem for Swedish com-panies is recruiting enough workers with the required skills, not reducing headcounts. As for employees, their feeling of security is founded on their qualifications and skills. Whereas school students in Sweden are shown by international surveys to have no better than average attainments by age fifteen, twenty years later (at age thir-ty-five) they are among the best trained in the world, thanks to a continuing education system that offers training on all subjects for all ages. The Swedish state stands back from industrial relations, let-ting its social partners define the rules for the functioning of the economy; its role is more that of arbiter and backstop. For instance, the state is responsible for checking that there is no discrimina-tion; (sometimes) financing training programmes offered by those social partners; and guaranteeing a reliable safety net of income, shelter, and health care on condition that the recipients of such benefits continue actively looking for work. This approach results in trade unions being tough negotiators while also accepting the idea that what is good for companies, even restructuring, is good for their members.

The contrast with its intrusive and micromanaging French coun-terpart could hardly be more marked. The Scandinavian model is founded on a high level of trust between management and work-ers; this feature appears to have been generally ignored by French labour market reformers. At the same time, French political lead-ers engaged with this vital question of trust in a parallel process: the labour market reforms that Macron prioritised at the start of his presidency were accompanied, and even marginally preceded, by a fresh drive to improve ethical standards in public life. There seems to have been some intuition at work here that since changes to workers' conditions would involve some sacrifice, at least in the short run, the proponents of such reforms must command a higher degree of trust than had ever been accorded to the scandal-ridden French political class.

The scandals during the Hollande presidency (such as the Cahuzac affair, which we reviewed in chapter 1) and the resulting reforms
from 2013 onwards amounted to the start of a culture change
(Aukrust and Weiss-Andersen 2019, 161). Macron built on this
foundation. The first month of his presidency produced a new law
(known as 'Sapin II'), roughly equivalent to the US Foreign Corrupt
Practices Act. The next package of legislation, designed to improve
ethical standards in public life, followed two months later (August
2017), with a strapline that emphasised public confidence in politicians (*lois pour la confiance dans la vie politique*). Macron described
this law on 'raising moral standards in public life' (*loi de moralisation de la vie publique*) on a government website called 'Confidence
in Public Action': 'this legislation will help to restore citizens' trust
in their elected representatives and in the democratic life of our
country, not least by increasing transparency so as to call time on
practices that the French will not put up with any longer.'

Aukrust and Weiss-Andersen note how the words 'confidence'
and 'trust' replaced the language about 'transparency' that had
been used in presenting similar initiatives in the previous political cycle (Aukrust and Weiss-Andersen 2019, 162). With this new
emphasis on trust, a cornerstone of general health in political economy, France's political leadership was latching on to the reality of
the Scandinavian model as opposed to evoking a Nordic utopia.
There were, however, two problems with this, in principle, encouraging departure.

The first was that this quest to improve public trust in politicians
succumbed rapidly to a new round of corruption scandals. On the
same day that Macron unveiled his new moralisation bill, prose-
cutors announced an investigation into suspected wrongdoing by
Richard Ferrand, who was the general secretary of Macron's *En
Marche!* party and who had just been appointed minister of territorial cohesion. It turned out that six years earlier, when Ferrand
was running a health insurance fund for public sector workers, he
had rented office space for the fund from his partner. She was then
able to secure a business loan on the basis of the rental income
and the renovations to the premises that were carried out by the
health fund, which increased the value of the property. The next
scandal came with an ironic twist, as it involved François Bayrou,
the newly appointed justice minister and leader of the centrist party
Mouvement Démocrate (MoDem). Bayrou had backed Macron in the

presidential election, and his party's campaign platform had majored in cleaning up politics. Yet just as Bayrou was beginning his ministerial task of piloting the new moralisation law through parliament, *Le Canard enchaîné* revealed on 14 June 2017 that MoDem had created a fictitious job in its offices, exposing the party's hypocrisy.

The second flaw in Macron's focus on trust was that it was not integrated into the design of the main substantive reform policies, especially with regard to the labour market. These reforms, taking in the pension system, unemployment insurance, and collective bargaining, were first and foremost undertaken – as I have already noted – to tackle the unemployment problem; their most powerful inspiration was geopolitics, a consideration rather distant from typical Scandinavian concerns. Overcoming structural unemployment and improving the economy's performance – and hence public finances – were seen as crucial to getting France an equal place at the negotiating table with Germany in order to advance towards a more federal monetary union and a more dynamic Europe.

The core agenda of Macron's labour reforms was to devolve hitherto centralised collective bargaining to the level of industry sectors or even individual companies. This more horizontal approach would give employers greater flexibility in managing relations with the workforce in their own firms. That same goal underlay many of the long series of labour market reform efforts (as reviewed by Charmettant 2017) that were a feature of all four preceding presidencies. Socialist administrations naturally tilted the balance towards worker security. For instance, the government led by Lionel Jospin during the presidency of Jacques Chirac restricted the scope for redundancies on economic grounds (i.e. firms having to reduce staff because of a business turndown) and also instituted individual training entitlements. By the time of the next Socialist government (under the Hollande presidency in the 2010s) the problem of unemployment had become so pressing as to force a shift in emphasis. Reforms in this period did allow more flexibility in setting wages, and they permitted wage bargains to be sealed with the approval of a simple majority of workers in union-run ballots (Porta 2019). However, restrictions on firing workers were maintained. The most ambitious of the Hollande-era labour market reforms – known as the El Khomri Law – focused on shifting collective bargaining down to individual company level. This reform sparked widespread, and often violent, street protests. Macron's main contribution to this story was to make it easier for firms to fire workers. This was the single most important element in the labour market reforms that he forced through in the first year of his presidency. Also of note was the new institution of a 'company referendum', designed to enable collective agreements to be directly endorsed by the workforce. Finally enacted in March 2018, these measures comprised five ordinances including thirty-six measures aimed at lightening the Labour Code, which was considered too rigid. Yet the printed 2019 version of the Code still ran to 3,784 pages and weighed 1.5 kilograms; the 1985 version weighed 500 grams (Greef-Madelin and Paya 2020).

The irony of Macron adding ninety pages to the already voluminous Labour Code was not the only problem with his labour market reforms. There was, of course, criticism from the left that was coherent in its own terms. As stated by legal scholar Jérôme Porta, while there may have been no doubt that the reform amounted to 'a profound transformation of the architecture of the regulation of subordinate employment relationships', evidence cast doubt on its necessity (Porta 2019, 96).

It turns out that the Labour Code restrictions on dismissing employees, now relaxed by Macron, were not the central issue for employers. The main obstacles were, and are, costs – meaning the burden of payroll taxation – and skills shortages. These conclusions emerged from a thorough study undertaken by INSEE (the national accounts agency) (Dortet-Bernadet 2017). This study, published in December 2017, investigated the main obstacles to hiring employees under permanent (CDI) and fixed-term (CDD) contracts by interviewing managers from 10,000 companies in all sectors (services, manufacturing, construction). It found that skills shortages were the main obstacle (cited by 32 per cent of respondents). The second most frequently cited problem – by a quarter of respondents – was general economic uncertainty, followed by the burden of taxation and social security contributions in third and fourth place (22 per cent and 17 per cent). A mere 12 per cent cited the legal risks around dismissals as being a pressing concern.

We looked at these problems of taxation and training in the previous chapter. Here, it is sufficient to add that the OECD has emphasised in numerous reports that to boost job creation and growth, France needs to promote equality in access to good education and training opportunities. The OECD stresses that a higher share of young people and adults in France have poorer literacy and numeracy skills than in most OECD countries, and it identifies specific areas where skill shortages are particularly acute. These are IT and electronics, engineering and technology, teaching, and training and management, as well as areas such as verbal ability and complex problem solving. In contrast, sales and marketing or consulting skills are in surplus.

On this evidence, then, the labour market and industrial relations reforms that culminated in Macron's flagship measures were aimed at the wrong target. This shortcoming is quite separate from the possibility that these reforms were counterproductive in their own terms. For instance, Dominique Méda refers to a study carried out by the ILO (2015), covering 119 countries, which shows that 'deregulating work contracts systematically generates a drop in the employment rate and a rise in unemployment' (Méda 2016, 17–18).

The problem of wayward targeting brings us back to the question of trust. It is not just in the area of political corruption that French reformers need to build more public trust (regardless of the failure of their efforts to date in that area), but above all in the area of labour relations. Long before that INSEE study was published, Thomas Philippon showed that the institutional constraints of labour laws and the level of social charges (payroll taxation) on companies account for no more than 30 per cent of the variation observed in the employment rates of the twenty most advanced economies. The remaining 70 per cent is explained by the quality of social relations in individual firms. In France, that quality is poor. The damage caused by high unemployment extends from the associated economic dislocation and social deprivation to the spiral of 'fear and loathing' among workforces that it engenders. Philippon favours more neutral legislation that encourages competence and talent at the top of SMEs. Improved SME access to capital markets would usefully supplement family funds to finance their growth. He makes a powerful case for encouraging social dialogue, in both private and public organisations, between more representative trade union organisations and more inclusive employers' organisations. Improvements in the quality of social relations in the firm would help restore trust between companies, employees, and the state; improve employee welfare; and, ultimately, boost the overall performance of the economy (Philippon 2007). Hervé Charmettant also insists that solutions worth exploring include giving workers more voice, not only by supporting trade unions but also by shifting corporate governance norms towards the German practice of including employee representatives on companies' supervisory boards. He cites studies that show how companies' economic and social performance, and therefore their ability to stabilise and develop quality employment, are linked to the degree of employee participation (Charmettant 2017). Trust is a key component in the quality of labour relations and therefore in the performance of a firm (Blanchard, Jaumotte, and Loungani 2014).

In joint research I conducted on the backgrounds of members of supervisory boards of 'blue chip' companies in France and Germany (using 2015 data), one notable finding was the greater variation in educational background and the more conventional business career tracks of German company directors compared with their French counterparts. The number of German directors who had started their career in the civil service was negligible (there was only one such, and his first job had been in a regional tax authority). In addition, there was no pattern of certain higher education institutions shaping corporate careers in Germany like there is in France. It seems a considerable proportion of German directors are highly educated, with 55 per cent holding a PhD, although the educational background of a small but significant 15 per cent of directors was an apprenticeship (reflecting the contingent of directors drawn from the ranks of employees). In German firms, the main selection criterion for directors is relevant technical qualifications, or, in the case of worker–directors in private sector manufacturing, trade union experience. In the French case, directors have typically run through the high ranks of the civil service before being parachuted to boardroom positions. Directors with this kind of background are most common in sectors that are highly dependent on regulation, such as banking or energy (Granville, Martorell-Cruz, and Prevezer 2018). The overlapping career trajectories and connections of senior French regulators and company directors have been shown to have a detrimental effect on both management and regulation. This worst-of-both-worlds picture is particularly prevalent in the banking sector (Pollin and Gaffard 2014). Most CEOs and supervisory board chairs of major French banks previously held senior civil service posts, giving them easy access to the political and regulatory authorities and allowing the banking industry to exercise effective lobbying strategies (Creel, Labondance, and Levasseur 2015).

It is worth taking a closer look at the shortcomings of French trade unions touched on in these studies, as they highlight the importance of trust in labour relations. Countries like France, where trade unions are unrepresentative and ineffective, are characterised by a lack of trust between employers and employees (Philippon 2007). Trade unions play a central role in Nordic-style flexicurity. The strength of trade unions in countries such as Denmark, Finland, and Sweden does not, however, lead to the confrontational style seen in France. Instead, Nordic trade unions facilitate workforces' active role in decision making and work-related issues, covering both the employed and the unemployed as well as skills and jobs. Labour market experts warn that the cooperative relationships between unions and management embedded in the Nordic model (but largely absent in France) cannot simply be wished into being. Unlike in Denmark, French trade unions tend to focus on the interests of those in work, demanding higher wages and preventing layoffs even at the cost of lower overall employment.

The history of French industrial relations does not bode well for the development of a more collaborative 'Scandinavian' culture. France has a long tradition of labour militancy and the use of industrial action to achieve wider political goals. An important reason for this is the previously noted historic dominance of the state in labour relations. The benefits of trade unions have been weakened by their political polarisation: the General Confederation of Labour (CGT) was affiliated to the Communist Party until the 1990s, while the Confédération française démocratique du travail (CFDT) and Force Ouvrière (FO) were created as anti-communist alternatives to the CGT. French unions are simultaneously too strong and too weak: they bargain aggressively on behalf of a small minority and can block layoffs at the company level. They are fragmented and have too few members to cooperate and share responsibility with companies' management. Union opposition to change has resulted in rigidities that large businesses are better able to cope with than small businesses, which have increasingly resorted to foreign outsourcing and to the use of temporary contracts. A lack of effective union mediation to give workers more voice has contributed to an increasing recourse to social networks to mobilise for the redress of grievances. Social networks have proved particularly effective for organising protests based on petitions, as demonstrated by the yellow vests movement.

Two general factors underlie French trade unions' ineffectiveness. The first stems from their low membership. This makes them dependent on state funding rather than their own members' contributions. The unions' resistance to reform is not only ideological: substantial financial interests are also in play. For example, the fees they earn from managing supplementary pension pots offer an important background for understanding the militancy of their opposition to Macron's pension reform project (see below). The unions cannot afford to give up these subsidies, which the state trades in exchange for social peace, but this deal leads to poor accountability (OECD 2015, 27). In 2007, Nicolas Perruchot, a lawmaker elected in the Loir-et-Cher *département*, initiated a parliamentary commission of inquiry into trade union finances (Bonazza and Delattre 2012). The commission's findings were so controversial that only nine out of its thirty members approved the final text in 2011 – meaning that the report was not formally adopted and published (officially, it will only be eligible for release into the public domain after thirty years). However, large extracts of the report were leaked to conservative daily newspaper *Le Figaro*; the weekly news magazine *Le Point* followed suit by publishing a virtually unabridged version. The document paints a shocking account of trade union life, where the state connives with union officials at an annual cost to public finances of about €4 billion. In 2015, further scandals revealed by *Le Canard enchaîné* and *Le Monde* involved various cases of embezzlement of union funds by CGT and FO officials.

The second general feature of the French trade union movement concerns the lopsided distribution of its already sparse membership. On closer inspection, the aggregate unionisation of the workforce appears to be somewhat higher than the widely quoted level of 8 per cent. One official statistical and research agency estimated that the true number was 10.8 per cent in 2016, down from 11.2 per cent three years earlier (DARES 2018). Trade union membership in the public service remains twice as high as in the private sector (19.1 per cent versus 8.4 per cent), and women are on average less unionised than men (10 per cent versus 12 per cent) – a trend observed in both the public and private sectors. What is particularly ominous for the future of the trade unions is that the rate of unionisation decreases with the age of employees: 3.7 per cent of those under thirty years old belong to a union compared with 14.9 per cent of those aged fifty and over. The major obstacles to the unionisation of women and young people stem from the difficulties they face in becoming settled in the job market, as reflected in the phenomenon I noted earlier of their accounting for most temporary or fixed-term employment contracts.

Against this unimpressive backdrop, the trade unions were nevertheless able to seize the opportunity presented by Macron's pension reform proposals to regain a prominent position on the national stage. Work on this project began in May 2018. In principle, the reform was not that radical, as it envisaged retaining a pay-as-you-go system – that is, contributions paid by current employees would continue to fund the pension entitlements of current retirees. Yet it had two core objectives: first, in the name of fairness, to unify the plethora of existing pension schemes (more than 600 basic pension plans and 6,000 supplementary ones) into a single standard for the whole country; and second, to balance the system's budget (Assemblée nationale 2020).

Those who lost out due to that first goal were public sector workers who had enjoyed superior pension privileges. This applied generally, as the reform would align the pension entitlements of civil servants and other public sector workers with the less generous regime that had been established for private sector employees via a series of reforms since 1993. A key difference was that private sector pension benefits were calculated based on an employee's twenty-five highest-paid years of work, while the pensions of public sector workers (with 4.3 million such retirees in 2019, not counting the 1.2 million contract workers in the public sector) were based on what they had earned in the last six months of their careers. This blow to public officials was cushioned by the proposal to include their bonuses in the calculation base; however, for the many, such as teachers and researchers, who never receive bonuses, the government was forced to promise salary increases. The shift to a new universal system would entail particular losses for the most privileged of the forty-two *special* (public sector) regimes. Of those employed by these regimes, three stood out: workers on state railways (SNCF), on public transport utility for Paris (RATP), and in the electricity and gas industries (IEG).

Two key features of the reform that affected everyone were the move to a points-based system for determining the size of pension payments and an increase in the pensionable age. The proposed points system reflected the reform's strategic goal of transparency and fairness: the future pension benefits of all employees in both the public and private sectors, and regardless of any special existing dispositions, would be linked to the number of days worked in their lifetimes. Hitherto privileged groups stood to lose out from this change too. These included seamen, lawyers, and even employees of the national opera.

As for the retirement age, the reform aimed to increase this by stealth to sixty-four years from the existing sixty-two years and one month (which, in turn, was the result of the multi-year implementation of a reform brought in by Nicolas Sarkozy in 2007, when the pensionable age had been sixty years). Macron's reform left the official age of retirement unchanged at sixty-two years, while introducing the principle of a 'pivot age' of sixty-four years. This meant that those retiring before that age (i.e. at sixty-two or sixty-three) would receive lower pensions and, conversely, those who continued to work after the age of sixty-four would get more, with the discount or premium applied to pension payouts set at 5 per cent for each year the receiver was under or over that pivot age. The reform proposals maintained some of the early retirement privileges of the existing system, most notably those for employees in security-sensitive roles such as army personnel, police officers, customs officers, prison guards, and air traffic controllers. Their pensionable age would be fifty-seven, or even fifty-two, which is, incidentally, also the pensionable age of sewage workers recruited before 1 January 2022.

Turning to the reform's second – financial – objective, this took the form of the introduction of a 'golden rule': ensuring the overall financial balance of the pay-as-you-go pension system. The balance of income and expenditure must be positive or zero over five years, and at least a fifth of spending must involve some internal redistribution within the system in favour of poorer pensioners. The adjustment required to eliminate the system's deficit would be achieved not by increasing contributions but by gradually raising the age at which full pension entitlements were paid out. The increases in that age threshold would be linked to rising life expectancy in accordance with a formula worked out in 2003; this advocated that two-thirds of longevity gains should be added to working lives and the remaining third should be added to the average length of retirement. A modelling exercise conducted by the Pensions Guidance Council (Conseil d'orientation des retraites – COR) and published in late 2019 showed no more than mild losses to future retirees in four different scenarios. The drop in the ratio of the number of contributors to the number of retirees (1.7 active workers per retiree in 2010 falling to 1.6 active workers per retiree in 2030) should be offset by the increase in the average retirement age (by a total of fourteen months over the fourteen years from 2016, to reach sixty-three years and three months by 2030). As for the income of retirees, the average pension for all retirees should represent between 47.1 per cent and 47.9 per cent of gross average employment income (down from 51.3 per cent in 2010). Overall, this report suggested that pension spending remained under reasonable control. Macron and his government might therefore have been better advised to shelve the financial aspects of the reform (centred on raising the pensionable age), the better to withstand the resulting social and political storm (COR 2019a).

On 5 December 2019, France was paralysed by a mass nationwide protest movement spearheaded by the CGT, FO, and youth organisations. The effects were felt mainly in the suspension of national rail and municipal public transport (especially in Paris), and included some power outages. Despite such privations, public opinion took an indulgent view of the protests, with two-thirds of respondents to a 19 December survey saying that they considered the strike action to be justified (Odoxa 2019). This attitude may seem surprising, given the cost to the public of the abovementioned privileged pension entitlements of people working in state-owned transport and energy utilities. An analysis published by COR in mid 2019 showed those privileged schemes accounting for half of the entire pension system's projected deficit by 2025. If the employees concerned had been subjected to the same conditions as private sector workers, the pension payouts made under their schemes in 2017 would have been €5.3 billion instead of the actual total of €11.4 billion. Only half of that total was funded by employee and employer contributions, with the deficit being financed by public contributions: state subsidies (that is, general subsidies) in the case of the RATP and SNCF, and a hypothecated user charge in the case of the IEG. The general taxpayer has thus been making a substantial contribution to the special pension regimes enjoyed by the employees of the SNCF, RATP, and IEG – amounting to, respectively, 62 per cent, 59 per cent, and 28 per cent of those schemes' total funding (COR 2019b).

Although it waned over time as the inconvenience caused by the strikes mounted, public support for the protests against Macron's pension reforms remained impressive. The reason for such sympathy may have been a public perception that regardless of whether such privileged pension arrangements are intrinsically justified, unilateral changes to those arrangements are akin to a breach of contract, and the workers concerned had just cause to object. Regardless, previous attempts by successive French governments to bring public sector pensions in line with the (less generous) private sector regime had all foundered on similar waves of protest. A notable example came in 1995, when Chirac's first prime minister, Alain Juppé, attempted to bring about such a convergence. The resulting weeks-long strikes by civil servants and transport workers in effect brought down his government, and a snap parliamentary election in 1997 ushered in five years of socialist administration. The only partial success in this area came in 2003, when François Fillon (later prime minister during the Sarkozy presidency, but then the minister responsible for pensions) managed to equalise the contribution periods required of public and private sector workers to gain pension entitlements. Yet public sector retirees' actual entitlements remained higher, and the special pension schemes survived.

The moral of this tale is that decades of social history cannot be erased by the stroke of an ambitious reforming pen. In the face of the protests, Macron's government was forced to water down its plans. One concession allowed certain special pension schemes to continue after the originally envisaged cut-off date of 2025. The beneficiaries here included airline pilots, lawyers, and doctors. With other special schemes (e.g. for police officers and railway workers) set to survive the reform or to be largely compensated by the public purse (as may be the case for schoolteachers), the final version of the reform can no longer repair the injustices of the current system. To enact this final version on 2 March 2020, the government ended up by resorting to its decree powers (under Article 49.3 of the constitution), bypassing the National Assembly. A few weeks later, the government declared that the whole undertaking would be suspended while the country dealt with the coronavirus emergency.

Looking back at these projects to reform labour relations and pensions points to the same overall conclusion: that the reforming energy was misdirected. What is the use of reforming the Labour Code when the fundamental reason for chronically high unemployment clearly has much more to do with France's education and tax systems? What is the use of a universal pension scheme for all employees if some receive benefits while others do not? The underlying and often overlooked problem is a lack of trust in society, which is itself a function of the root causes of high unemployment and the predicament of the working poor. The resulting spread of poverty and despair is the subject of the next section.

POVERTY AND DESPAIR

The broad survey in the previous section of developments in the labour market during the last three decades provides the necessary background for considering the associated increases in precariousness and wage inequality. In addition to the official unemployment rate that became the main spur for changes in public policy, other challenges that have emerged since the 1970s include the aforementioned rise in insecure temporary (fixed-term) jobs. Already well established before the advent of a 'gig economy' based on the digital revolution, this development has affected women, in particular, as well as the age groups at either end of the working population (fifteen- to twenty-four-year-olds and fifty- to sixty-four-year-olds), owing to successive pension reforms. Women predominate in non-voluntary part-time work, and the rate of underemployment among women is at least twice that of men at all ages (COR 2019a, 4).

In 2019, the monthly minimum wage (SMIC) came to €1,200 net per month and can be supplemented by allowances. The proportion of private sector employees whose wage income is below the annual SMIC is high among young employees and women. This is due to short-term unemployment and part-time work as well as people frequently entering and exiting the labour market or (for students) working during their studies. Among SMIC employees, 57 per cent work part time, and 15 per cent are on fixed-term or temporary contracts. About 5 per cent of employees are paid at a wage lower than the hourly minimum wage: apprentices, minors, holiday and leisure centre coaches, childminders, etc. Some of the self-employed have very small average monthly incomes, below the minimum wage (Observatoire des inégalités 2019). Other employees who support a family with a single minimum wage are also below the poverty line.

INSEE, like Eurostat (the EU's statistics office) and other European countries' national statistics agencies, measures income poverty relatively, while Canada and the United States use an absolute approach. With the relative terms approach, the poverty line is determined in relation to the distribution of income of the entire population. Eurostat and European countries generally define the poverty threshold at 60 per cent of the median income based on living conditions and employment levels. While France likewise favours this threshold, INSEE also estimates poverty rates according to other thresholds (40, 50 or 70 per cent of the median). According to 2016 data from INSEE (the most recent year available), France has 8.8 million people below the 60 per cent poverty line threshold and five million people below the 50 per cent poverty line threshold. That means a poverty rate of 14 per cent or 8 per cent, depending on the threshold used. In that year, these groups were living on a monthly income of less than €1,026 and €855, respectively (falling to €684 on the basis of a 40 per cent threshold).

Seven out of every ten people defined as poor on the basis of the standard 60 per cent threshold are either unemployed or have left the labour market; in many cases, these are pensioners and single women with children. The working poor are, for the most part, manual workers holding low qualifications such as the CAP, and part-time employees. The number of employed people with incomes below the poverty line stands at around 2 million (1.2 million at the 50 per cent threshold).

The Inequality Observatory (Observatoire des inégalités) highlighted a sharp increase in poverty in the wake of the GFC. Between 2006 and 2016, the number of poor increased by 630,000 at the 50 per cent threshold and by 820,000 at the 60 per cent threshold. Although most of that increase occurred in the first half of this period, the stabilisation of the poverty rate since 2012 is misleading because the GFC effect is spreading to the middle-income bracket (Observatoire des inégalités 2018). The median standard of living in 2016 remains lower than it was in 2011. This negative development has the further perverse effect that some of the people counted as poor in 2011 (based on that median income criterion) were no longer considered poor in 2016. The think-tank also drew attention to INSEE poverty data being silent about 'all those people who live slightly above the poverty line but who are at risk of rapidly slipping into poverty at any moment' (Guilluy 2019, 89).

The average income of the bottom 20 per cent of the population is almost five times less than that of the top 20 per cent. In Paris, inequalities are more flagrant: while the city's overall poverty rate is close to the national average of 14 per cent, the rate jumps to 40 per cent in its underprivileged neighbourhoods. The new millennium marked a turning point: poverty had fallen sharply in the 1970s and early 1990s, but the years since then have seen a reversal of that positive trend (Observatoire des inégalités 2018). Rising poverty ripples down the generations. Back in the 1970s, the incidence of poverty was highest among the elderly, while now it is the young who are the worst affected.

The money incomes that are the direct determinant of material living standards depend on a person's having educational qualifications, a supportive network of friends or family, the ability to master new technologies, and adequate housing. The Inequality Observatory remarks that 'school poverty' is so little mentioned in standard studies of poverty that there is not even a commonly accepted definition. Persistent inequalities in educational attainments have an impact on wage inequality and precariousness during a person's life. The OECD's cross-country PISA surveys, which provide quantified comparisons of the performance of education systems around the world, show that educational inequalities in France linked to social origin increased between the 2003 and 2012 surveys. The educational levels of both the worst performing and the poorest pupils deteriorated the most between 2007 and 2012 (COR 2019a, 8–9). In addition, 30 per cent of the entire adult population not in full-time education did not progress beyond the end of third-grade level in school (data from the 2017 INSEE CENSUS). In the thirty- to forty-nine-year-old age bracket, 13 per cent (more than two million people) have no qualifications at all, while 17 per cent have only the BEP or CAP at best (Observatoire des inégalités 2018.) Among the least educated, some are functionally illiterate or innumerate (7 per cent of eighteen- to sixty-five-year-olds, about three million people) (Hinnekint and Janin 2019). The education system fails to promote social mobility: more than two-thirds of the children of employees or workers are occupying the same position as their parents, and the share of managers' children following in their parents' professional footsteps is equally stable. One reason for this has been suggested by Bernard Maris: 'Families are looking for territorial optimization, that is finding a home in the right neighbourhood for getting their children into a good school – private or public; the school system which was supposed to unify the country has produced segregation and discrimination' (Maris 2016, 54).

The term 'poor housing' describes not only dwellings and amenities that are in a degraded condition, but also cramped living space.

The Inequality Observatory reports that four million people are poorly housed, exceeding INSEE's 2013 estimate that 3.8 million people were living in 'inadequate' or 'very inadequate' housing conditions. Among these poorly housed people, 143,000 are outright homeless, 332,000 people live in housing without running water, 934,000 live in overcrowded housing (a couple with two children in a two-room apartment, for example), while 69,000 people are accommodated with third parties apart from their own families.

A further illuminating survey by the Inequality Observatory reports that 12 per cent of those questioned by the Ministry of Solidarity (2016 data) said that they 'often feel alone', as did 24 per cent of the unemployed (twice as many as those in work). Moreover, the Inequality Observatory notes that 10 per cent of the population never connects to the internet, citing 2019 data from the Research Center for the Study and Observation of Living Conditions (known as *Crédoc* in French). Almost half (44 per cent) of people over seventy and 25 per cent of people on low incomes have no internet connection (based on 2017 data from Observatoire des inégalités 2019). A third of the population has never carried out administrative procedures on the internet. This is the case for 70 per cent of non-graduates compared with only 10 per cent of tertiary graduates. The elderly and the low-skilled are finding themselves excluded from services (private but also public) that are increasingly available only online (Observatoire des inégalités 2018).

Anne Case and Angus Deaton have noted that in the period from 1999 to 2015 there was a significant increase in the number of 'deaths of despair' among the less-educated part of the white population of the United States between the ages of forty-five and fifty-four. This phenomenon was consistent across the country rather than being concentrated in certain states. They define 'deaths of despair' as deaths from suicide, alcohol-related liver disease, drug overdoses, and obesity. They point out that while the opioid epidemic is significant, drug overdose deaths are not as numerous as suicides and alcohol-related deaths, taken together. They compare the situation in the United States with a selection of other rich countries (Australia, Canada, France, Germany, Sweden, and the United Kingdom), focusing on the forty-five- to fifty-four-year-old age group. The United States and these comparator countries were age-adjusted to this age group, taking 2010 as the base year and deriving single-year mortality data from the raw data. Based on these age-adjusted death rates, each comparator country experienced an average rate of decline of 2 per cent per year in deaths of despair between 1990 and 2015. The authors find that back in 1990, white Americans had much lower drug- and alcohol-related death rates and suicides than France, Germany, or Sweden. However, in the period from 1999 to 2015, and looking at the fifty- to fifty-four-year-old age group, the average annual percentage variation in all-cause mortality increased by 0.5 per cent, while that for drugs, alcohol, and suicide rose by 5.4 per cent. This compares unfavourably with, for example, France, where the corresponding figures declined by 1.3 per cent and 1.2 per cent. The study concludes that this deaths of despair phenomenon is peculiar to the United States and cannot simply be attributed to globalisation, new technologies, or individualistic values preached by capitalism, since the six comparator countries do not seem to exhibit the same mortality spike (Case and Deaton 2017).

Case and Deaton contend that their findings reflect a general deterioration in the lives of Americans without a university degree entering adulthood after 1970, and that this is an American evil primarily related to political choices. In other words, neither the Great Recession nor the structure of revenues can explain such a sharp upward variation in mortality. While recognising the role of economic decline, they dismiss outright the 'caricature' of attributing the mortality trend solely to changing economic conditions from 1999 to 2015. Instead, they identify anti-union laws and other norms that prevent workers from collectively defending their economic interests as the culprits. They mention the increasing control over the functioning of the labour market exerted by giant firms such as Apple, Walmart, and McDonald's. They cite the American health care system, which costs almost twice as much as that of other developed countries, on average, yet still fails to adequately treat the entire population.

The problem is that Case and Deaton compare the mortality of US white non-Hispanic (WNH) people with that of the equivalent age group and income bracket among the general population of their chosen peer group of countries, including France. However, as we saw in chapter 3, French statistics do not permit a precise comparison with the French equivalent of white non-Hispanic (FWNH) people. What results might emerge were it possible to compare US WNH with FWNH?

Table 4.2 compares suicide rates this century in thirteen countries. The first observation is that male suicide rates are much higher than female ones. The second observation is that the trend analysed by Case and Deaton is confirmed by World Health Organization (WHO) data, which shows the male rate of suicide as having continuously increased from 2000 to 2016. What the table also shows is that this trend starts to rise for Belgium, Finland, Greece, and the United Kingdom in the years after 2015 (WHO 2018).

France has one of the highest suicide rates in Europe, according to the latest report from the National Suicide Observatory (ONS): only a few countries of the former Soviet bloc, along with Finland and Belgium, record an even higher incidence of suicide. In 2015, 8,948 people voluntarily took their own lives in mainland France – that is twenty-four deaths per day, the equivalent of one every hour (Observatoire national du suicide 2018).

While suicide affects all ages, the suicide rate is significantly higher among the elderly, especially among men: 7.5 per 100,000 for men aged fifteen to twenty-four, 33.4 for men aged forty-five to fifty-four, and 59.4 for men aged over seventy-four. Although the suicide rate is relatively low between the ages of fifteen and twenty-four compared with that of other age groups, suicide was still the second leading cause of death after road accidents in this age group for 2015, representing 16 per cent of deaths. Suicide is the primary cause of death among thirty- to thirty-nine-year-olds.

Social exclusion is a central element of suicidal vulnerability, and having a job acts as a protective factor against it; hence, suicide is more frequent among the unemployed. The ONS also cites several studies which mention that, following the GFC, the rise in the unemployment rate was accompanied by an increase in the suicide rate among working-age men. The employed are not completely immune, however. The ONS identifies six conditions experienced at work that can have material health effects: the demands of the job itself, the emotional pressures of the workplace, the degree of autonomy and flexibility to manoeuvre, social relations, value conflicts, and job insecurity. The risk of suicide decreases in line with higher income levels and education but increases steadily with age. Among men, it is the lower socio-professional groups that are most affected, while the single most important factor for women is being unemployed (though young women in general are also more vulnerable). The professions most frequently quoted for being at risk

Table 4.2   Age-standardised suicide rates (per 100,000 population), 2000–2016.

Country	Gender	2016	2015	2010	2000
Austria	Male	17.5	18.2	19.5	25.2
Austria	Female	5.7	5.3	5.4	7.9
Belgium	Male	22.2	21.6	24	27.3
Belgium	Female	9.4	8.9	9.8	10.6
Finland	Male	20.8	19	25.3	32.8
Finland	Female	6.8	5.7	8	10.7
France	Male	17.9	18.5	21.8	25.1
France	Female	6.5	6.7	8.1	9.3
Germany	Male	13.6	13.9	15.3	18
Germany	Female	4.8	4.9	4.6	5.4
Greece	Male	6.1	5.8	4.6	4.5
Greece	Female	1.5	1.5	0.6	1.2
Ireland	Male	17.6	17.6	17.6	19.3
Ireland	Female	4.2	4.2	5	4.4
Italy	Male	8.4	8.2	8.3	9
Italy	Female	2.6	2.5	2.3	2.8
Netherlands	Male	12.9	12.9	11.6	11.4
Netherlands	Female	6.4	6.4	4.8	5.3
Portugal	Male	14.3	14.3	14.4	9.2
Portugal	Female	3.8	3.8	4.2	2.1
Spain	Male	9.3	8.7	8.1	10.4
Spain	Female	3.1	3	2.2	3
UK	Male	11.9	11.6	10.6	12.7
UK	Female	3.5	3.7	3.2	3.8
US	Male	21.1	20.5	18.6	16.5
US	Female	6.4	6.3	5.2	4.1

Source: WHO 2018.

are health care workers, teaching and administrative staff, farmers, prison guards, and police officers (Loriol 2019).

Household incomes are another area in which Europe in general, and France in particular, may compare less favourably with the United States than has been suggested by Case and Deaton. They argue that purchasing power has not diminished for European countries since 2007, but this assertion is contradicted by the results of research conducted by the OFCE, an independent agency for forecasting, researching, and evaluating public policies. As previously noted in chapter 1, their data shows a 1.2 per cent decrease in the real personal disposable incomes of French households for the period from 2008 to 2016 (Madec *et al.* 2018). Although the state of French statistics does not allow for a true comparison, the data reviewed here indicates that the social problems studied by Case and Deaton are not, after all, peculiar to the United States. The frequency of suicide associated with socio-economic factors can be high even in a country, like France, that is reputed for its good health care system (though, as in the United States, the French system lacks effective trade union representation).

The yellow vests movement and the Covid-19 pandemic have underlined the importance of the proper functioning of French institutional and political systems. A fruitful rethinking of contemporary democracy needs to focus less on reshuffling responsibilities and more on the way in which power is exercised. The damaging effects of the gulf between the political powers that be, in their civil service cocoon, and the general public have been laid bare by both episodes, but particularly the coronavirus epidemic. The workers who enabled the country to survive through 'lockdown' were those who lacked status and qualifications but who showed dignity and courage, risking their lives because the state was unable to provide the most basic equipment necessary for their protection.

The issue touched upon in the conclusion of this chapter is a guaranteed income (or universal basic income – UBI), which offers a way to eliminate poverty and foster economic fairness and freedom. This is an old debate that has been put back on the agenda to ensure a decent living standard for the 'invisibles' by NGOs and think-tanks engaged in the fight against poverty. In particular, Noam Leandri and Louis Marin from the Inequality Observatory have proposed a version of UBI that could be applied uniquely to the very poor (those at the 50 per cent threshold – i.e. people with incomes of less than half the median level) (Leandri and Maurin 2019).

PROSPERITY FOR ALL

In 1963, convinced that 'machines must win', economist Robert Theobald wrote in *The Nation*: 'Unemployment rates must … be expected to rise. This unemployment will be concentrated among the unskilled, the older worker and the youngster entering the labour force. Minority groups will also be hard hit. No conceivable rate of economic growth will avoid this result' (Theobald 1963,

393–4). The solution proposed by Theobald was the introduction of a 'guaranteed income'. Many researchers since have shared his fear that automation will accelerate the trend towards precarious jobs and incomes (Frey 2019). Rising inequality, expensive welfare programmes, and accelerating automation (of service provisions as well as production) explain today's renewed interest in introducing a guaranteed income. In the United States, for instance, one of the candidates for the 2020 Democratic Party presidential nomination, Andrew Yang, ran on a platform that included this policy.

At the same time, automation entails productivity gains, as the price of wage-free robots is limited to maintenance costs. The productivity gains generated by the digital economy could be used to offer a guaranteed income either through direct cash payments or through a negative income tax (NIT). Underpinning this argument is a belief in abundance: a belief that technological progress will generate enough wealth to grant everyone in rich societies a decent standard of living (Diamandis and Kotler 2012). The idea is that transitioning to a digital and collaborative economy will make the social protection system developed after World War II obsolete.

Since the surge of globalisation and technological change at the end of the twentieth century, income and wealth have become increasingly concentrated in the upper wage bracket of the population, a group who are highly mobile and difficult to tax. This leaves the least qualified workers, whose income is fixed, with little prospect of sufficient wage income as well as the burden of extra taxation. Advocates of a guaranteed income argue that as neither paid employment nor the existing welfare system can secure a decent livelihood for low-skilled workers, a guaranteed income will provide a cushion against poverty (Standing 2011). However, this raises the question of the definition of poverty: 'If poverty is the lack of money, the provision of money should end poverty. But if poverty is the lack of a job, and the discipline and self-respect that go with it, transferring money may only gloss over the poverty problem' (Munnell 1986, 12).

The proposals on guaranteed incomes vary widely, in line with their authors' political sympathies. They range from a UBI via versions of NIT to a universal 'demogrant' – that is, a grant based on demographic criteria such as age and gender (Ackerman, Alstott, and Van Parij 2005). UBI is defined as a payment made to all citizens from birth to death, regardless of their (in)activity. NIT envisages all citizens completing tax returns, with those whose income is below a defined threshold of net taxable income receiving payments ('negative taxes') that would top up their incomes to that threshold. NIT aims to simplify and de-bureaucratise the welfare state in such a way that it could be gradually phased out as people start to earn more. The negative taxes would be paid directly into the bank accounts of individuals, instead of being distributed to them through social programmes. The income tax credit variant advocated by Nobel Prize-winning economist James Tobin proposed a minimum income system whereby each household was to be granted a basic credit at a level varying with family composition, which each family could supplement with earnings and other income taxed at a uniform rate (Tobin 1968). In the 1960s and 1970s in the United States, the concern was that social welfare programmes were discouraging people from working and making them dependent. For many scholars, NIT represented an attractive alternative. The political authorities, however, maintained 'a deadly fear that some potential workers [would] choose laziness even at the expense of income' (Tobin 1968, 113).

Four separate experiments were conducted to measure people's reaction to such a scheme. These pilot projects, carried out in the period 1968–82, each lasted between three and nine years, with sample sizes ranging from 1,357 to 4,800 households. The random assignment of treatment participants and control groups was an important feature of those four experiments. Various combinations of guaranteed payments and tax rates were applied to test their effects on labour supply, family stability, and other issues. While the rigour of the methodology may be questioned (Rossi and Zellner 1986), most experts concluded that guaranteed income did reduce work effort, but to a lesser extent than expected by its opponents (Burtless 1986), and that the results of these experiments were significant. It was the first time that randomised, controlled trials were used to test the effectiveness of an economic policy measure (Munnell 1986). This technique would be used in most subsequent experiments: the complexity, both conceptual and administrative, highlighted by these experiments continues to inform attempts to investigate the feasibility of implementing an NIT at local, regional, and national levels. For instance, in the early experiments, many families were receiving benefits worth more than the experimental payments, raising doubts about the robustness of the results. In later experiments, some of these failings have been corrected by increasing the income payments; however, doing so makes the project less affordable on a national scale.

Since these early experiments, other scientific evaluations have been made. In 2010, in the central Indian state of Madhya Pradesh, a basic income project started that covered twenty villages. The findings were conclusive. They included an increase in both economic activity and savings, and an improvement in housing, health, and schooling (SEWA Bharat 2014). Finland carried out a guaranteed income experiment in 2017–18. This was the first nationwide trial (rather than focusing on just one area), and it was randomised: 2,000 recipients of a basic income were selected through random sampling from among those who in November 2016 had received an unemployment benefit; the control group consisted of another 2,000 unemployed people who had also been in receipt of benefits at that time. The recipients were paid a monthly tax-exempt basic income of €560 regardless of any other income they may have had or whether they were actively looking for work. The experiment was mandatory. For two years, the group's life choices and outcomes were compared with the experiences of the control group. The survey was carried out by phone interviews immediately before the experiment was concluded. The average response rate to the survey was 23 per cent (31 per cent for the recipients of a basic income and 20 per cent for the control group). The results released in 2019 cast light on individual experiences with economic well-being, financial control, stress, and trust (Kela 2019).

Those who received a basic income as part of the experiment took a more favourable view of their well-being compared with the members of the control group. A total of 55 per cent of the basic income recipients reported their state of health as being good or very good; this number was 46 per cent for those in the control group. Relative to the control group, the basic income group also described their financial situation more positively, saying that they had experienced less stress and fewer financial worries than the control group. In addition, they expressed a greater trust in other people and in societal institutions, such as political parties and the courts, and figures, such as politicians and police officers. This relatively high level of trust felt by basic income recipients applied across the board – that is, there was not a single institution or figure towards which the control group expressed greater trust. This finding remained robust even after allowances were made for individuals' age, gender, family circumstances, and so on. It was also reflected in the observation that the basic income recipients participated no less than the control group in regional adminis-tration programmes designed to facilitate the reintegration of 'customers' into the labour market (despite having a reduced in-centive to do so). No perverse incentive effects could be seen in the unemployment register data either, which, for the first year of the experiment, suggested that the basic income experiment did not have any effect on employment. In other words, the basic in-come recipients were as likely to have become gainfully employed as the members of the control group.

Inspired by the way insurance systems are built on pooling and counterparty contracts, a team of researchers has proposed an affordable guaranteed income scheme based on blockchain tech-nology. They call it the DUBI-SPEC: decentralised universal basic income (DUBI) built from a smart personal equity contract (SPEC) (Potts, Humphreys, and Clark 2018). Before the development of the modern insurance industry and the introduction of the welfare state, economic risk was managed through informal arrangements within a defined community. Potts, Humphreys, and Clark offer an example of such a risk diversification strategy involving a SPEC, where two or more people agree to 'swap' a fixed percentage of their incomes with each other at set dates in the future. Introduced by computer scientist Nick Szabo, smart contracts 'combine proto-cols with user interfaces to formalise and secure relationships over computer networks' (Szabo 1997). The SPEC would therefore be ex-ecuted automatically using blockchain technology, which would coordinate the contracts, calculate the transfers, and make the pay-ments. The advantage for public authorities would lie in the fiscal burden of social security being considerably reduced, making it pos-sible for governments to afford adequate guaranteed incomes for all those without resources.

As this discussion reveals, the proposals in favour of having a guar-anteed income raise many questions. Should such programmes be applied to all or reserved for citizens only (i.e. excluding non-natu-ralised immigrants)? How much income would be guaranteed, and on what criteria? What would be the cost of such a programme, and who would pay for it? Cost is clearly one decisive factor, and affordability would ultimately depend on the sustainable sufficiency of the redistributable wealth coming off the productivity gains brought about by the digital economy.

The Swiss seem to have decided that a guaranteed income would be unaffordable. In June 2016, Switzerland was the first country to hold a referendum on paying a universal allowance every month to all Swiss and foreigners living in the country for at least five years, whether or not they already had a job. The amount of this income remained to be fixed, but the group behind the initiative suggested distributing to each adult and minor an unconditional monthly income. Most of the cost would have been funded by the abolition of various social security benefits, with a residual shortfall having to be funded via taxation. Supporters of this Swiss UBI project suggested the introduction of a tax on electronic payment transactions, which, set at 0.2 per cent, would generate sufficient funds to finance the measure in its entirety. Still judged too expensive, the proposal was rejected by 77 per cent of voters (*Le Monde* with AFP 2016).

The question of guaranteed incomes seems set to become an ever more urgent policy debate in the face of growing economic inequality and social degradation. Its proponents argue that the security of a guaranteed income will provide people with the opportunity to train and develop their skills, which will ultimately benefit society. Some argue that the guaranteed income should replace all other welfare transfers, including unemployment payments, pensions and social security, child support, tax subsidies, and so on, to simplify and to reduce the cost of the welfare and tax systems. Others strongly oppose the replacement of the multitude of social benefits by a unique guaranteed income. In France, the social protection system provides a plethora of cash and in-kind benefits administered by various public agencies. This system is costly and ineffective, and it excludes large groups of the relatively poor. Yet its abolition in favour of a single guaranteed income would face strong opposition from trade unions and civil servants, who may be expected to resist any simplifying reform that would make one or more state agencies redundant.

This debate is far from closed. At time of writing, future experiments with basic income are planned in other European countries. But what this chapter has attempted to show is that restoring the dignity of workers will require a fundamental overhaul of society and its economic principles. This must include creating an infrastructure to harness the power of data to deliver services and subsidies in real time and to give a voice to workers. The digital economy may be a source of abundance, but it also poses risks to privacy, freedom, and employment. This topic is the focus of our next chapter.

5

The Knowledge Commons

Français, vous n'êtes pas coupables, vous ne devez rien ; le chômage, la catastrophe urbaine, le déclin de la langue, ce n'est pas vous ; le racisme, ce n'est pas vous, contrairement à ce qu'on veut faire croire. Vous n'êtes pas coupables. Retrouvez ce sourire qui fut l'envie des voyageurs pendant des siècles, 'au pays ou Dieu est heureux'.

[People of France, you are not to blame or under some obligation for the problems of unemployment, urban social decay, the degradation of language. None of that is you. And racism – that's not you either, contrary to what they would have you believe. Bring back the smile that was the envy of travellers over the centuries to 'the country where God is happy'.]

Bernard Maris (Maris 2014, 13)

On 2 January 2015, economist Bernard Maris mailed his publisher some pages from his book, including the above excerpt. The following week, he was murdered by Islamist terrorists in the *Charlie Hebdo* killings. Maris would have been proud of the way the nation came together to admire its true heroes during the Covid-19 pandemic, when France was in what President Macron called a 'state of war' (on Monday 16 March 2020 at 8 p.m. in a television address). These heroes were not the people wielding technocratic power and influence, Macron's 'lead mountaineers', whose high status is taken to denote high achievement. Instead, they were people whose low status (and incomes) would normally make them invisible. These champions of courage and resilience, who earned well-deserved praise and respect for their efforts throughout the crisis, included not only health care workers but also supermarket cashiers and shelf-stackers, hauliers, farmers, garbage collectors, and more, all of whom are vital to the basic functioning of the economy and society.

A year earlier, many of these individuals had actively joined or passively supported the yellow vests' campaign to get the attention of the 'great and good', only to be greeted with fearful contempt. The authorities under Macron's martial-toned leadership sent this army to the front line without the necessary equipment or a clear plan of action. The historic event of a national lockdown at the height of the epidemic highlighted for a few weeks not only the inequalities but also the distortion of social values in France – and public demand to address such problems is set to dominate political life and policy debates after the pandemic crisis has finally passed.

A root cause of such problems is the instinct of the governing bureaucracy, and the political class that overlays it, to denigrate ways of thinking that deviate from established orthodoxies. Any challenges from below can only stem from *wrong* ideas, with their errors being variously diagnosed according to where each high-placed critic is situated on the political spectrum (Haidt 2012). Thus, the yellow vests have fallen prey to 'deranged' populism and other equally ill-defined ideas deemed to be pernicious and orchestrated by pariah intellectuals (including economists). A common tactic to discredit such opponents is to claim that they are sold to, or manipulated by, fashionable bogeymen like Russia. This is what Maris had to say on the matter: 'The elites never encourage the French: "France falling", "does France have a future?", "French melancholy", "suffering in France", "French misfortune" … There are countless books that denigrate and make the French feel guilty. In 1940, the elites blamed the people for their own incompetence and guilt' (Maris 2016, 125).

The government's public line during the Covid-19 pandemic showed how prescient Maris was to highlight the persistence of this habit of blaming the French for failing their leaders. The press pounced on a line spoken by one presidential adviser in March 2020, who claimed that Macron had been forced to impose more stringent social distancing because of the public's excessive 'spirit of enjoyment' – a quotation from Marshall Pétain's infamous address to the French people in August 1941 constrasting that decadent spirit with the needed 'spirit of sacrifice' (*Sud Ouest* 2020). In early April 2020, the rationale offered by the official government spokesperson for the shortage of masks was that 'people do not know how to wear them correctly' (*Mediapart* 2020).

The governing establishment always faults the people as if hoping by that means to spare itself (Girard 1978). This habit of deflecting responsibility must also contribute to another of its failings: that of not learning lessons. It fails to see that it is caught in a cobweb of received notions, exemplifying the psychological phenomenon of groupthink. Persistent problems are attributed to failure to realise some bureaucratic utopia – the cause of European sovereignty remains a core favourite, although one of the most long-standing adepts of that cause in the ranks of the French ruling class, Jacques Attali, has more recently upgraded the aspiration to world government (Attali 2011). Such figures have been consigned by American–Lebanese thinker Nassim Nicholas Taleb to the category of 'intellectual yet idiot' (IYI), whose distinguishing characteristic is ignorance of the extent of their idiocy:

> The IYI pathologises others for doing things he doesn't understand without ever realising it is his understanding that may be limited. He thinks people should act according to their best interests and he knows their interests, particularly if they are 'rednecks' or from the English non-crisp-vowel class who voted for Brexit. When plebeians do something that makes sense to themselves, but not to him, the IYI uses the term 'uneducated'. What we generally call participation in the political process, he calls by two distinct designations: 'democracy' when it fits the IYI and 'populism' when plebeians dare to vote in a way that contradicts IYI preferences (Taleb 2019, 124–5).

Taleb's polemical book on this theme was published in 2018, just before the dawn of the yellow vests movement; but his description fits France's professional intellectuals and the technocrats in power like a glove. However lacking in creativity and independence of mind, they are supremely confident in the rectitude of their ideas – for, after such training as they have had, who would gainsay them? 'Only the mediocre' is the answer of these Jupiterians. Almost a century earlier, Keynes, with his inimitable brilliance, expressed a similar thought: 'Madmen in authority, who hear voices in the air, are distilling their frenzy from some academic scribbler of a few years back. I am sure that the power of vested interest is vastly exaggerated compared with the gradual encroachment of ideas' (Keynes 1936, 383, quoted in Rosa 2006, 342).

I know the power of groupthink at first-hand, having fallen for it myself upon coming out of my classical economics training. It took me years of study and reflection to begin questioning my long-held conventional notion that excessive labour market regulation is the main barrier to employment. Now I see that the problem lies elsewhere. Many outdated notions are still in play. This backwardness is the main hazard of the groupthink of the officials at the top of France's centralised state administration. These insiders are wedded to ideas, visions, and principles that were valid in the 1950s environment of state-led post-war reconstruction, but which stifle present-day aspirations for individual freedom and creativity. This seems like a contemporary version of the traditional French stand-off between Ancients and Moderns. In the seventeenth century, this was a literary dispute (the Ancients championed Greek and Latin texts). In today's political economy debates, the power-wielding Ancients have fallen behind the present state of economic evolution, while the Moderns are accused by the ruling establishment of being backward and uneducated. France seems eternally doomed to be fighting the last war, as in the notorious Maginot Line. This is certainly the view of my uncle, whose reaction to the ideas I was developing for this book had me believing he was an unsung philosopher: 'That's nothing new! In 1939, we were told that we French were the cleverest and strongest – and with the best army in the world, they said … but nine months later the Germans were parading down the Champs Élysées and the politicians had fled Paris!'

I did not find it hard to understand the hopes, or even the enthusiasm, that greeted Macron's election in 2017. His predecessor, François Hollande, styled himself as a 'regular guy president', to the amusement of many of my friends in Britain and the United States. I found myself feeling ashamed that Hollande was the head of state – the same feeling, I realised, that many Russian friends had had about Boris Yeltsin after his drunken public escapades, while I myself continued to admire Yeltsin for leading Russia out of the Soviet system. Returning to the subject of Macron, his inherently refreshing youthfulness and energy were accompanied by a genuine awareness of the frontiers of the knowledge economy that are the main subject of this chapter. Yet that awareness, and its associated policies, have proven to be harnessed not to the process of horizontal knowledge communities supplanting state and corporate hierarchies, but instead to that same anachronistic groupthink about the desirable prowess of the state, whether at the national or European level.

This rigid ideology found itself up against the formidable impulse and novelty displayed by the yellow vests movement, and then by millions of individuals during the pandemic. Like all ideas about the ordering of societies and political beliefs, those championed by the French state as the (only) alternative to the 'barbarians [yellow vests] at the gates' were not developed in a vacuum. They emerged instead from day-to-day constraints and opportunities, and especially from the heat of historical events: a pandemic, for instance, or a change of regime such as that heralded by the fall of the Berlin Wall in 1989. These events did not take place because some nefarious conspiracy led to the Covid-19 pandemic, or somebody in Berlin was suddenly inspired by some intellectuals to destroy the wall. Such turning points occur because the state of play has been altered; because new technologies and other scientific advances have made redundant the economic systems that were previously workable and sustainable. This is highlighted by Yuval Noah Harari in his best-selling book *Sapiens: A Brief History of Humankind.* Here, he identifies a series of revolutions – cognitive, agricultural, scientific, industrial, information, and, finally, the biotechnological revolution (Harari 2015).

French economist Jean-Jacques Rosa has elaborated very persuasively on how the 'information revolution shapes business, states, and nations'. His central argument is that technological advances have reduced the cost of using markets relative to that of using state hierarchies. The result is a greater decentralisation of economic decision making. As small businesses overtake large companies at the forefront of technological and economic development, this alters the way people think about their lives. The attitudes and norms that best promote the success of the economy change accordingly. The standards of obedience and respect for the rules handed down by overweening centralising bureaucracies are supplanted by the spirit of individualism and entrepreneurship. Technological advances change the environment in which individuals evolve and articulate their preferences (Rosa 2006, 346).

The Covid-19 epidemic highlighted the value of self-determination and national self-sufficiency, notably in the health care and pharmaceutical sectors. However, while such trends may commonly be regarded as a backlash against globalisation, they are also inherent in the very fabric of globalisation and technological change. In this vein, Covid-19 illuminates a process that was already taking place, only less visibly (Rosa 2006, 356–7). Part of this process consists in behavioural adaptation. The abundance of information fuels its own dissemination, and that dissemination of information decentralises power, weakens hierarchies and liberates individuals by promoting a horizontal organisation stimulated by consensual and collaborative dialogues. In this new environment, the organisational structures of the state and companies must adapt. Societies will demand more compact bureaucracies delivering public goods in closer interaction with their customers, i.e. firms and households. This interactive provision of more and better services at lower cost will hinge increasingly, if not exclusively, on the opportunities created by the digital technology revolution. If technological transformations are the engine for such change, the catalyst will often be a crisis.

The world of the French utopian technocrats has been shattered by Covid-19. As the pandemic gripped the continent, the European motto '*In varietate concordia*' (United in Diversity) was, in effect, replaced by 'Every State for Itself'. The experience of 'lockdown' (or *confinement*, as it is known in France) has finally made those holding state power in France (and her counterparts in peer group countries) aware of how much their authority is ebbing away. As already presaged by the yellow vests movement, this vacuum has been filled by local communities, which are much more visible to people than the discomfited central state authorities.

This chapter explores the potential of digital technology to promote decentralisation and empower horizontal networks within society at the expense of traditional central bureaucracies placed above societies. At points the discussion will necessarily be general, with some focus being turned to the United States, where this technological revolution began and is now being dominated by Big Tech companies. I see this discussion as being acutely relevant to France, in the sense of this revolution being both an opportunity and a threat. The social implications of the developing knowledge economy have positive potential for treating the pathologies of the French political economy described in this book. Having said that, information technologies and digital tools might turn out to be another instrument for aggravating those pathologies.

Another hazard is the facile belief that technological progress and its consequent improvement of material circumstances equates to human happiness. Harari's broad historical sweep serves as a powerful caution against this delusion. Yet the potential of this modern technology-driven knowledge economy is greater than a boost to material living standards. The next section looks closely at the various fears surrounding this new economic paradigm as well as the reasons why some observers see this new phase as portending a more humane future. This is followed by a reflection on the changes brought about by the knowledge economy in business entrepreneurship, the 'knowledge commons' and finally public policy.

MAKING SENSE OF THE KNOWLEDGE ECONOMY

French economist Dominique Foray has formulated this neat summary of the characteristics of the knowledge economy: 'The proportion of knowledge-intensive jobs is high, the economic weight of information sectors is a determining factor, and the share of intangible capital is greater than that of tangible capital in the overall stock of real capital' (Foray 2006, ix).

This description captures the reasons why the knowledge economy gives rise to both hopes and fears. Knowledge represents a public good since its use does not involve exclusive, or zero-sum, rivalry (Arrow 1962). In other words, once the cost of producing knowledge has been incurred, it can be used without limit or additional costs, and its unauthorised use is difficult to prevent. However, because the costs of producing original knowledge can be considerable, far higher than imitating an existing discovery, incentives such as patents exist to discourage illegal transfer and production. An initial difficulty is to identify whether knowledge creation is a discovery or an invention. Foray, once again, clears this up: 'Much knowledge is produced by invention, that is, it does not exist as such in nature and is "produced" by man. Other types of knowledge stem from discoveries, that is, the accurate recognition of something which already existed but which was concealed. ... In terms of incentives, one can claim an intellectual property right on an invention, not a discovery' (Foray 2006, 14).

Patents are contested not only for the specific reason that the purported original knowledge has been discovered rather than invented, but also because of their general negative effects. One such criticism hinges on an ironic reversal of the concept of the 'tragedy of the commons', a term coined by American biologist and philosopher Garrett Hardin to denote the destruction of exhaustible resources by unregulated access and exploitation (Hardin 1968). From this perspective, overlapping patent claims in the hands of different owners may produce a 'tragedy of the anticommons', in which people underuse scarce resources because too many owners can block each other (Heller and Eisenberg 1998). Other general problems with patents include the duplication of research as well as the emergence of ethical questions, notably in the pharmaceutical sector (Granville and Leonard 2002).

This is not to say that a knowledge product requires no resources beyond the inventor's brain. On the contrary, the knowledge economy is built on extensive capital of all kinds – social, financial, and physical. This point is well made by American political scientist Matthew Hindman in his book *The Internet Trap*: 'Scale economies dominate whether the heavy machinery is refining data or iron ore' (Hindman 2018, 163). Still, in the knowledge economy, the proportion of intangible capital is higher than that of tangible capital, and products from the knowledge economy are susceptible to imitation (Haskel and Westlake 2017). While imitating a product is not open to everyone, the cost of doing so is considerably less than that of innovating: it suffices for the imitator to have sufficient knowledge and an investment base, the R&D innovation costs having been covered by the innovator. Knowledge is difficult to control, as it leaks to potential imitators through the different stages of production and product marketing. Building knowledge involves collaboration between firms, academe, and government, and across countries. Information about new discoveries is diffused by routine communication, allowing for imitation and innovation, and resulting in a self-sustaining expansionary process catalysed by the prospect of new markets and pressures to reduce costs. Although regulatory regimes can slow down the flow of information (for the sake of rewarding discoverers of knowledge and encouraging future discoveries), they cannot stop it. As Foray puts it, 'Making knowledge exclusive and controlling it privately are difficult and costly. Knowledge continuously escapes from the entities producing it' (Foray 2006, 15). This leads to what he calls the 'comedy of the knowledge commons' (Foray 2006, 16), reflecting the contrast between knowedge being non-exclusive and cumulative while physical resources are 'tragically' exhaustible. This comedy may be one of the reasons today's economists are so enthusiastic about the knowledge economy: a zeal matched only by the scepticism demonstrated by their elders in the early 1990s (Gordon 2000).

In the 1980s, sociologists announced a new stage of civilisation, to be propelled by the knowledge economy, understood as an amalgamation of science and production (Schement and Lievrouw 1987). At the dawn of the IT revolution, economists took up the running by arguing among themselves about how to measure the impact of the internet on economic growth (Solow 1998). This academic controversy revolved around questions on how to account for knowledge in economic performance, given the difficulty of measuring continuous improvements in technology, and on how new knowledge is assimilated in human capital (Lucas 2003). Now that the reality and scale of the new knowledge economy is visible to all, Foray remarks that 'the new economy debate can only be viewed with a degree of amusement ... this debate will mainly be remembered for the clash between the ultra-optimists and their relatively crude economic thinking, and the sceptical macroeconomists who, despite their usual rigor and prudence, have an extremely partial and truncated view of the impacts of new technologies' (Foray 2006, 47).

Against this backdrop of four decades of knowledge economy development being driven by new information technologies, the Covid-19 pandemic crisis provided a sobering case study of the lag in institutional and social dynamics required to make the most of this development's potential to enhance general welfare. The fact that this crisis was caused by a novel virus maximised the importance of producing, coordinating, and then applying all types of knowledge about this pathogen. This unexpected challenge demonstrated how the effectiveness of the all-important knowledge response hinges on avoiding the typically French phenomenon of vertical political and bureaucratic power stifling the more horizontal process by which new research and the lessons of new experience are diffused and assimilated.

The pandemic crisis has provided what amounts to a controlled test of how far France, along with its peer group countries, has travelled along this path of fostering a broad social and economic environment that supports innovation as a holistic process grounded in 'transparent democracy' (Park 2014). Under the most scrutiny was the performance of the state in facilitating and coordinating pharmaceutical research, where decisive breakthroughs depend on effective cooperation between (inter)national bureaucracies as well as research networks comprising academic and commercial teams and, ultimately, individuals.

Another characteristic of knowledge is that it is cumulative: we learn by doing. A substantial body of academic research demonstrates the contribution of this knowledge process to, for example, improvements in manufacturing processes and therefore overall productivity (Granville and Leonard 2002). During the pandemic, this expertise has been acquired by many citizens, whose daily contact with the virus has accumulated to boost our understanding of the pathogen's characteristics. The challenge for policymakers lies in tapping into and spreading that cumulative knowledge. This would improve the effectiveness of the response to the pandemic, and bonds of trust and confidence could be strengthened.

At time of writing, the jury is out on whether France will walk away from this a freer, more united country. The first signs have not been encouraging, as the traditional vertical power impulses seem to have prevailed. While the severity of the crisis may well justify authoritarian lockdowns, this experience nevertheless exemplifies the limitations in the modern world of applying the Hobbesian paradigm of unlimited obligation to the sovereign state in return for physical survival. These limitations extend beyond the mediocre performance of France, as the most objective comparative measure – the deviation throughout the pandemic of all-cause mortality from long-term averages ('excess deaths') – has revealed. The pandemic has aggravated a long-standing obstacle to overcoming the country's blockages: namely, the lack of public trust in institutions. At the height of the lockdown in mid April 2020, a public opinion survey conducted by Odoxa barometer for the National Mutual Hospital (Mutuelle nationale des hospitaliers) showed that the French did not trust the Ministry of Health (51 per cent) or the government (64 per cent). More than three-quarters of French people (76 per cent) as well as hospital professionals (81 per cent) said they believed that the state had failed and could have done better to prevent the spread of the epidemic and resulting mortality (Odoxa 2020). A survey of 13,426 people in nineteen countries about 'vaccine hesitancy' found that French (along with Russian and Polish) respondents were the most reluctant to take any widely available vaccine against Covid-19 – and the authors of this study attributed such reluctance to weak trust in governments (Lazarus et al. 2020).

The hardening of the French public's chronic distrust in government, a recurrent theme of this book, is ominous not only for

Table 5.1   Trust in institutions (men and women), 2019 (in per cent).

	UK		France		Italy		Germany	
	M	W	M	W	M	W	M	W
Business	51	44	55	45	56	51	54	40
Government	45	39	35	29	46	40	45	35
NGOs	49	45	60	52	41	47	49	38
Media	41	33	39	33	42	47	50	39
Trust index	47	40	47	40	46	46	50	38

The trust index is the average per cent trust in NGOs, business, government, and the media. 'TRU_INS. Below is a list of institutions. For each one, please indicate how much you trust your institution to do what is right using a nine-point scale where one means that you "do not trust them at all" and nine means that you "trust them a great deal".' 1,150 respondents, 18+, per country. All fieldwork was conducted between 19 October and 16 November 2018. *Source:* 2019 Edelman Trust Barometer.

meeting the continuing challenges arising from the Covid-19 pandemic, both in public health and socio-economic spheres, but also for the country's general prospects. Table 5.1 summarises the results of the 2019 Edelman Trust Barometer, showing that France had a lower level of trust in both the government and the media than the United Kingdom, Italy, and Germany did.

Table 5.2 shows data collated by Canadian–American economist Michael Spence (recipient of the 2001 Nobel Memorial Prize in Economic Science) and American economist David Brady which confirms that France's score on trust is among the lowest in its peer group.

This evidence of relatively poor public confidence will not surprise readers who have made it this far through the book. The French state's response to the pandemic provides a general illustration of the vicious cycle that is continually aggravating this problem of trust. The government wanted to keep centralised control over the distribution of protective equipment (e.g. masks, gloves) as well as the development of the perfect antigen test. This tension between official delays or hesitations and the urgency of effective action and public reassurance may be traced back to the mid 1980s scandal in which, as a result of culpable negligence by the authorities, HIV-contaminated blood products ended up being used for medical treatments (Chauveau 2011). That episode left its mark on French society and helped to instil a distrust in the political authorities that has since become encrusted.

Table 5.2   Trust in political elite and in institutions (in per cent).

	UK		France		Italy		Germany	
Political elite (PE)	A	D	A	D	A	D	A	D
People are represented by PE	8	71	10	67	19	70	16	60
PE have nation's interest at heart	11	66	13	58	23	60	17	54
PE are corrupt	55	15	65	10	66	16	46	27
Institutions	A lot	None	A lot	None	A lot	None	A lot	None
Trust in media	2	35	2	30	5	18	11	19
Trust in church	9	46	5	18	9	30	6	40
Trust in police	25	8	17	6	29	5	37	4
Trust in business	6	14	3	10	10	6	6	13
Trust in trade unions	8	26	4	23	4	27	15	12
Trust in EU	9	36	4	25	9	21	13	17

A: agree. D: disagree. *Source:* Spence and Brady 2020, survey conducted in July 2019 by the Hewlett Foundation, the Hoover Institution and YouGov.

Another lesson of the pandemic experience that is relevant to this discussion of changes in social and political structures linked to the knowledge economy is the so-called digital divide. The heightened importance of digital connectivity during the lockdown highlighted the exclusion of a large part of the population due to age, income, and area of residence. There are institutional and political failures that will limit people's capacity to benefit from the knowledge economy even once optimal (broadband) connectivity and diffusion of necessary hardware and software (personal computers, tablets, smartphones, etc.) has been achieved. Other preconditions for successful knowledge transfer are secondary technical education on top of basic literacy and numeracy. This was made clear by the closure of schools announced by the government on 16 March 2020. Teachers quickly mobilised to set up distance education, but they encountered serious difficulties. For a start, 12 per cent of households have either no home internet connection or one of poor quality (Bossuet 2020). Many teachers themselves lacked adequate digital connections and IT equipment in their homes as well as the unlimited telephone plans needed to maintain reliable contact with families. Tools such as virtual classes proved to be complex, and digital textbooks were found to be incomplete. Many pupils experienced similar problems, including a lack of private space, which was combined, for some, with a lack of family support to help them with

Table 5.3   2019 Global Innovation Index – subcategory: infrastructure.

		Finland	France	Germany	Sweden	Switzerland
3	Infrastructure	12	11	13	2	3
3.1	Information and communication technologies (ICTs)	16	10	15	12	19
3.1.1	ICT access	52	16	6	17	10
3.1.2	ICT use	17	14	22	6	2
3.1.3	Government's online service	8	4	17	14	35
3.1.4	Online e-participation	1	13	23	19	41
3.2	General infrastructure	13	29	26	4	28
3.2.1	Electricity output	10	20	22	7	30
3.2.2	Logistics performance	10	16	1	2	13
3.2.3	Gross capital formation	66	59	91	39	55
3.3	Ecological sustainability	42	31	29	10	3
3.3.1	GDP per unit of energy use	96	46	34	57	6
3.3.2	Environmental performance	10	2	13	5	1
3.3.3	ISO 14001 environmental certificates	18	46	41	7	21

Source: Statistics Time, 2019 Global Innovation Index, https://www.globalinnovationindex.org/analysis-indicator.

their home-based distance schooling. At the national level, Minister of National Education Jean-Michel Blanquer estimated that the education system had 'lost' 5 to 8 per cent of pupils in lockdown. (Blanquer 2020). The main reason for this may not have been problems with IT infrastructure, however: the Global Innovation Index (GII) data in table 5.3 shows France ranking in a respectable eleventh position in the infrastructure subcategory, above Germany (thirteenth) and even Finland (twelfth).

French sociologist Dominique Pasquier has examined the reasons for disappointed hopes about the benefits of the internet as a path towards a more horizontal democracy. He argues that the causes of the digital divide run deeper than a lack of equipment or poor access to the network, stating that they are ultimately social and cultural in nature (Pasquier 2019). This divide may be bridged over time, as suggested by the way that spontaneous social movements such as the yellow vests have made use of social networks to promote horizontal democracy. The successful adaptation of the knowledge economy, it seems, hinges on the people concerned having 'contact with the ground' (Taleb 2019, 7).

In general, however, there are strong grounds for Pasquier's thesis that the education required to promote an inclusive knowledge economy is not about 'how to use a computer', an area in which most pupils will probably know more than their teachers, but about teaching children and students 'how to learn' (Foray 2006, 236). Reducing the digital divide means nurturing creative thinking, which rests on developing expertise, information processing strategies, and personality characteristics in a positive learning environment (Hunter, Bedell, and Mumford 2007). An uplifting environment – in the workplace as well as in schools – comprises freedom, positive challenges, supervisory and organisational encouragement, and workgroup support. The negative counterparts to these concepts are organisational and management obstacles due to rigid controls, constrained procedures, internal politics, risk-averse management, and excessive workload pressure. Pasquier concludes that the education system should not be based on distrust and the stigma of failure, but on the notions of perseverance despite difficulty and of learning from setbacks. This will establish a feeling of trust and collaboration from a young age. Progress depends on changing France's perception of teachers from wielders of authority, giving insubordinate pupils the chance to earn peer-group respect, to conduits of knowledge and purveyors of an ethos that will accompany children throughout their lives. A part of that ethos would involve a healthy source of authority, including that of the state, based on the respect felt by the community.

This positive environment that would be conducive to the optimal development of the knowledge economy does not correspond to the picture that emerges from a persuasive assessment of the French education system by journalist Peter Gumbel. In his account, the system is good at producing people who can write long and well-argued reports on what should or should not be done, but it is not so good at producing people who know how to take decisions or how to make things happen (Gumbel 2013).

Creativity is hard to define, but it might be summed up as the articulation of a set of thoughts as innovative ideas and concepts that are of value to the person who imagines them (or others). The development of these ideas and concepts into some form of real-isation is also key. Creativity touches all forms of human activity and endeavour, whether in science, technology, engineering, and mathematics (STEM); the arts and entertainment; or services and business. The concordance of creativity and innovation (the tangible materialisation of creativity) determines the future economic performance of an enterprise and, ultimately, of an economy. However, creativity and innovation do not develop in a vacuum. The development of creative thinking begins even before children enter school, when families encourage their offspring to play. The capacity for creative thinking increases with each stage of life and schooling as students expand the concepts they have learned and rearrange them into new ones. These skills and abilities are gradually developed to enable creative ideas to be transformed into new processes and products. Such innovative and valuable creative ideas can spring from anywhere: for instance, studying another person's ideas, trying to solve a problem that naturally occurs, bypassing a constraint or cultivating interests and passions. Creative people are moved by curiosity and passion; their reward is to do what they love (Amabile 1997). This love is fed by learning and methods that help the subconscious to generate ideas, such as relaxing activities that silence the censorship of the conscious mind, which can sometimes prevent innovative ideas from germinating. This curiosity and love cannot be promoted by pressure or force, which will generally have the perverse effect of discouraging any creative thinking (Amabile 2012).

But how can a nation develop these skills if, as observed by French historian Jean-Baptiste Noé, its official textbooks portray the innovator as a person bent on obtaining 'suspect' profits and exploiting the 'masses' (Noé 2013)? How can innovation be promoted if pupils are not taught that it is a key driver of improved living standards, and that behind innovations stand entrepreneurs? The failure to convey that entrepreneurs play an important role in innovating and creating jobs has deep consequences for the values and behaviour transmitted to young people, which, in turn, affects creativity, innovation, and ethics. The message is that it is more moral to seek a protected, risk-averse job in the public service than to risk everything to do what one loves. This lack of exposure to risk means that failure is rarely perceived, let alone used, as an opportunity to learn and develop.

The French love knowledge and high-tech: a passion supported by a long-standing scientific and technical tradition as well as an education system in which the teaching of STEM subjects has always remained strong. Yet ideas outside the 'model' are regarded with suspicion: groupthink has shaped a fixed, unquestioned way of thinking, bolstered by the 'cultural centralisation' in Paris of 'the nation's major intellectual bodies – from the state to the great educational institutions, academies, publishing houses, and organs of the press' (Hazareesingh 2015, 10). Neither collaboration nor initiative is encouraged. Instead, the education system is oppressive, undermining self-confidence (Gumbel 2010). This explains why some of the ablest products of the education system prefer to work outside France and are eagerly tapped by world-leading tech firms for their highly valuable quantitative skills. A good example of this phenomenon is the career of French–American computer scientist Yann LeCun. He may have started life in France, but he is currently scientific director of AI at Facebook and professor at the Courant Institute of Mathematical Sciences at New York University. He is recognised as one of the pioneers of artificial neural networks, having received (with his two colleagues Geoffrey Hinton and Yoshua Bengio) the Turing Award – the equivalent of the Nobel Prize for computer science – in 2018.

As we saw in chapter 3, the concentration of political power reflected in the tradition of the centralised state tends to mute individual initiative and voices. The knowledge economy, composed of intangible goods and AI, rests on individual creativity and ingenuity, and it requires openness to new ideas. None of that sits comfortably with the technocrats of the Fifth Republic, aloof from worker cooperation and ignorant of risk, but confident in the way they allocate the large redistributed contents of the taxpayer's purse. Having said that, in October 2015, then Prime Minister Manuel Valls (who had the distinction of not being an ENA graduate) launched an international communication campaign, *Creative France*, which bore the slogan: 'Creativity: a quintessentially French trait'. The campaign was designed to send a strong signal to the outside world: 'French bashing is over, now is the time for pride' (Valls 2015)! This campaign, over a period of eighteen months, targeted ten priority countries to be enlightened about the superlative creativity of France. For instance, on the website of the French Embassy in Wellington, New Zealand, one could read:

French ingenuity is rooted in creativity and innovation. For centuries, our thinkers, writers, artists, researchers, and scientists have worked to uplift and better humanity, to help the world make progress and live in freedom, to spread ideas and forward-thinking ideals. From Molière to Matisse, from Nicolas-Joseph Cugnot to Luc Montagnier, the French have shared their country's greatest, most universal achievements with the world. Today, new generations are taking up the baton and carrying on this tradition of creative genius that forms part of our national identity. ... International observers are spot on in their assessment of France as the world leader in creativity.

The means adopted by Manuel Valls to propel this message seem close to the technique of 'conscious autosuggestion' developed by French pharmacist Émile Coué (1857–1926). In this spirit of 'goal communication', the campaign's instigators appear to have believed that repeatedly telling the targeted countries that France was a world leader in creativity would mean that after eighteen months, and with a bit of imagination, this would be the reality.

Unfortunately, the assessment of many 'international observers' differed. The Global Creativity Index 2015 statistics, compiled by the Martin Prosperity Institute, placed Australia first, followed by the United States and New Zealand, with France lagging behind in sixteenth position. France has been ranked tenth in the Global Innovation Index (GII) and fifteenth in a 2017 survey of global innovation conducted by the World Intellectual Property Organization (WIPO), coming behind Switzerland, Sweden, the Netherlands, the United States, and the United Kingdom. The abovementioned GII, developed jointly by Cornell University, INSEAD, and WIPO, includes seven categories: institutions, human capital and research, infrastructure, market sophistication, business sophistication, knowledge and technology outputs, and creative outputs. Each of these categories contains various subcategories covering all together more than eighty indicators, reflecting a broad vision of innovation. In the annual ranking for 2019, France was placed sixteenth, unchanged from the previous year and far behind its peer group countries (see table 5.4).

The World Bank lists four pillars that a country must have to take part in the knowledge economy: an educated and skilled population, technology infrastructure, a regime that encourages technology

Table 5.4 2019 Global Innovation Index.

	Finland	France	Germany	Sweden	Switzerland
Indicator					
Global Innovation Index	6	16	9	2	1
Innovation input subindex	7	16	12	4	2
Innovation output subindex	7	14	9	3	1
Index					
1. Institutions	3	19	16	9	12
2. Human capital and research	2	11	3	6	7
3. Infrastructure	12	11	13	2	3
4. Market sophistication	27	12	20	14	7
5. Business sophistication	5	19	12	1	2
6. Knowledge and technology outputs	9	15	10	2	1
7. Creative outputs	13	16	10	7	1

Source: Statistics Time, 2019 Global Innovation Index, https://www.globalinnovationindex.org/analysis-indicator.

and entrepreneurship, and a network of public and private research organisations. In the GII's 'business sophistication' subcategory (table 5.5), Switzerland and Sweden lead, with France lagging far behind. Despite France's fascination with Sweden and its ilk, noted earlier, the differences between these nations in terms of education, research, and business environment seem forbiddingly wide.

In the previous chapter, we saw the features of Swedish-style governance that contrast so favourably, in this context, with French traditions. These start with limited vertical hierarchies in firms, leaving well-trained staff with ample autonomy and capacity for initiative within their teams, who are thereby able to adapt quickly to shifts in demand. The Swedish state lets its social partners define the operating rules of the economy. Sweden is one of the most advanced countries regarding AI research and project implementation. Yet the Swedish state did not decide on a big strategy, and nobody expected it to declare the D-Day of a great era devoted to AI. Instead, the government limited itself to asking the social partners to prepare a strategy. The conclusion of their work was that the way in which the state could best support the development of AI was by training the workforce. As a result, Swedish companies moved rapidly, collaborating with other firms and consulting with trade unions. These considerations highlight the importance

Table 5.5   2019 Global Innovation Index – subcategory: business sophistication.

		Finland	France	Germany	Sweden	Switzerland
5	Business sophistication	5	19	12	1	2
5.1	Knowledge workers	6	15	13	2	3
5.1.1	Employment in knowledge-intensive services	10	16	17	5	3
5.1.3	GERD performed by business enterprise	10	13	7	4	5
5.1.4	GERD financed by business enterprise	15	20	7	14	10
5.1.5	Females employed with advanced degrees	5	21	51	12	28
5.2	Innovation linkages	4	26	10	2	3
5.2.1	University/industry research collaboration	5	30	6	9	3
5.2.2	State of cluster development	17	20	2	12	3
5.2.3	GERD financed by abroad	35	51	60	55	41
5.2.4	Joint venture/strategic alliance deals	10	30	32	5	13
5.2.5	Patent families filed in at least two offices	3	14	9	1	4
5.3	Knowledge absorption	12	17	22	6	3
5.3.1	Intellectual property payments	37	14	51	16	6
5.3.2	High-tech imports	60	23	37	59	90
5.3.3	ICT services imports	4	22	25	6	1
5.3.4	Foreign direct investment, net inflows	31	85	86	55	13
5.3.5	Research talent in business enterprise	20	14	15	4	25

Source: Statistics Time, 2019 Global Innovation Index, https://www.globalinnovationindex.org/analysis-indicator.

of making deep changes in governance and culture at every level, without which pumping public funds (and therefore current or future taxation) into the digital economy, while welcome, will not suffice. For France, given the rigidities of its political economy (which we have been viewing from various angles), the challenges will be immense.

The wide-ranging skills mix required for the development of a dynamic knowledge economy poses two threats to labour markets:

the replacement of jobs through automation and the creation of low-skilled jobs. Dominique Méda stresses that the 'Uberization' of society allows those offering and those requesting a service to connect directly through online platforms, which, while creating new jobs (at Uber, at Airbnb, and at proliferating e-commerce platforms), is destroying jobs in traditional organisations (taxi companies, hotels, and shops). These regulated professions are watching their monopolies and protections disappear (Méda 2016, 12). It was no accident that Uber's network of drivers and users were violently attacked by the powerful Parisian taxi corporation.

Innovation – whether technological, organisational, institutional, or conceptual – creates uncertainty about the future of the rights and expectations anchored in individuals. Every innovation generates uncertainty as to the effects of its adoption on a group's relative position by threatening that group's acquired rights and established expectations; this leads entire segments of the workforce, employers, and investors to feel mutual suspicion or hostility. The previous chapters have analysed the feelings of hopelessness, the economic insecurity, and the lower standards of living suffered by those who feel left behind, as if the Republic has other, more pressing concerns than their predicament. For years, editorials in newspapers, books, and pamphlets have depicted the predicament of rural people, suburban dwellers, and blue-collar workers either romantically or critically – and sometimes even contemptuously. A reaction from below has materialised, as we have seen with the *gilets jaunes*, whose movement has several counterparts in peer group countries such as the United States (as powerfully related by Princeton social scientist Robert Wuthnow in his 2018 book *Rage in Rural America*). This is a resistance against the perceived causes of declining living standards and status: the transfer of production to low-wage countries, and threats from either outside (through migration) or within (through failings of governance that in France amount to a betrayal of the proclaimed values of the Republic).

The sharpening of such grievances may cut two ways. While discontents will make societies more receptive to change, they may also breed suspicion that the practical effect of such change will only be to entrench existing disadvantages. In the first Finlay Lecture delivered at University College Dublin in April 1933 – a historic turning point in political and economic orientations – Keynes depicted this tension as a fundamental 'perplexity': 'The decadent international

but individualistic capitalism, in the hands of which we found ourselves after the war, is not a success. It is not intelligent, it is not
beautiful, it is not just, it is not virtuous – and it doesn't deliver the
goods. In short, we dislike it, and we are beginning to despise it.
But when we wonder what to put in its place, we are extremely per-
plexed' (Keynes 1933, 183).

Perplexity bordering on hostile suspicion of changes associated with the knowledge economy is liable to spread well beyond
the existing ranks of the yellow vests. American economist Richard Baldwin warns that the feelings of abandonment and despair
currently expressed by the periphery will soon be shared by many
white-collar workers in the service industry, who will find themselves marginalised by what he calls 'globotics': a combination of
globalisation and armies of increasingly skilled but always zero-wage
robots. The increase in computing power observed since the 1980s
has been translated into many tasks being performed by machines,
working twenty-four hours a day, seven days a week, and threatening many service sector workers, who have been relatively sheltered
until now. Therefore, part of the population is bound to react negatively against the knowledge economy because they feel that their
jobs and their social gains are being threatened, or that protected
market positions are in jeopardy.

Robots can produce the same product anywhere, whenever it is
required, calling into question many conventional notions about
comparative advantage (King 2017, 189). Firms will have fewer reasons to relocate in search of a low-cost workforce without social
protection. Machines can be reproduced at will and at minimal
cost. They do not go on strike or indulge in absenteeism (such as
fake sick leave) or demand better working conditions. Migrant labour can be replaced by locally produced machines that do not
require retraining. These trends should incidentally allay concerns
about demographic weakness in many advanced countries (an area
where France is in a better position than its European peers, notably Germany).

Baldwin highlights the 'explosive progress' phase of the digitech
revolution, which is leaving many 'unaware of how fast the changes
are coming or living in denial' (Baldwin 2019, 90). The jobs of
the future will require qualities such as creativity, empathy, intuition, leadership, and an ability to face the unknown, all of which

are remote from automated digital learning. This conclusion makes him optimistic about the future, as he believes that 'the sense of belonging to a community will rise and people will support each other' (Baldwin 2019, 264). Baldwin's optimism seems to be the perfect answer to the widely remarked upon demoralisation of the French and their craving for some recognition of the cultural reality of their community. This aspiration was well expressed by Stephen King, who called it 'the re-emerging influence of history, geography and religious belief in shaping values in different parts of the world' (King 2017, 115).

The technocrat's life would be easier if, once the Covid-19 crisis has passed, business as usual were to resume. Yet it is far from certain whether people will readily take up their previous routines: commuting on crowded public transport or booking dream vacations on beaches at the farthest ends of the earth. Shocks like this pandemic can displace normality: those previously entrenched activities that are, according to the mimetic theory developed by French anthropologist René Girard, the key to understanding much human behaviour (Girard 1978). Within a few weeks of a lockdown being implemented in Europe and North America in March 2020, many white-collar workers had discovered that their regular physical presence in the workplace was no longer necessary, and that their daily commute had therefore become redundant. Meanwhile, the state, managers of companies, and directors of educational institutions were jumping to the complacent conclusion that their employees could carry on 'business as usual' in a virtual environment. In reality, complex adaptations were, and are, required across the board.

The question is whether the French tradition of governance can become 'Swedish' in the sense of facilitating a highly flexible adaptation to the knowledge economy. We have seen in previous chapters the obstacles on this path: centralisation; relentless bureaucratic intervention fuelled by the notion of tax-and-spend as both first and last resort; distrust of entrepreneurship and success; the cult of the chief; and a penchant to regulate and exert social control in ways that generate unemployment and a lack of fulfilling work. All of this stokes chronic discontent, criticism that frequently borders on the nihilistic, and protests that most often end in violence. Still, any progress whatsoever through such thickets will unleash the country's deep creative potential, which is the subject of the following section.

THE STATE AND THE ENTREPRENEUR
IN THE KNOWLEDGE ECONOMY

As mentioned in chapter 1, France has always had a liberal tradition in the 'classic' sense of favouring individual liberty and initiative over state encroachment. This flame has been kept alight by some feisty voices such as, in the political arena, Alain Madelin (Madelin 1997) and, among economists, Pascal Salin (Salin 2000). They have both noted the paradox of a country producing some of the greatest liberal thinkers in history becoming one of the least liberal of the large Western-type countries.

It took the policies of Socialist president François Hollande to provoke something more than books and speeches from liberal-minded public figures: that is, an effective and organised reaction from entrepreneurs. It felt as if the old discussion about wealth needing to be created before any of it can be redistributed had completely passed by the Hollande team and the cohort of officials that produced his administration's detailed policies. One example of this was a tax reform that followed Hollande's election in 2012. At the time, headlines announced a 75 per cent marginal rate of tax to be placed on personal incomes exceeding €1 million per year. More significant in the end was a proposal to tax capital gains on the sale of shares in privately held companies at the same rate as personal incomes. This change would have nearly doubled the effective tax rate on entrepreneurs. There was also a strong sense of unfairness, as this form of capital gain would have been taxed more heavily than art transactions, real estate investments, and even profits on the sale of securities listed on public exchanges. With this single proposal, the French government was eliminating the one tangible reward for building new companies, creating innovation, and providing employment.

The proposal triggered an online revolt, mounted by a group of entrepreneurs calling themselves *Les Pigeons* (the word *pigeon* in French being slang for dupe). The movement attracted 75,000 founders of start-ups and their supporters, who changed their profile pictures to pigeons across the web in a social media campaign that forced the government to beat a hasty retreat (less than a week after the policy was announced). The spokesperson of the pigeons movement, Jean-David Chamboredon, a graduate of Polytechnique and the executive chairman of an ISAI investment fund financed by web entrepreneurs, told the *Tribune* newspaper that entrepreneurs were quite indifferent to the wealth tax, as 'you're either going to go into tax exile or you aren't'. However, he said that the proposed capital gain tax changes signified a total misunderstanding by bureaucrats of the world of enterprise: 'For example, an entrepreneur who sells his company, after 10 years of work, 10 years of uncertainty, of ups and downs, of 70-hour work weeks ... would have to pay 45 per cent (income tax rate) + 15.5 per cent of Social Contributions in total i.e. over 60 per cent. We can only read from that proposal an anti-capitalist and anti-economic mindset that destroys entrepreneurial dreams with an almost sadistic approach' (Chamboredon 2012).

Les Pigeons started a fashion during the Hollande presidency. The Bees (*Abeilles*) movement won a similar battle against the *Marisol-tax* (which drew its name from then Minister of Health Marisol Touraine), which required companies to subscribe to the mutual health insurance chosen by the social partners in their sector. The Constitutional Council struck down the law in question in December 2013. There were also the Chicks (*Poussins*), defending the status of sole traders, who obtained some redress from Hollande's government. They were followed by more online movements whose results were not so successful – such as the Sparrows (*Moineaux*), defending novice entrepreneurs; the Sheep (*Moutons*), campaigning for improvements in social security arrangements for the self-employed; and the Fleeced (*Tondus*), deciding not to pay the social security contributions due from them as employers on the grounds that they considered this burden of payroll taxation to be excessive (this particular group were told by the courts that they were being legally fleeced). These different movements were all expressing French entrepreneurs' frustration at decades of state policies that weighed on budding ventures with burdensome regulations and taxation (Raymond 2014).

As a result, even before Hollande left office, the political atmosphere shifted in favour of supporting new entrepreneurs. Macron latched onto this trend. He seems to have understood that urgent change was needed in the way that the state machine related to new businesses. This conclusion emerges from an analysis by political scientist Carla Ibled of four important Macron speeches made on this theme between June 2017 and February 2019 (Ibled 2019). Macron's vision had 'Swedish' and even classically liberal features.

He advocated a 'facilitating' and 'supportive' state that would target and calibrate its interventions, simplify regulations, reduce the tax burden on companies, and reduce the 'cost of failure'. Macron's stated goal was to limit the individual's dependence on state benevolence. Individuals should instead protect themselves through 'training and retraining': it was for the state to protect them from adverse economic conditions. All this seemed well suited for the development of the knowledge economy. Viewed from another angle, however, this vision combined the worst of both worlds in the sense of championing the state while ducking its responsibilities. Thus, the 'start-up nation' catchphrase became the 'start-up state'. Macron's whole tone was martial and confrontational. He evoked a civilisational war between the backward forces of yesterday and the 'progressive' and enlightened forces of tomorrow. The nation must win this 'battle', he exclaimed. His bellicose tone had a messianic tinge: France was called to lead in today's 'civilisational and cultural challenge'. Weaker brethren were, by implication, irrelevant or a burden to this vanguard of the new 'republican order'. Here, the liberal vision turned to indifference: responsibility for failure or success was now seen as resting with the individual, not with the market or the state. It was ironic that Macron's martial state would soon be turned physically on the yellow vests.

For all its deviations from the 'Swedish' model, Macron's rhetoric and policies gave some hope to entrepreneurs. Instead of being demonised, they found themselves cast by him in the leading role of his start-up nation. However, the wave of new and creative entrepreneurship that was highlighted by the *Pigeons* movement and later championed by Macron did not materialise out of thin air. The process dated back to the 1990s, when the liberalisation of financial markets made equity and venture capital financing more accessible to smaller innovative firms than had ever been seen before. Tax incentives, grants, contracts, and loans were provided to encourage R&D in all kinds of firms. Collaborative research between SMEs, large firms, and public research organisations started to be encouraged to create competitiveness clusters (Liu and Laperche 2015). In a sign that even the technocrats had been infected with start-up mania, 2012 saw the merger of the Caisse des Dépôts et Consignations and the EPIC BPI-Groupe to create Bpifrance; this was mandated to finance venture capital funds for young entrepreneurs alongside similar vehicles created by large industrial companies such as Total and AXA.

Yet this was far from being a state-led process. The lean years following the Great Recession and the euro sovereign debt crisis stimulated new ideas, with help from the inherent dynamism supplied by digital technology's ability to reduce costs and facilitate exchange (Goldfarb and Tucker 2019). France was no laggard when it came to the peer-to-peer (P2P) online platforms that underpinned the 'sharing economy', contributing dynamic homegrown brands such as the car-sharing start-up BlaBlaCar. This new generation of twenty-first-century entrepreneurs amounts to a latter-day Free French, driven to create their own firms to escape the hierarchical structures and rigid career paths of the civil service and big corporations. The start-up nation got its start not because of any decisions by the state or its president, however messianically inclined, but because of the very reasons mentioned by Jean-Jacques Rosa – namely, a societal adaptation to the opportunities and demands of the knowledge economy. There is anecdotal evidence that a growing number of children of the caste of senior state officials are steering away from their parents' career paths of power and privilege and are instead turning to enterprise in the new knowledge economy.

A stand-out role model and active promoter of a new and more creative economic culture is Xavier Niel, a leading French tech entrepreneur. Niel had already started and successfully sold his first venture by the age of nineteen. By the time he reached his forties, he decided to take the lead in the development of the country's tech ecosystem – not something that could be left to the government to provide. In 2013, he founded, with former executives of the Epitech school, a unique educational institution called Ecole 42, in order to form entrepreneurial talent. He followed this by setting up Station F, a start-up business incubator, in 2017.

The idea behind Ecole 42 was born out of frustration with the traditional education system, which was, and is, failing to deliver the skills required by the digital economy, such as searching and filtering information to create projects in collaboration with other students. Its name alludes to the answer ('42') given by the Deep Thought supercomputer to the ultimate question of 'life, the universe and everything' in Douglas Adams's *The Hitchhiker's Guide to the Galaxy* (Adams 2007). Now organised in four campuses (three in France, and one in Silicon Valley), Ecole 42 is the anti-Jacobin school *par excellence*: no previous degrees or predefined skills are required. Access is means-blind and truly meritocratic (60,000 to

80,000 students apply every year for 1,000 places). There are no traditional teachers or printed books. Open 24/7, the school provides an environment for self-organised P2P training and project-based learning. All students must qualify for an internship conditional on validating several projects (in which they retain the intellectual property rights) and passing five exams (Ranger 2018). Graduates get jobs before or on completion of courses lasting three to five years, with annual drop-out rates in the range of only 5–15 per cent. Study is framed as a series of quests and achievements, using the language of gaming to avoid making students feel too disheartened if they fail the first few times – a problem already mentioned as being typical of the traditional French education system, where students suffer from failure stigmatisation. This is one of many ways in which Ecole 42 overturns some of the worst drawbacks of French educational culture as well as other characteristic national pathologies such as excessive centralisation. In an inspired move, Niel chose to locate one of the Ecole 42 campuses in a middling-to-small town, Angoulême (population 42,000). Such towns are typical in peripheral France and, as the yellow vests movement showed, have often been overlooked by state policy.

Niel's enthusiasm provided inspiration not only for budding young entrepreneurs, but also for the country's youthful president as he set out to improve the business climate. There was certainly room for such improvement in governmental and bureaucratic attitudes towards entrepreneurs.

Another important subcategory in the previously mentioned GII is 'institutions'. As shown in table 5.6, France was given a low nineteenth place here, with strikingly bad scores for political and operational stability, government effectiveness, and regulatory quality.

The poor performance of France in those areas indicates that Macron was misdirecting his combative energies. The main threat to the progress represented by the knowledge economy agenda is not 'backward forces' in society, as he states in his speeches, but the obstructionism of officialdom reaching up to the most senior levels. The high bureaucratic caste will aim to see off any change that threatens the settled order over which it presides. A caricatural case of this reflex from the early Macron period was the derailment of his commitment to abolish the ENA, announced at the height of the yellow vests unrest. In the area we are focused on here – Macron's efforts to improve the business climate and encourage an

Table 5.6   2019 Global Innovation Index – subcategory: institutions.

		Finland	France	Germany	Sweden	Switzerland
1	Institutions	3	19	16	9	12
1.1	Political environment	5	22	13	9	2
1.1.1	Political and operational stability	15	32	18	12	4
1.1.2	Government effectiveness	4	21	11	8	2
1.2	Regulatory environment	5	20	23	13	6
1.2.1	Regulatory quality	8	26	11	10	7
1.2.2	Rule of law	1	19	16	3	4
1.2.3	Cost of redundancy dismissal	31	41	89	57	31
1.3	Business environment	1	21	15	·14	44
1.3.1	Ease of starting a business	39	27	88	16	62
1.3.2	Ease of resolving insolvency	2	26	4	16	43

Source: Statistics Time, 2019 Global Innovation Index, https://www.globalinnovationindex.org/analysis-indicator.

entrepreneurial renaissance – the main exhibit is the PACTE Act. Enacted in the spring of 2019, this legislation had the stated goal of 'Giving businesses the means to innovate, transform, grow and create jobs'.

A core focus of the law was to streamline the web of regulation and financial burdens that tightens around companies as they get bigger. This burden runs on a broad spectrum, from general payroll taxation (social security contributions) via mandatory internal regulations and election of staff representatives to the provision of work canteens, anti-sexual harassment officers, and holiday vouchers. When a company's headcount exceeds certain defined thresholds, more such constraints and costs kick in. As things stood, 199 obligations of all kinds were spread over forty-nine thresholds. In 2018, the government decided it was time to create some order out of this mess. It came up with an 'action plan', reflected in the PACTE Act's consolidation of those forty-nine headcount thresholds into just three levels: 11, 50, and 250 employees. By simplifying the obligations linked to each of these levels, the law aimed to create a legal environment that was more favourable to the development of SMEs. The reform included a more business-friendly definition of when a company would be deemed to have passed a threshold. Instead of this being the moment when it hired one more employee over the

defined threshold number (deterring new hires, especially of a fif-
tieth employee), the new law provided that the headcount would
have to remain stably above the threshold level for five consecutive
years before a company would be counted in the higher bracket
(and thus subject to more onerous regulation and taxation). The
downward crossing of the threshold for a single year resets this five-
year period to zero.

Encouraging as all that might seem, a detailed investigation by
two journalists – Marie de Greef-Madelin and Frédéric Paya – revealed that the real picture was much less pretty (Greef-Madelin
and Paya 2020). As it turned out, officials had ensured that complex
exceptions remained after all. Some of these may seem like caricatures of triviality worthy of Georges Courteline's immortal comic
satire on French bureaucracy, *Messieurs les ronds de cuir* (Courteline
1993). Thus, the abolished twenty-employee threshold was retained
for the purpose of obligations relating to disabled workers (who
must comprise 6 per cent of the workforce of companies of this
size). More seriously, there would still be, for a transitional period,
intermediate headcount thresholds between the three basic levels
of 11, 50, and 250. Most seriously of all, the new five-year reference
rule for calculating the number of employees – harmonising and
automating headcount calculations under the Social Security Code
based on social insurance declarations – would coexist with other
calculation methods specific to certain pieces of legislation.

Greef-Madelin and Paya also noted that as soon as the bar of eleven
employees is crossed, various taxes and charges cease to be proportional to the number of workers and actual payroll amounts. In this
higher bracket, for example, a flat 8 per cent surcharge is applied
to employers' contributions to fund the Supplementary Provident
Scheme (a defined contribution pension scheme). Another extra
charge is the contribution rate of 1 per cent of the payroll (compared with 0.55 per cent previously) to participate in continuing
vocational training and transport costs. Other charges – these are
all taxes by another name – include a contribution of up to 0.5 per
cent of the wage bill (compared with 0.1 per cent previously) for the
National Housing Aid Fund, and an additional 0.45 per cent of the
payroll for the Construction Investment Fund.

These worthy efforts to improve the quality of regulation might
have deflected attention from still more important areas. In research
published in 2011, INSEE investigated to what extent regulation

based on headcount thresholds was preventing companies from growing (or, in other words, was aggravating the problem of corporate 'dwarfism' that prevents the greater efficiency which flows from businesses' scaling up, in turn slowing the overall growth in productivity that is the ultimate key to improved living standards across the board). The conclusion of the modelling work in this research was that the impact of such regulation was marginal. A complete smoothing of all such thresholds would have resulted in the share of companies with fewer than ten employees in the total number of companies decreasing from 91.9 per cent to 91.5 per cent (Ceci-Renaud and Chevalier 2011).

As implied by that critical scrutiny of the PACTE Act, the burden of taxes and levies combined with other financial pressures amounts to an even more serious obstacle to creative entrepreneurship than the complex regulatory tangle. Some oblique evidence for this comes from a 2019 survey conducted by France Digitale (an association of start-ups that emerged from the *Pigeons* movement) of its 356 member companies. Over half the respondents in this barometer survey highlighted the mismatch between the skills they required and those coming out of the French education system. The survey also revealed that their dependence on local recruitment is now much greater due to the deterrent of high French taxes on hiring overseas workers (tax is most likely the more powerful factor here than, for example, the language barrier, as this is virtually non-existent in the French tech world, where English is the working language). Another recurring theme of that survey was inadequate access to finance (Audry and Sebag 2019).

Successive French governments have come up with a battery of research and tax credits designed to help start-ups get off the ground, and various programmes have been introduced to encourage young entrepreneurs to settle in France. But the sums involved are modest – a problem flagged over many years by entrepreneurs themselves and various iFrap reports. This was another of the problems addressed by the PACTE Act, which introduced a standardised funding arrangement platform for people setting up new businesses and allowed more flexible use for this purpose of established savings and life insurance investment products. Despite such myriad new measures, French entrepreneurs' access to long-term institutional investment capital, allowing the mobilisation of significant sums over time, remains insufficient compared with that of their

Table 5.7   2019 Global Innovation Index – subcategory: market sophistication.

		France	Germany	Sweden	Switzerland	Israel	UK	US
4	Market sophistication	12	20	14	7	16	4	1
4.1	Credit	33	28	19	9	37	10	1
4.1.1	Ease of getting credit	87	40	77	66	54	29	3
4.1.2	Domestic credit to private sector	26	39	15	4	48	14	3
4.2	Investment	25	79	30	21	14	6	7
4.2.1	Ease of protecting minority investors	35	68	30	93	21	14	47
4.2.2	Market capitalisation	14	31	n/a	1	21	n/a	5
4.2.3	Venture capital deals	5	20	17	10	3	4	1
4.3	Trade, competition, & market scale	6	4	29	26	34	5	1
4.3.1	Applied tariff rate, weighted mean	23	23	23	20	50	23	18
4.3.2	Intensity of local competition	8	18	25	23	24	9	3
4.3.3	Domestic market scale	10	5	38	36	50	9	2

Source: Statistics Time, 2019 Global Innovation Index, https://www.globalinnovationindex.org/analysis-indicator.

peers in the United States, the United Kingdom, and China, as the former spokesperson of the *Pigeons,* Jean-David Chamboredon, has declared in various press interviews (L'Opinion 2019).

The challenge here boils down to achieving the scale that would give this pioneer movement real weight in the development of France's economy and society. The main problem may not be with the availability of early stage venture funding as such. Returning once again to that 2019 GII data, table 5.7 shows that while the United States unsurprisingly leads the ranking for venture capital deals, France is not doing too badly, coming in fifth position: well ahead of its continental European peers this time.

In 2013, Aileen Lee, the founder of Cowboy Ventures, came up with the moniker 'unicorn' for venture capital-backed new companies ('with big dreams ... to build things that the world has never seen before') that reach valuations of more than US$1 billion (Rodriguez 2015) – a nod to the rarity of this outcome. As of May 2020, 471 unicorns had been recorded, about half of which came from the United States; Silicon Valley-based capital accounted for over a third of global start-up funding. The entrepreneurs who took part in that France Digitale barometer expressed their frustration with the French government, and with Europe more generally, for the lack of concerted cooperation and integration taking place between countries: such cooperation is required for companies to grow beyond the start-up phase. They also feared that Europe would prioritise regulating and taxing the digital economy over helping large tech companies to emerge.

This challenge raises an important general question about the desirability of scaling up tech companies. In *The Great Reversal: How America Gave Up on Free Markets*, published in 2019, Thomas Philippon, a French academic economist who has taught for many years in the United States, argues that the authorities – and, in particular, competition ('anti-trust') regulators and enforcers – in America have fallen asleep at the wheel. This has led to the rise of corporate 'gigantism', where huge firms use their commercial clout and lobbying power to build up ever larger market shares to the detriment of wages, investment, and innovation – all of which widens inequalities. Philippon contrasts the American picture with the European one: in the latter, more out of countries' and firms' mutual suspicions than as the result of any inherent virtue, there has been more effective official action against the threat of monopolies and market abuse (Philippon 2019).

Philippon's thesis that 'America gave up on free markets' has been questioned by US economist Tyler Cowen in his *Marginal Revolution* blog (Cowen 2019). Cowen acknowledges the existence of undesirable regulatory barriers to new entrants in markets such as health care and cable television, and he agrees in general that the American economy could be more dynamic and competitive. However, he argues, this does not mean that monopoly power has increased in an economically significant way in a wide variety of sectors. Cowen rests his case on a variety of studies – one in particular, in which the authors distinguish between the emergence of larger firms at the national level and the concentration in local markets, where changes in the competitive environment have the greatest economic impact (Rossi-Hansberg, Sarte, and Trachter 2018). The authors conclude that large firms reduce local concentration and therefore most likely increase competition in product markets. Their results help to reconcile the observation of a growing concentration at the national level with the more mixed data on increasing mark-ups and profits. Virtually no theory of product market competition associates a decrease in concentration with an increase in margins or an increase in profits. The rising trend in national concentration is not, in itself, necessarily a concern for anti-trust policy. By decreasing local concentration, the growth of the top firms has likely increased local competition and therefore helped to improve the quality and reduce the prices of a large share of products.

While Philippon's general thesis about the growth of monopoly power in the US economy might seem overdone, it could apply more specifically to the tech sector, where the high concentration achieved by the Big Tech giants is particularly visible.

Concern about the monopoly power of Big Tech may to some extent be supported by the data reported in table 5.8, which shows how these giants consistently rank among the top ten global companies measured by the market valuation of their equity. Related to this question of Big Tech's market power is a broader debate about whether such concentration at the frontiers of technology that transform societies might be a price worth paying. This question emerges from a pioneering work on evolutionary economics by American economists Richard Nelson and Sidney Winter undertaken in the 1980s. They drew on the ideas of the great Austrian political economist Joseph Schumpeter (Schumpeter 1942) in a way that is relevant to the knowledge economy (Nelson and Winter 1982). These authors put forward the 'Schumpeterian hypothesis' of a market structure comprising large companies with a considerable degree of market power being the price that society must pay for a rapid technological advance. This thesis is potentially controversial in the present context of 'techlash' (i.e. the backlash against Big Tech coming from both public authorities and public opinion). In early 2020, the US Federal Trade Commission (FTC) initiated an investigation into five leading Big Tech firms (Google, Microsoft, Facebook, Amazon, and Apple) regarding their use of personal data owned by the many and various smaller companies that they had acquired during the preceding decade (FTC 2020).

Along with parallel investigations by authorities at various levels in the United States and Europe, this enquiry will most likely drag on for many years. Wherever the correct balance may lie in this debate about the positive and negative effects of the technological progress and monopoly power associated with Big Tech, the social benefits that we can expect to flow from the new 'knowledge commons' will

Table 5.8   Evolution of the ten largest firms by market capitalisation.

Year	Description	Top company	Who dominates the top ten?
1999	Dotcom bubble	Microsoft ($583B)	Five tech companies in the mix
2004	Post-bubble	GE ($319B)	Diverse mix of companies by industry
2009	Financial crisis	PetroChina ($367B)	Six non-US companies make list
2014	$100 oil	Apple ($560B)	Last year for oil companies, tech starts ascending
2019	Big Tech era	Microsoft ($1,050B)	Seven companies are tech
		Amazon ($943B)	
		Apple ($920B)	
		Google/Alphabet ($778B)	
		Facebook ($546B)	
		Berkshire Hathaway $507B)	Diversified holding
		Alibaba ($435B)	
		Tencent ($431B)	
		Visa ($379B)	Financial
		Johnson & Johnson ($376B)	Consumer goods

PwC reports on the ranks of the largest public companies based on their market capitalisation in US dollars. The analysis compares values between March of each year and excludes exchange-traded funds and closed-end funds. *Source*: https://www.visualcapitalist.com/a-visual-history-of-the-largest-companies-by-market-cap-1999-today/; Bloomberg with PwC 2019.

be far from automatic. The next section of this chapter looks at the precarious potential of the knowledge economy – centred as it is on the production and distribution of a public good – to promote a more flourishing society.

THE COMEDY OF THE KNOWLEDGE COMMONS

We came across the phrase used in this section heading at the start of this chapter. The writer who coined it stresses that it is up to political decision makers to fully understand the importance of the public dimension of the knowledge economy, to make sure that the comedy does not turn into a tragedy (Foray 2006, 245). The advent of the knowledge economy has accentuated the immemorial imperative of getting people to cooperate, since cooperation is essential to the reproduction and enlargement of knowledge. John Stuart Mill advocated cooperative ownership, envisioning that workers' shared ownership in the firms they worked for would bring about 'the healing of the standing feud between capital and labour; the transformation of human life, from a conflict of classes struggling for opposite interests, to a friendly rivalry in the pursuit of a common good to all; the elevation of the dignity of labour; a new sense of security and independence in the labouring classes; and the conversion of each human being's daily occupation into a school of the social sympathies and practical intelligence' (Mill 1994, 153). Mill's vision always had an economic dimension, and he believed that the 'school of social sympathies' stemming from workers being made partners in production would also 'increase the productiveness of labour' (Mill 1994, 153).

In France, a century later, this style of thinking was echoed at the pinnacle of the state by de Gaulle, who championed the idea of co-operation between employers and employees. As the General put it: 'The condition of the workers? It is largely about the dignity of the working class. When their dignity is recognized ... the condition of the workers improves. The question of the working class is, along with nuclear disarmament, one of the great questions of our time' (Peyrefitte 2000, 1434, quoted in Jackson 2018, 703).

This French version of Mill's vision revolved around the term *participation* (de Gaulle 1970, 148). Historian Lucette Le Van-Lemesle traced this aspiration back to the first plans for national reconstruction in the dark days after the defeat of 1940 (Le Van-Lemesle 1990). Alain Peyrefitte in *Le Mal français* offers an account of how de Gaulle's thinking evolved from an initial concentration on rebuilding the state and the nation to a realisation of the need to address the question of how society itself was structured, starting with its administrative framework. He saw the resistance of the administrative caste to measures, which for him were crucial for the public good, but the logic of the system was too strong even for the General (Peyrefitte 2006). In documenting this episode, Le Van-Lemesle collected first-hand testimony about de Gaulle's determination to uphold his vision against all odds. This resulted in the signing on 17 August 1967 of three *ordinances* on participation that related to 'employee participation in the fruits of business expansion'. De Gaulle regarded these orders as a first step towards participatory management, where employees and employers would share responsibility; they also marked a turning point towards shared decision making based on common stakeholder interests. For the first time, the law required companies with 100 or more employees to provide the latter, in addition to their wages, with a share of the profits left over after a reasonable return had been paid out to stockholders. Employees also became entitled to transparent information about their firm's financial position. For firms with fewer than 100 employees, participation was not mandatory, but the workers could negotiate voluntary participation agreements (Le Van-Lemesle 1990). (In 1990, the threshold for compulsory participation was to be lowered from 100 to 50 employees; this rule was further modified by the PACTE Act in 2019.)

François Seydoux recalled that de Gaulle, via his 'supreme message' of May 1969, intended to break with a tradition of several centuries, and even with the policies of his own government, which, from Prime Minister Georges Pompidou downwards, and with the backing of most trade unions, resisted these ideas of shared decision making based on common stakeholder interest. He wanted the state to apply and extend to all citizens the principle of participation by renouncing part of its own power. This reversed the secular vector of French history towards the centralisation of administrative power. The specific measures on decentralisation and the reform of the Senate were rejected by voters in a referendum in 1969, after which de Gaulle resigned. Like all visionaries, he was too far ahead of his time (Seydoux 1977).

Le Van-Lemesle noted that in the 1980s an increasing number of SMEs with fewer than 100 employees were signing participation agreements, mainly in the sectors where the proportion of highly qualified labour and managers was significant, and where the added value compared with the wage bill was strong, such as in financial and professional services, research, health care, building materials, and entertainment. For her, writing in the late 1980s, participation was no longer a utopia, dreamt up by a great man tired of power, but a necessity. Her observations in this 1990 study about the ethos of participation point forward to the importance of creative and social intelligence in the knowledge economy as it would develop in subsequent decades. Writing about the prospect of ever more rapid automation, Richard Baldwin summarises the concept of an intelligence that cannot be replaced by robots, which was articulated by Swedish–German economist Carl Benedikt Frey and British machine learning scholar Michael Osborne (Frey and Osborne 2013, 2018): 'Typical workplace tasks that draw on social intelligence are negotiation (getting people to cooperate and reconcile differences) and persuasion (getting people to agree on ideas, ways of doing things, etc). It is also important in tasks like assisting and caring for people, providing emotional support, and the like' (Baldwin 2019, 245).

The intrinsic and relative merits of employee share ownership (ESO) schemes (either through shares or cooperatives) have been much debated by scholars and policymakers. Researchers have highlighted evidence of positive transformations in industrial relations in employee-owned businesses (EOBs) and ESO environments, where workers feel more motivated to raise productivity (Pérotin and Robinson 2002; Conyon and Freeman 2004). The costs related to absenteeism and managerial oversight should also be lower due to peer management, as employees will take more responsibility for themselves – and for each other – in this arrangement, acting as an internal management guard rail against free riders. Other benefits linked to co-owned firms include reducing labour turnover, improving retention of key employees, rooting firms to their communities and maintaining higher-than-average levels of trust, leading to better life satisfaction (Helliwell and Huang 2008).

As more firms listed their shares in the equity capital market, shares started to be used as a basis for employee remuneration. Collective ownership of a company's shares by employees is known in France as *Fonds commun de placement d'entreprise* (FCPE). In 2006, the *FCPE de reprise* (employee buyout mutual fund) was introduced to allow employees to take over their employer company under preferential conditions; however, very few cases were reported. The distribution of stock options for employees of large listed companies (included in the CAC-40 national 'blue chip' index) was typically limited to a handful of the most senior executives (Culpepper 2008).

As for cooperative ownership, this has a long history in France (Desroche 1989). It has taken various forms, involving entrepreneurs, artisans, farmers, and retail traders. Cooperatives have been organised around consumers (typically banks, such as Crédit coopératif, Banques populaires, and Caisse d'épargne) and employees: this has been seen in a variety of sectors and with well-established legal forms of organisation, making for an alphabet soup of acronyms such as SCOPs and SCICs (Société cooperative et participative and Société coopérative d'intérêt collectif). In theory, cooperatives seem to be a good way of satisfying the aspiration for more horizontal social relations and better representation, as they render the employee a co-entrepreneur, involved in operational management, who shares in the success of the company. The reality, however, can be quite far from the theory (Carluer-Lossouarn 2008).

De Gaulle's vision of employers and employees moving from an adversarial relationship to one of partnership for the sake of the common good was fired by his almost mystical notions about the French nation and its paths to greatness. But there was also a streak of modernity in the way he sought to shift from the traditional conflict-ridden top-down approach by appealing to society's collective intelligence. Part of the inspiration was straightforwardly democratic. A pioneering formal rationale for universal suffrage came from mathematician and philosopher of the Enlightenment Condorcet (1743–94). It was based on the following probabilistic argument: since the average citizen has less than a one in two chance of being wrong, the sum of all citizens' votes has very little chance of being wrong. This demonstration, known as Condorcet's jury theorem, is reflected in present-day discussions about the 'wisdom of crowds' that lie at the heart of the potential which the knowledge economy can unleash (Yu, Chai, and Liu 2018).

Conducting fundamental research on this collective ethos was the life's work of Elinor Ostrom, an American economist and winner of the 2009 Nobel Memorial Prize in Economic Sciences. She established through her study of micro local organisations that there is no need for a 'tragedy of the commons' since participation in the commons creates the mutual obligation necessary to respect the rules defined by the collectivity (Ostrom 2015). She identified eight such rules, relating to access, monitoring, self-enforcement, and conflict resolution, as necessary to avoid the negative 'externalities' to which the commons may be exposed. She does not deny that the commons can be prone to negative behaviour, but she argues that an optimal state of organisation can be reached without an over-enforcement of property rights. Ostrom also observed that the common institutions that have best adapted to technological change did so thanks to a bottom-up approach to organisation. The key factors identified by Ostrom are the same organisational principles found on the internet and in the knowledge economy. This is at least true for what we saw Hindman label as the 'imagined internet', where digital commons offer a democratised space in which the 'invisibles' can express themselves, and where small technology firms have the potential to supplant larger incumbents. The digital commons contributors are often volunteers living on different continents who are not subject to the authority of a boss. It is not greed that leads them to contribute, but an ethic of freedom and equality, often with a strong commitment to user empowerment and privacy. By interacting, and even competing, the group shares information and collectively resolves problems. This improves group members' chances of finding answers. The reason it works is that the crowd comes to wisdom by finding consensus in the answers that stand the test of joint scrutiny for error or tendentiousness. Thanks to crowdsourcing, individual actions combine to shape projects and help achieve shared goals.

Perhaps the most direct enactment of the comedy of the knowledge commons in the new digital technologies is the open source software movement. The peculiarities of software development have enabled programmers to achieve much greater efficiency by releasing an original version of some new software program into the 'wild' and allowing people around the world to contribute to its improvement. The alternative 'closed source' approach involves a company creating software using internal talent and keeping the source code of the program locked up. In his book *The Cathedral and the Bazaar,* Eric Raymond describes closed source as a cathedral development model and open source as a bazaar development model (Raymond 2001). A cathedral is centrally planned: creation takes a long time and is not open to change. A bazaar is lively and consists of a variety of buyers and sellers. If the bazaar needs to be moved, this can be done quickly, and changes in preferences can also be rapidly accommodated. The famous example of an open source operating system for personal computers is Linux, created in 1991 by Finnish–American software engineer Linus Benedict Torvalds. Its advantages over Microsoft's proprietary Windows operating system include lower cost (it is protected from private appropriation by a general public license) and greater security against possible breaches of confidentiality. In contrast to Microsoft's huge in-house teams of researchers and developers, Linux succeeds in gathering and exploiting the IQs of thousands of users across the internet for free (Foray 2006, 178). It is particularly encouraging that France has become part of the trend of increasing take-up of Linux by the public sector, with users including the French police, the *gendarmerie,* and the defence ministry (Commission européenne 2018).

This comedy of the knowledge commons also has a dark side, which has likewise found fertile ground in France. The story of Big

Tech plays out in the daily lives of rich (and not so rich) countries in ways that few have the inclination or practical scope to evade (save China, except that it has its own Big Tech). The emergence of the Cloud has enabled businesses to outsource their hardware and network infrastructure for a modest monthly fee, saving them the cost of building technology infrastructure in-house. The Covid-19 pandemic and the associated shift by millions of office workers to remote working with video conferencing accelerated migration to the Cloud. Collaboration tools such as Microsoft Teams and Google Meet have become cogs in the larger Cloud-based ecosystem of businesses. The combination of the first-mover advantage and network effects has been a huge boon for the Big Tech firms. Dominated by Amazon Web Services (AWS), Microsoft Azure, and Google Cloud, the Cloud has reinforced Big Tech's dominance based on the value of networks. This ballooning effect has been swollen by the absorption of smaller tech firms – a process that may have slowed the pace of technological innovation (Greenspan and Wooldridge 2018, 197–8). The ability of Big Tech firms to collect more data than anyone else and to achieve economies of scale and scope has virtually assured them total market dominance. Data is monitored and exploited, allowing the personalisation of ads and content without conscious authorisation (Mulgan 2018, 206). Social relationships are mediated by platforms like YouTube, Twitter, Facebook, Instagram, etc. With most advertising dominated by the Big Tech platforms, most news media and journalism have become similarly dependent. This applies also to the most successful online news providers such as Buzzfeed, Huffington Post, Vice, and Vox.com (Hindman 2018, 168).

This background will be familiar to many readers, but it warrants rehearsing to drive home the risk of digital technology being misused by state authorities. Since all tech stories seem to start in the United States, here is Matthew Hindman on the background of the Snowden affair in 2013: 'State surveillance … is closely intertwined with the power of big digital firms. The NSA's capabilities have piggybacked upon the networks, tools, techniques of companies like Google, Facebook, and Verizon. The NSA's infrastructure copies digital giants' data warehouses, it depends critically on software architectures that Google and Facebook developed, and it even hires former Facebook staff. And, of course, the biggest digital firms increasingly serve as a one-stop-shop for all kinds of personal data:

email, browsing history, location data, and increasingly even credit card purchase data. The temptation for governments to use this data through legal or covert means is strong' (Hindman 2018, 175–6). Edward Snowden revealed not only state surveillance but also the dark side of Facebook.

This lesson of the Snowden affair was borne out by scandalous revelations in early 2018 that the personal data of millions of Facebook users had been collected without consent by Cambridge Analytica, to be used mainly for political advertising purposes. Silicon Valley investor Roger McNamee recounts a moment of revelation during a congressional hearing in April 2018, contained in this question put by Kathy Castor, a Democratic representative from Florida, to Facebook's founder and CEO, Mark Zuckerberg: '[B]ut you're following Facebook users even after they log off of the platform and application, and you are collecting personal information on people who do not even have Facebook accounts. Isn't that right?' (McNamee 2019, 211)

The Snowden affair highlighted the extent of the surveillance carried out by US state agencies on the online world. This prompted European governments to seek ways of protecting their own online spaces from such surveillance – in particular, by developing the GAIA X European Cloud project (Farrell and Newman 2019). In the area of realising sovereignty in the digital technology field, therefore, the French establishment has determined that this goal can only be successfully pursued at the European rather than the national level. Since the Snowden affair, the German position has similarly evolved towards the pursuit of European digital sovereignty. However, this policy orientation does not in itself resolve the tension between private companies and public institutions reacting in different ways to the ethos of knowledge communities oriented towards cooperation. Such experiences can, however, lead to lessons being learnt – or, in the language of the tech world, to the 'adaptive evolution of organizational practices' (Foray 2006, 186–7). A clear example of this adaptive evolution was visible when the president of Microsoft, Brad Smith, declared in 2020 that 'Microsoft was on the wrong side of history when open source exploded at the beginning of the century, and I can say that about me personally'. He was referring to former Microsoft CEO Steve Ballmer, who in 2001 compared Linux to 'a cancer that attaches, in the sense of intellectual property, to everything it touches'. Smith said he took pride in Microsoft being 'the largest contributor to open source projects in the world as far as businesses are concerned'. He also stated his view that the Cambridge Analytica scandal had marked a political turning point, forcing the digital giants to change their ways to escape sanctions from the authorities (Tung 2020).

All of this highlights the attitude that institutions require to exploit the new forms of social coordination and innovation offered by digital technologies. These knowledge communities are a form of organisation that places openness of knowledge, cooperation, trust, and the rules of reciprocity at the heart of the economy (Foray 2006, 187). The discussions we are having about them reflect a realisation that industrial production and technology should be geared towards meeting human needs in the sense of promoting overall well-being that is not limited to material living conditions. Geoff Mulgan nails the problem: 'We are in the midst of revolution after revolution in technologies that are founded on the ultimate commons – information and knowledge. But these are being squeezed into organizational models designed for the sale of baked beans and cars. Instead, we need to match the imagination of the technologies with a comparable social and organizational imagination' (Mulgan 2018, 213).

The ENA does not train technocrats in the principles of complex systems and chaos theory. The ideas of Henri Poincaré on the fateful consequences of a butterfly flapping its wings might have helped them to better handle the GFC. Even if it was a bat rather than a butterfly that was the alleged source of Covid-19, the chaos it created left the 'untouchables' vulnerable. Social media defies the high priests of the official press: through their kaleidoscopic vignettes of life, social network communications echoed a society in deep disarray.

The comedy of the knowledge commons will play on in public institutions, quietly and subtly, calling into question an order established by centuries of centralised governance. This new Velvet Revolution, as in the overthrow of communist tyranny in Czechoslovakia in 1989, is a transition of power without violence. Ill-suited to a hierarchical leadership favouring a caste of untouchables, the striving knowledge commons can run like a reforming thread through society. The experience of the Covid-19 epidemic highlighted for many the importance of national autonomy and repatriating production, mainly, but not only, in the health care sector. The reasons that Keynes gave in 1933 for this aspiration seem valid today: 'the policy of an increased national self-sufficiency is to be considered, not as an ideal in itself, but as directed to the creation of an environment in which other ideals can be safely and conveniently pursued' (Keynes 1933, 185).

A natural benefit of the comedy of the knowledge commons is improvements in understanding and responses – thanks to the mingling of knowledge communities – in relation to phenomena affecting society such as pandemics, innovations, and financial crises. Such progress stems from a new paradigm in research that has formed since the 1980s, of which the essence is interdisciplinary exchange. This way of thinking draws its strength from the theory of evolution and complex sciences, and insights from that theory are then applied by scholars and thinkers in physics, biology, environmental sciences, economics, history, philosophy, mathematics, literature, and psychology (Epstein 2014; Kahneman 2012; Kirman 2010; Wilson and Kirman 2016). The whole approach is supported by the application of mathematical methods, ranging from dynamic systems to game theory, as well as new economic and social interpretations of the results. This results in a collaboration between interdisciplinary academics and experts in digital technology and software, providing a multiplicity of points of view that can lead to a more precise representation of the complexity of human behaviour. Of particular relevance to the political economy themes covered in this book is the New Approaches to Economic Challenges (NAEC) initiative, aimed at working towards a better understanding of complex, dynamic, and interconnected challenges in order to assist the OECD in formulating policy recommendations (Hynes, Naumann, and Kirman 2019). This NAEC team includes not only academics but also analysts from central banks and public administrations, and they are joined by researchers from some Big Tech firms such as Google. The supporting techniques used are simulations capable of capturing 'non-linear dynamics' – that is, developments that do not appear predetermined – like the diffusion of technology and information. The complexity of the economic system that such knowledge communities model then emerges as the simulation progresses. The model is not conceived and controlled by some grand team leader: instead, the economic process and macroeconomic properties emerge through the interactions of individual agents. The difficulty is that despite the increase in computing power available today, it is hard to build an agent-based model (ABM) on a scale corresponding to a country, not to mention the world. In time, however, machine learning will generate ever-greater data capacities.

It is not state institutions that will conceive such ideals; rather, it is the institutional environment that can help people to solve problems, just like in Ostrom's commons. Yet applications of digital technology by the state, even if well intentioned as opposed to aimed at covert surveillance, can all too easily traduce the spirit of the knowledge commons. France has produced a perfect example of this: the system developed by theoretical physicist Eric Bonabeau using evolutionary algorithms to design the mail delivery routes of the French post office.

In 2010, the French postal agency *La Poste* became a public limited company (SA) (with the state retaining a majority shareholding) and was mandated to optimise profits. In 2005, *La Poste* had hired Bonabeau's firm Icosystem to spend a week eliminating delivery route network faults in a small town two hours north of Paris (Roush 2006). After a few days, a persistent network of routes began to emerge; the program had found a solution. When the new routes were put into practice, the postal delivery workers apparently said they were happier or less unhappy than before. Journalist Nicolas Bérard recorded his rather different findings, based on numerous interviews with postal workers about their lives under the algorithm named GeoRoute (Bérard 2018).

La Poste enters a maximum of information into the software, which takes care of planning and timing everything. The slightest movement is timed, and each action is framed. *La Poste* explains that its algorithm allows for an accurate assessment of the duration of the mail delivery tour. Based on this assessment, GeoRoute maximises the productive delivery time of each tour: for example, it allows one minute and thirty seconds to deliver a registered letter, six seconds to have a door opened, one second per step when there are stairs, and so on. It evaluates the speed of movement on each POS (portion of track), between two PREs (delivery points), depending on the means of transport used and other equally poetic parameters. Each mailbox environment must correspond to more than fifty defined criteria: Is there a 'no junk mail' sticker? Is there a dog that disrupts the distribution of mail? Is it the box of a private or business address, an INH (uninhabited dwelling), or an RS (second home)? Besides its love of acronyms, the problem with the software is its inhuman intelligence. The lived experience of the

street, its traffic, the weather, or the mood of Monsieur X, who, depending on the day, may want to talk with the postal worker for
twenty minutes: the software is ignorant of all these things. Such factors affecting delivery workers' time, previously ignored or taken for
granted, were now designated as 'dead time' and eliminated. The
absurdity of the operation is absolute. The postal employee is transformed into a robot, dehumanised and soulless.

THE STRUGGLE BETWEEN PRIVACY AND SECURITY

The knowledge economy can potentially point in one of two dir-
ections: utopia or dystopia. Richard Baldwin and those who hope
that the knowledge commons will prove to be an uplifting comedy foresee a humane society, where workplaces will foster united
communities and local production and craftsmanship (Baldwin
2019, 262). However, technological changes have also long been associated with dystopia. This threat was famously imagined in two
masterpieces of dystopian literature – George Orwell's *1984*, which
depicts the use of technology for constant surveillance of human
behaviour, and Aldous Huxley's *Brave New World*, which reflects on
the social consequences of genetically manipulating humanity on a
large scale. This last theme was taken up in Yuval Noah Harari's *Sapiens* (2015), mentioned earlier, which offers a premonition that the
biotechnological revolution will end in our species being supplanted
by biodesigned post-human cyborgs capable of living eternally. For
Harari, most technological revolutions, including the agricultural
revolution, are a Faustian bargain in which humans, by renouncing
living in synergy with nature, lose their soul and humanity.

The question of surveillance was at the heart of the concerns
voiced by philosopher Michel Foucault, who viewed the public
provision of health care as a new way of monitoring individuals
(Foucault 1994). He may have been shocked had he lived to see
the law of 23 March 2020 imposing a state of health emergency,
restricting collective and individual freedoms, prohibiting travel
outside the home, and arbitrarily extending provisional restrictions. While those lockdown measures were a hasty reaction to an
epidemic involving a life-threatening disease, they were followed
by more systematic plans for monitoring society in the form of the
track-and-trace system designed to identify the contacts of people
testing positive for Covid-19. The problem of the trade-off between

protecting privacy and freedoms on the one hand and offering protection against threats such as terrorism or pandemics on the other hinges on big data: extremely large data sets that may be analysed computationally to reveal patterns, trends, and associations, especially those relating to human behaviour and interactions. This new source of wealth is made available to the private and public sectors more or less voluntarily by users.

In *Of Privacy and Power*, American political scientists Henry Farrell and Abraham Newman explain that with the advent of consumer credit, revolving credit cards, and tourism and airline companies, individuals started to leave traces of data about their daily activities. This data has proliferated with social media and the advent of the smartphone. With the emergence of facial recognition technology, biometrics, and location information, individual actions translate into data, which is fed into machine learning processes that analyse and predict behaviour and can be used to manipulate it. Governments rely on the private sector to collect data that is then used to monitor citizens, including citizens from other countries. The authors add that 'there is no magical solution that would resolve the struggle between privacy and security. And the discussion has hardly begun' (Farrell and Newman 2019, 169). Applying that view from America to France, the interim conclusion can only be that France is on the cusp of both comedy and tragedy.

Conclusion

In this book, I have drawn on the thorough research and original thinking of many writers to develop and refine my own sense of what ails France. By frequent, direct quotation from their writings, I have tried not only to let their own words do better justice to their thinking than my descriptions could manage, but also to echo the fine French tradition of the *salon*. Inspired by models from Italy (that cradle of French culture and civilisation), *salons* were where the conversations of thinkers began to be nurtured, starting in the seventeenth century and flowering in the eighteenth-century Enlightenment. The freedom of spirit and thought for which the Enlightenment is justly celebrated is reflected in the pride of place given to *liberté*, followed by *égalité* and *fraternité*, in the motto of the French Republic that encapsulates its social contract.

Debating is a real art of living, and the revival of the symposia of antiquity in Renaissance Italy was intrinsic to that rebirth which is most often associated with the glories of the visual arts. Liberty in a state and a society will wither without free debate. In those Parisian houses where the likes of Madame Geoffrin would host encyclopaedists Diderot and d'Alembert, or adventurer and playwright Beaumarchais, the philosophy of the Enlightenment, which reacted against all kinds of institutionalised restraints, was brought to life (Orsenna 2019). Its first target was the Church and its doctrines; next in line was the royal state. The philosophy forged in that ferment was materialist, leading to a revolutionary fervour to perfect human society by an alternative route to the one that had been laid down by established religion (Colander and Kupers 2014, 113). Yet this dominant, enlightened revolutionary tradition would itself come to resemble a religion to many of its adepts – the French intellectuals, so many of whom, in the two centuries following the bloody upheaval of the French Revolution, would take up the cause of revolutionary communism, with a notable passion for the messianic and millenarian impulse that would produce bloodbaths in twentieth-century Russia and China. In the political sphere, the state achieved its ambition of supplanting the Church and, as it did so, continued the work of the preceding centuries of centralising royal power as well as the related quest of disposing of large portions of the nation's wealth (Tocqueville 1985).

As the horrors of the twentieth century receded and the West won the Cold War, much of the intelligentsia became conformist, the acolytes of a state-centred oligarchy. This betrayal of the spirit of free debate was camouflaged by political partisanship. However, the noisy debates of this French cohort of Nassim Taleb's 'intellectuals yet idiots' (IYIS), which became a staple of the established TV networks, were a sham. Only approved ideas were admitted. This establishment rounds on dissenting voices with a vehemence that betrays fear and insecurity. The IYIS have ghettoised French society both spatially and intellectually: spatially in terms of the populations of invisible people confined to the suburbs and the peripheral territories; and intellectually in terms of praising those with 'correct' ideas and consigning those with 'incorrect' notions to the disreputable margins, where they are considered to be deluded or deplorable. The offending ideas are typically denounced as extreme right wing (Jean-Paul Sartre championed the slogan that opponents can only be on the right – *pas d'ennemis à gauche*). This is especially so when discussion turns to the question of traditional national identity in the face of mass immigration or the state's ambition to promote a European identity as a way of projecting its power. It would appear that the king – now reincarnated as a tight Parisian oligarchy – sits uneasily on this throne.

Such unease and fear are shared by millions of French people outside the Parisian political and media hothouse. After achieving prosperity, a natural goal is to hold on to what has been acquired (the French word for acquired – *acquis* – has a specific connotation of entitlements that enhance living standards). It is no wonder that anti-establishment politicians of the left and right have abandoned electoral commitments to take France out of the European monetary union, lest that serious but, as I have argued, beneficial step frighten too many voters away. Yet, as recent election results have shown, the fear of such change is being overcome by frustrations and resentments. Stagnating living standards have upended the previously treasured assumption that the young generation would live better than its parents. The millions of working poor who felt forgotten and ignored rose up as the yellow vests. As this feeling that 'we can't go on like this' gathers force, it will be accompanied by an ever-stronger sense of being free to seek and apply new solutions.

Historian Walter Scheidel wrote in *The Great Leveler* that there were four horsemen of levelling inequality: mass mobilisation warfare, transformative revolutions, state collapse, and – presciently in this book, which was published in 2017 – pandemics. 'We cannot be certain that the coming years will be free of the violent shocks that have punctuated history since the dawn of civilization. There is always a chance, however small, that a big war or a new Black Death might shatter the established order and reshuffle the distribution of income and wealth' (Scheidel 2017, 442).

The Covid-19 pandemic has had a cathartic effect. It has galvanised aspirations and frustrations on the fault lines of social and political institutions, the role of the state, the place of the nation in Europe, and the survival of the European model and the common currency. Despite taxing and spending over half the value of the country's annual output, the French state has proved unable to provide basic protective equipment for those caring for the sick and doing essential jobs at the height of the epidemic. A desire for change, a deep dynamism, and a creative effort by everyone – especially by those who have long been neglected and invisible – has been revealed.

The various strands of thinking in this book converge on the best treatment for the ailments of France lying in what Richard Baldwin called a new localism that should reinforce community ties (Baldwin 2019, 262). A conventional final flourish might have me advocating or hoping for the political and bureaucratic establishment to reinvent itself through a self-denying agenda of transferring power and resource allocation decisions to regions, towns, and districts. My actual conclusion is a bit different. The social and political reaction to structural economic setbacks and dislocations will *force* a more local orientation, regardless of whether those holding the central levers of power prefer to resist or facilitate this movement. The happier scenario of facilitation might entail incremental steps or grand departures in the French manner, such as the replacement of the

Fifth Republic's unitary state with a federal model. A multitude of individual initiatives during Covid-19 have seemed to support such a localising tendency. Thousands of Parisians rediscovered the rest of the country during the weeks of lockdown in 2020 under glorious spring skies – a spectacle which reminded me of the intuition of Bernard Maris: 'All of a sudden, the despised provinces – never forget that the word province means a country that has been conquered – are getting themselves a makeover whereas Paris remains a city of dirt and noise, stressful and inaccessible as speculative money drives out its inhabitants' (Maris 2016, 129).

Recentring the country on its component localities will give citizens what social scientists would call greater 'agency', while poets might call it a chance to breath a freer air. To continue in that poetic vein, the French show so many signs of gasping for breath. For me, Christine Kelly's *Face a l'Info* talk show on CNews is the most authentic contemporary version of the Enlightenment *salons*. I am not alone in this opinion. Since its launch in 2019, the show has attracted an audience of millions, especially 'provincials', whose online feedback makes it clear that they enjoy this liberating change from the stitled language of the long-entrenched studios. A free exchange of contending ideas is the wellspring of overall freedom, without which, as the great nineteenth-century conservative romantic Chateaubriand said, 'there is nothing in the world'. Like any economist, I enjoy debating trade-offs. Any real debate about the trade-offs between *liberté* and her sisters *egalité* and *fraternité* presupposes an underlying freedom – and this for me is a kind of ontological proof of freedom's primacy. But that is a discussion for another day. In France, the art of conversation is so specific and unique that, as reported by journalist Vincent Mongaillard, the *Festival des conversations* has applied to be included in UNESCO's inventory of 'intangible cultural heritage' along with other hallmarks of French civilisation such as the gastronomic meal and the carnival of Granville in the Manche *département* that juts out from the coastline of Normandy into the English channel, as if the land itself were striving for freedom.

References

Abdelgadir, A., and V. Fouka. 2020. 'Political Secularism and Muslim Integration in the West: Assessing the Effects of the French Headscarf Ban'. *American Political Science Review* 114 (3): 707–23.

Ackerman, B., A. Alstott, and P. Van Parij. 2005. *Redesigning Distribution: Basic Income and Stakeholder Grants as Alternative Cornerstones for a More Egalitarian Capitalism.* New York and London: Verso Books.

Adams, D. 2007. *The Hitchhiker's Guide to the Galaxy.* New York: Random House Publishing Group.

AFP. 2018. 'France to Overhaul Baccalaureate in Tricky School Reform'. *The Nation,* 29 January.

Aghion, P., Y. Algan, P. Cahuc, and A. Shleifer. 2010. 'Regulation and Distrust'. *Quarterly Journal of Economics* 125 (3): 1015–49.

Alesina, A., E. Glaeser, and B. Sacerdote. 2001. 'Why Doesn't the United States Have a European-Style Welfare State?' Brookings Paper on Economic Activity 2, 187–278, September.

Algan, Y., P. Cahuc, and A. Zylberberg. 2012. *La fabrique de la défiance … et comment s'en sortir.* Paris: Albin Michel.

Algan, Y., C. Landais, and C. Senik. 2012. 'Cultural Integration in France'. In *Cultural Integration of Immigrants in Europe,* edited by Y. Algan, A. Bisin, A. Manning, and T. Verdier, chapter 2. Oxford: Oxford Scholarship Online.

Algan, Y., C. Malgouyres, and C. Senik. 2020. 'Territories, Well-being and Public Policy.' *Les notes du conseil d'analyse économique* 55 (January): 1–12.

Allcott, H., and M. Gentzkow. 2017. 'Social Media and Fake News in the 2016 Election'. NBER Working Paper 23089, April.

Amabile, T.M. 1997. 'Motivating Creativity in Organizations: On Doing What You Love and Loving What You Do'. *California Management Review* 40 (1): 39–59.

– 2012. 'Componential Theory of Creativity'. Harvard Business School Working Paper 12(096), April.

Amara, F., C. Carsin, J.-M. Charpin, D. Knecht, D. Ientile, I. Rougier, N. Le Ru, and P.-A. Pottier. 2016. 'Evaluation de politique publique: La Mobilité géographique des travailleurs'. Report, Inspection Générale des Finances and Inspection Générale des Affaires Sociales, January, http://www.igas.gouv.fr/IMG/pdf/2015-095R.pdf.

Antiprince. 2018. 'Manifeste de la commune Blockchain'. Manifesto, Antiprince, http://www.antiprince.org/wp-content/uploads/2018/03/Manifeste-de-la-Commune-Blockchain.pdf.

Armingeon, K., and K. Guthmann. 2014. 'Democracy in Crisis? The Declining Support for National Democracy in European Countries, 2007–2011'. *European Journal of Political Research* 53 (3): 423–42.

Aron, R. 1965. *Démocratie et Totalitarisme.* Paris: Gallimard.

Arrow, K.J. 1962. 'The Implications of Learning by Doing'. *Review of Economic Studies* 29: 155–73.

– 1972. 'Gifts and Exchanges'. *Philosophy and Public Affairs* 1 (4): 343–62.

Assemblée nationale. 2020. 'Projet de loi instituant un système universel de retraite'. Document, 29 February, http://www2.assemblee-nationale.fr/static/15/pdf/2623-6.pdf.

Attali, J. 2011. *Demain, qui gouvernera le monde?* Paris: Fayard.

Audier, F., M. Bacache, P. Courtioux, and J. Gautié. 2012. 'The Effects of Pay Reforms and Procurement Strategies on Wage and Employment Inequalities in France's Public Sector'. EWERC Working Paper, Manchester Business School.

Audry, C., and F. Sebag. 2019. 'Social and Economic Performance of French Digital Business Startups'. Barometer, Digital France and EY.

Aukrust, K., and C. Weiss-Andersen. 2019. 'Is France Becoming More Scandinavian? The Utopia of Scandinavian Virtue in France from Chirac to Macron'. *Utopian Studies* 30 (2): 146–73.

Bachofen, B. 2012. 'La nation, la patrie, le pays. La question de l'appartenance politique chez Rousseau'. *Annales Jean-Jacques Rousseau* May: 266–98.

Bagnai, A. 2016. 'Italy's Decline and the Balance-of-payments Constraint: A Multicountry Analysis'. *International Review of Applied Economics* 30 (1): 1–26.

Bagnai, A., B. Granville, and C.A. Mongeau Ospina. 2017. 'Withdrawal of Italy from the Euro Area: Stochastic Simulations of a Structural Macroeconometric Model'. *Economic Modelling* 64: 524–38.

Balassa, B.A. 1961. 'Towards a theory of economic integration'. *Kyklos* 14 (1): 1–14.

Baldwin, R. 2019. *The Globotics Upheaval.* London: Weidenfield and Nicolson.

Banque de France. 2020. Taux d'endettement des agents non financiers - Comparaisons internationales 2020T1. Report, 26 August, https://www.banque-france.fr/statistiques/credit/endettement-et-titres/taux-dendettement-des-agents-non-financiers-comparaisons-internationales.

Barbier, J.-C., and M. Knuth. 2010. 'Of Similarities and Divergences: Why There Is No Continental Ideal-type of "Activation Reforms"'. CES Working Papers 75.

Barbier, M., G. Toutin, and D. Levy. 2016. 'L'accès aux services, une question de densité des territoires'. *INSEE Premiere* 1579, January.

Bard, P., and J. Bayer. 2016. *A Comparative Analysis of Media Freedom and Pluralism in the EU Member States*. Brussels: European Parliament's Committee on Civil Liberties, Justice, and Home Affairs (LIBE), European Union.

Barjon, C. 2018. 'Macron chasse les journalistes du palais de l'Elysée'. *Nouvel Observateur*, 21 February.

Barro, R.J. 1974. 'Are Government Bonds Net Wealth?' *The Journal of Political Economy* 82 (6): 1095–117.

Barruel, A. 2005. *Mémoires pour servir à l'histoire du jacobinisme*. Chire-en-Montreuil: Editions de Chiré.

Baruch, M.O. 2008. 'Les élites d'État dans la modernisation'. In *De Gaulle et les élites*, edited by S. Berstein, P. Birnbaum, J.-P. Rioux, and M.O. Baruch, 95–111. Paris: La Découverte.

Bas, P. 2019. *Les chemins de la République*. Paris: Odile Jacob.

Bastiat, F. 1998. *The Law*. Irvington-on-Hudson, New York: Foundation for Economic Freedom.

Bastié, E. 2018. 'Ces intellectuels victimes du politiquement correct à l'université'. *Le Figaro*, 21 December.

Baverez, N. 2004. *La France qui tombe*. Paris: Perrin.

Bayart, B., and E. Egloff. 2019. *Le piège, enquête sur la chute de Carlos Ghosn*. Paris: Calmann-Lévy.

Bazot, G. 2014. 'Financial Consumption and the Cost of Finance: Measuring Financial Efficiency in Europe (1950–2007)'. Working Papers halshs-00986912, HAL.

BBC HARDtalk. 2014. 'Cooperation Just as Important as Competition in Capitalism'. *BBC*, 24 June, https://www.bbc.co.uk/programmes/p021jr93.

BBC News. 2020. 'Griveaux Paris Race: Sex Video Prompts Macron Ally to Step Down', *BBC*, 14 February, https://www.bbc.co.uk/news/world-europe-51502424.

Becker, G.S. 1974. 'A Theory of Social Interactions'. *Journal of Political Economy* 82: 1063–93.

Beetsma, R., and M. Giuliodori. 2010. 'The Macroeconomic Costs and Benefits of the EMU and Other Monetary Unions: An Overview of Recent Research'. *Journal of Economic Literature* 48 (3): 603–41.

Behaghel, L. 2008. *Poverty and Social Exclusion in Rural Areas – Final Report Annex I – Country Studies. France.* Brussels: European Commission.

Belke, A., and C. Dreger. 2013. 'Current Account Imbalances in the Euro Area: Does Catching Up Explain the Development?' *Review of International Economics* 21 (1): 6–17.

Bénabou, R. 2013. 'Groupthink: Collective Delusions in Organizations and Markets'. *Review of Economic Studies* 80: 429–62.

Bénabou, R., F. Kramarz, and C. Prost. 2009. 'The French Zones d'Éducation Prioritaire: Much Ado About Nothing?' *Economics of Education Review* 28: 345–56.

Benchoufi, M. 2011. 'Quand Mitterrand refusait les Mac de Steve Jobs ... et autres symboles d'une France qui peine à innover'. *Atlantico*, 8 October.

Benda, J. 2003. *La Trahison des clercs.* Paris: Grasset.

Bénilde, M. 2017. 'The Creation of Emmanuel Macron'. *Le Monde diplomatique*, May.

Bennhold, K. 2006. 'France's Murky Mix of School and Scandal'. *New York Times*, 15 May.

Bensoussan, G. 2015. *Les territoires perdus de la République.* Paris: Fayard Pluriel.

Bérard, N. 2018. 'Ciel! La poste a algorithmé mon facteur'. *L'Age de faire*, 10 August, https://lagedefaire-lejournal.fr/ciel-la-poste-a-algorithme-mon-facteur/.

Berdah, A. 2018. 'Macron à un jeune chômeur: "Je traverse la rue, je vous trouve du travail"'. *Le Figaro*, 16 September.

Berger, H., and A. Ritschl. 1995. '*Germany and the Political Economy of the Marshall Plan, 1947–52: A Re-Revisionist View*'. In *Europe's Post-War Recovery*, edited by B. Eichengreen, 199–245. Cambridge: Cambridge University Press.

Birnbaum, P. 1977. *Les sommets de l'État. Essais sur l'élite du pouvoir en France.* Paris: Le Seuil.

– 1998. *La France imaginée. Déclin des rêves unitaires?* Paris: Fayard.

Blanchard, O., F. Jaumotte, and P. Loungani. 2014. 'Labor Market Policies and IMF Advice in Advanced Economies during the Great Recession'. *IZA J Labor Policy* 3 (2): 1–23.

Blanquer, J.-M. 2020. 'Décrochage scolaire: "Nous avons perdu entre 5 et 8% des élèves" affirme Blanquer'. *AFP*, 31 March.

Bloom, N., C. Genakos, R. Sadun, and J. van Reenen. 2012. 'Management Practices across Firms and Countries'. NBER Working Paper Series 17850, February.

Bloomberg with PwC. 2019. *Global Top 100 Companies by Market Capitalisation.* London: PWC.

Blyth, M. 2013. *Austerity, the History of a Dangerous Idea.* Oxford: Oxford University Press.

Bonazza, P., and M. Delattre. 2012. 'Argent des syndicats: l'intégralité du rapport Perruchot'. *Le Point,* 16 February.

Boniwell, I. 2017. 'Le Paradoxe francais'. *Psychologies* 2017: 16–17.

Bordo, M.D., and H. James. 2014. 'The European Crisis in the Context of the History of Previous Financial Crises'. *Journal of Macroeconomics* 39: 275–84.

Bordo, M.D., and L. Jonung. 1999. 'The Future of EMU. What Does the History of Monetary Unions Tell Us?' NBER Working Paper Series 7365, September.

Bossuet, K. 2020. 'L'enseignement à distance, cruel accélérateur des inégalités sociales'. *Marianne,* 7 April.

Boulo, F. 2019. *La ligne jaune.* Bouzigues: Indigène éditions.

Bourdieu, P. 1977a. 'Cultural Reproduction and Social Reproduction'. In *Power and Ideology in Education,* edited by J. Karabel, and A.H. Halsey, 487–511. New York: Oxford University Press.

– 1977b. *Outline of a Theory of Practice.* Cambridge: Cambridge University Press.

– 1989. *La noblesse d'état, grandes écoles et esprit de corps.* Paris: Les Editions de Minuit.

Bove, A. 2020. 'Politics without Romance? The Pursuit of Consent in Democracy'. *History of European Ideas* 46 (3): 325–40.

Brunnermeier, M.K., H. James, and J.-P. Landau. 2016. *The Euro and the Battle of Ideas.* Princeton and Oxford: Princeton University Press.

Buiter, W. 2015. 'Unemployment and Inflation in the Eurozone: Why Has Demand Management Failed So Badly?' Presentation, 22 May, ECB Forum on Central Banking, Sintra.

Buiter, W., E. Rahbari, and J. Michels. 2011. 'The Implications of Intra-Euro Area Imbalances in Credit Flows'. *Centre for Economic Policy Research Policy Insight* 57 (August): 1–14.

Burrows-Taylor, E. 2017. 'Why Schools Are to Blame for the French Being So Glum'. *The Local,* 24 October, https://www.thelocal.fr/20171024/where-do-the-french-get-their-glum-attitude-to-work.

Burtless, G. 1986. 'The Work Response to a Guaranteed Income: A Survey of Experimental Evidence'. In *Lessons from the Income Maintenance Experiments*, edited by A.H. Munnell, 22–52. Boston: Federal Reserve Bank of Boston and the Brookings Institution.

Caillaud, C. 2018. 'Le gouvernement mise sur le développement du coworking'. *Le Figaro*, 19 September.

Cairncross, F. 2002. 'The death of distance'. *RSA Journal* 149 (5502): 40–2.

Camus, A., and Union Culturelle Gréco-Français. 1956. *'L'avenir de la civilisation européenne – entretien avec Albert Camus'*. Athènes: Union Culturelle Gréco-Français.

Carluer-Lossouarn, F. 2008. *Leclerc: Enquête sur un système*. Rennes: Éditions Bernard Gobin.

Case, A., and A. Deaton. 2017. 'Mortality and Morbidity in the 21st Century'. Brookings Papers on Economic Activity, spring.

Ceci-Renaud, N., and P.-A. Chevalier. 2011. 'Les seuils de 10, 20 et 50 salariés: un impact limité sur la taille des entreprises françaises'. *INSEE Analyses*, 2 December.

Chaffanjon, C. 2018. 'Emmanuel Macron et la presse, histoire d'un mépris'. *Vanity Fair*, 24 August.

Chamboredon, J.-D. 2012. 'Une loi de finances anti-start-up?' *La Tribune*, 28 September.

Chanel, G. 2015. 'Taxation as a Cause of the French Revolution: Setting the Record Straight'. *Studia Historica Gedanensia* VI: 65–81.

Chari, V.V., and P.J. Kehoe. 2008. 'Time Inconsistency and Free-Riding in a Monetary Union'. *Journal of Money, Credit and Banking* 40 (7): 1329–35.

Charmettant, H. 2017. 'État des lieux de la protection de l'emploi en France: L'essentiel préservé … jusqu'à maintenant'. Working Papers halshs-01616862, HAL, https://halshs.archives-ouvertes.fr/halshs-01616862/document.

Chauveau, S. 2011. *L'Affaire du sang contaminé (1983–2003)*. Paris: Les Belles Lettres.

Chauvel, L. 2006. *Les classes moyennes à la dérive*. Paris: Seuil.

Chen, R., G.-M. Milesi-Feretti, and T. Tressel. 2012. 'External Imbalances in the Euro Area'. IMF Working Paper 236, September.

Coenen, G., R. Straub, and M. Trabandt. 2012. 'Fiscal Policy and the Great Recession in the Euro Area'. *American Economic Review: Papers and Proceedings* 102 (3), 71–6.

Coignard, S., and R. Guibert. 2012. *L'Oligarchie des incapables*. Paris: Albin Michel.

Colander, D., and R. Kupers. 2014. *Complexity and the Art of Public Policy: Solving Society's Problems from the Bottom-up.* Princeton and Oxford: Princeton University Press.

Colliard, J.-É., and C. Montialoux. 2007. 'Une brève histoire de l'impôt'. *Regards croisés sur l'économie* 1: 56–67.

Collier, P. 2014. *Exodus, Immigration and Multiculturalism in the 21st Century.* London: Penguin Books.

– 2018. *The Future of Capitalism, Facing the New Anxieties.* London: Allen Lane.

Colosimo, J.-F. 2019. *La Religion française.* Paris: Editions du Cerf.

Commission européenne. 2018. *Stratégie numérique de la commission européenne. Une Commission transformée numériquement, centrée sur l'utilisateur et fondée sur les données.* Communication C(2018) 7118 (final). Brussels: Commission européenne.

Commission of the European Communities. 1990. 'One Market, One Money: An Evaluation of the Potential Benefits and Costs of Forming an Economic and Monetary Union'. *European Economy* 44 (October): 1–341.

Connexion journalist. 2019. 'Amnesty International Condemns French Anti-vandal Law'. *The Connexion,* 30 January.

– 2020. 'Make sense of: Maisons de Services in France'. *The Connexion,* 29 January.

Constitute. 2020. 'France's Constitution of 1958 with Amendments through 2008'. Constitutional Law, July, https://www.constituteproject. org/constitution/France_2008.pdf?lang=en.

Conway, P. 1995. 'Currency Proliferation: The Monetary Legacy of the Soviet Union'. *Essays in International Finance, International Finance Section* 197 (June): 1–75.

Conyon, M., and R. Freeman. 2004. 'Shared Modes of Compensation and Company Performance: UK Evidence'. In *Seeking a Premier Economy: The Economic Effects of British Economic Reforms, 1980–2000,* edited by D. Card, R. Blundell, and R.B. Freeman, 109–46. Chicago: University of Chicago Press.

COR (Conseil d'orientation des retraites). 2019a. 'Note de présentation générale: Évolution des inégalités intragénérationnelles'. Report, 11 July, Conseil d'orientation des retraites.

– 2019b. 'Note de présentation générale: Perspectives des retraites en France à l'horizon 2030'. Report, 21 November, Conseil d'orientation des retraites.

Corak, M. 2013. 'Income Inequality, Equality of Opportunity, and Intergenerational Mobility'. *Journal of Economic Perspectives* 27 (3): 79–102.

Cordazzo, P., and N. Sembel. 2016. 'Un "désordre" dans la catégorisation: le classement statutaire atypique de diplômés du superieur sans domicile'. *Economie et Statistique* 488–9: 69–85.

Cornut-Gentille, F. 2014. 'Rapport d'information, déposé en application de l'article 146 du règlement par la commission des finances, de l'économie générale et du contrôle budgétaire relatif à l'école polytechnique'. Report, 30 September, Assemblée nationale.

Cour des comptes. 2013. 'Rapport public annuel'. Report, https://www.ccomptes.fr/fr/publications/le-rapport-public-annuel-2013.

– 2015. 'Rapport public Thématique, le logement en Ile-de-France: donner de la cohérence à l'action publique'. Report, https://www.vie-publique.fr/sites/default/files/rapport/pdf/154000246.pdf.

– 2019. 'Rapport public annuel, Les communes défavorisées d'île de France: des difficultés structurelles appelant des reformes d'ampleur'. Report, https://www.ccomptes.fr/system/files/2019-02/08-communes-defavorisees-ile-de-France-Tome-1.pdf.

Courteline, G. 1993. *Messieurs les ronds de cuir*. Paris: Flammarion.

Cowen, T. 2019. 'The Great Reversal: How America Gave Up on Free Markets'. *Marginal Revolution*, 29 July.

Creel, J., F. Labondance, and S. Levasseur. 2015. *Le secteur français dans la crise. L'Economie Française 2016*. OFCE, 97–103. Paris: La Découverte.

Culpepper, P.D. 2008. 'Capitalism, Coordination, and Economic Change: the French Political Economy since 1985'. In *Changing France. French Politics, Society and Culture Series*, edited by P.D. Culpepper, P.A. Hall, and B. Palier, 29–49. London: Palgrave Macmillan.

DARES – Études et statistiques. 2018. *La syndicalisation*. Report, https://dares.travail-emploi.gouv.fr/dares-etudes-et-statistiques/statistiques-de-a-a-z/article/la-syndicalisation.

Davezies, L. 2012. *La crise qui vient, la nouvelle fracture territoriale*. Paris: Le Seuil.

Davies, J.C. 1962. 'Toward a Theory of Revolution'. *American Sociological Review* 27: 5–19.

Dedieu, F., B. Masse-Stamberger, B. Mathieu, and L. Raim. 2014. *Casser l'euro, pour sauver l'Europe*. Paris: Les liens qui libèrent.

De Gaulle, C. 1970. *Mémoires d'espoir. Le renouveau*. Paris: Plon.

De Grauwe, P. 2013. 'The Political Economy of the Euro'. *Annual Review of Political Science* 16: 153–70.

De Guigné, A. 2018. 'La France championne d'Europe de l'impôt'. *Le Figaro*, 27 July.

Deharo, A. 2018. 'Les niches fiscales battent des nouveaux records en 2018'. *Capital*, 17 December, https://www.capital.fr/economie-politique/les-niches-fiscales-battent-des-nouveaux-records-en-2018-1309058.

Delalande, N. 2011. *Les Batailles de l'impôt. Consentement et résistances de 1789 à nos jours*. Paris: Seuil.

Delhommais, P.-A. 2013. 'Les français sont-ils paresseux?' *Le Point*, 25 April.

Delwarde, E., and R. Lough. 2019. 'Macron Hopes Debate Can Quell French Unrest. So Did Louis XVI'. *Reuters*, 11 January.

Demais, A. 2014. *Rose sang*. Paris: Archipoche.

De Ménil, G. 2007. *Common Sense. Pour débloquer la société française*. Paris: Odile Jacob.

Denord, F., and S. Thine. 2015. 'Que sont les énarques devenus, étude inédite portant sur la carrière de 1215 anciens passés par les bancs de l'École nationale d'administration (ENA) durant les trois dernières décennies (1985/2015)'. Etude ENA/EHESS.

Denord, F., P. Lagneau-Ymonet, and S. Thine. 2011. 'Aux diners du Siècle, l'Elite du pouvoir se restaure'. *Le Monde diplomatique*, February.

Descoings, R. 2009. 'Préconisations sur la réforme du lycée. Paris, Lycée pour tous'. Report, 2 June, http://media.education.gouv.fr/file/06_juin/35/9/rapportconsultationlycee_60359.pdf.

Desroche, H. 1989. *Solidarités ouvrières. Sociétaires et compagnons dans les associations coopératives (1831–1900)*. Paris, Edition de l'Atelier.

Deville, C. 2015. 'Le non-recours au RSA des exploitants agricoles, L'intégration professionnelle comme support de l'accès aux droits'. *Politiques sociales et familiales* 119 (March): 41–50.

De Waal, F. 2000. *Chimpanzee Politics: Power and Sex among Apes*. Baltimore, MD: Johns Hopkins University Press.

Diamandis, P.H., and S. Kotler. 2012. *Abundance: The Future Is Better Than You Think*. New York: Free Press.

Dobbin, F. 2004. 'How Institutions Create Ideas: Notions of Public and Private Efficiency from Early French and American Railroading'. *L'Année de la Régulation* 8: 15–50.

Dogan, M. 2003. 'Is There a Ruling Class in France?' In *Elite Configuration in the Apex of Power*, edited by M. Dogan, 17–89. Leiden: Brill.

Donzeau, N., and Y. Pons. 2019. 'En 2017, l'emploi public est quasiment stable malgre la diminution des emplois aides'. *INSEE Premiere* 1741, March.

Dormois, J.-P. 2004. *The French Economy in the Twentieth Century*. Cambridge: Cambridge University Press.

Dornbusch, R. 1996. 'Euro Fantasies'. *Foreign Affairs* 75 (5): 110–24.

Dortet-Bernadet, V. 2017. 'La moitié des entreprises signalent des barrières à l'embauche'. *INSEE Focus* 106, December.

Draghi, M. 2012. 'Verbatim of the Remarks Made by Mario Draghi'. Speech by Mario Draghi, president of the European Central Bank, at the Global Investment Conference in London, 26 July, European Central Bank, Frankfurt am Main.

Dryancour, G. 2019. 'Reply to *The Euro is Doomed*'. *Inférence* 4: 3.

Ducoudré, B. 2019. *Emploi et Chômage. L'économie française 2020. Un éclairage macroéconomique très accessible*. OFCE. Paris: La Découverte.

Dudouet, F.-X., and H. Joly. 2010. 'Les dirigeants français du Cac 40: entre élitisme scolaire et passage par l'État'. *Sociologies pratiques* 2 (21): 35–47.

Egger, P.H., S. Nigai, and N.M. Strecker. 2019. 'The Taxing Deed of Globalization'. *American Economic Review* 109 (2): 353–90.

Eichengreen, B. 1992. *Golden Fetters: The Gold Standard and the Great Depression, 1919–1939*. Oxford: Oxford University Press.

– 2006. *The European Economy since 1945: Coordinated Capitalism and Beyond*. Princeton: Princeton University Press.

– 2010. 'The Euro: Love It or Leave It?' *VoxEU.org*, 4 May.

Eichengreen, B., and J. Frieden. 1994. 'The Political Economy of European Monetary Integration: An Analytical Introduction'. In *The Political Economy of European Monetary Unification*, edited by B. Eichengreen and J. Frieden, 1–21. Boulder: Westview Press.

Eluard, P. 1958. 'Liberte'. In *Anthologie thematique de la poesie francaise*. edited by M.-P. Fouchet, 215–17. Paris: Seghers.

Epstein, J.M. 2014. *Agent Zero: Toward Neurocognitive Foundations for Generative Social Science*. Princeton and Oxford: Princeton University Press.

Escafré-Dublet, A. 2014. *Mainstreaming Immigrant, Integration Policy in France: Education, Employment, and Social Cohesion Initiatives*. Brussels: Migration Policy Institute Europe, August.

Etzkowitz, H., and L. Leydesdorff. 1995. 'The Triple Helix – University-Industry-Government Relations: A Laboratory for Knowledge-Based Economic Development'. *EASST Review* 14 (1): 14–19.

EU Reporter correspondent. 2018. 'Macroeconomic Imbalance Procedure (#MIP): Well-designed but Not Implemented Effectively, Say EU Auditors'. *EU Reporter*, 24 January.

Eurofund. 2016. 'Sixth European Working Conditions Survey'. Overview Report, Publications Office of the European Union.

Europe 1. 2019. 'Macron lui avait dit de "traverser la rue pour trouver du travail": un an après, qu'est-il devenu?' *Europe 1*, 22 September, https://www.europe1.fr/economie/quest-devenu-jonathan-lhorticulteur-qui-devait-traverser-la-rue-pour-trouver-du-travail-3920798.

European Commission. 2014. 'Fourth Alert Mechanism Report on Macroeconomic Imbalances in EU Member States'. Fact Sheet, 28 November, European Commission.

– 2015. *Education and Training Monitor 2015 France*. Brussels: European Union.

– 2019a. *Autumn Fiscal Package: Commission Adopts Opinions on Euro Area Draft Budgetary Plans*. Brussels: European Union.

– 2019b. *Launch of the International Association of Trusted Blockchain Applications – INATBA*. Brussels: European Union.

Eurostat. 2018. *How Many Hours Do Europeans Work per Week?* Brussels: European Commission.

Farrell, H., and A.L. Newman. 2019. *Of Privacy and Power. The Transatlantic Struggle over Freedom and Security*. Princeton and Oxford: Princeton University Press.

Feldstein, M.S. 1997 'The Political Economy of the European Economic and Monetary Union: Political Sources of an Economic Liability'. *Journal of Economic Perspectives* 11 (4): 23–42.

Fernández-Villaverde, J., L. Garicano, and T. Santos. 2013. 'Political Credit Cycles: The Case of the Eurozone'. *The Journal of Economic Perspectives* 27 (3): 145–66.

Finkielkraut, A. 2019. *A la première personne*. Paris: Gallimard.

Floux, F. 2016. '100 Molenbeek en France? Ceux qui nuancent ces propos n'osent pas dire la vérité'. *20 Minutes,* 29 March.

Fondation travailler autrement. 2018. 'Mission Coworking – Faire ensemble pour mieux vivre ensemble'. Report, 19 September, https://www.fondation-travailler-autrement.org/2018/09/19/mission-coworking-faire-ensemble-pour-mieux-vivre-ensemble/.

Foray, D. 2006. *The Economics of Knowledge*. Cambridge, MA and London: MIT Press.

Fosse, S. 2020. 'Opinion. France Télécom comptera davantage que les "gilets jaunes"'. *Les Echos,* 2 January.

Foucault, M. 1994. *Pouvoir et corps. Dits et Ecrits*. Paris: Gallimard.

Fourastié, J. 1979. *Les Trente Glorieuses, ou la révolution invisible de 1946 à 1975*. Paris: Fayard.

Fourquet, J., A. Mergier, and C. Morin. 2018. 'Inutilité ou absence de reconnaissance: de quoi souffrent les salariés français ?' Paris: Fondation Jean Jaurès.

France Diplomacy. 2018. 'Europe – Franco–German declaration (19 June 2018)'. Meseberg Declaration: Renewing Europe's Promises of Security and Prosperity, https://www.diplomatie.gouv.fr/en/country-files/germany/events/article/europe-franco-german-declaration-19-06-18.

Franceinfo. 2020. 'Confinement: des McDonald's pris d'assaut en Ile-de-France après leur réouverture partielle'. *Radio France*, 21 April.

Frey, B.S., and A. Stutzer. 2000. 'Happiness, Economy and Institutions'. *The Economic Journal* 110 (466): 918–38.

Frey, C.B. 2019. *The Technology Trap: Capital, Labour and Power in the Age of Automation*. Princeton and Oxford: Princeton University Press.

Frey, C.B., and M.A. Osborne. 2013. 'The Future of Employment: How Susceptible are Jobs to Computerisation?' Working Paper, September, Oxford Martin School.

– 2018. '*Automation and the Future of Work – Understanding the Numbers*'. Oxford: Oxford Martin School.

Friedman, M. 1997 'Why Europe Can't Afford the Euro'. *The Times*, 19 November.

Froot, K.A., and K.S. Rogoff. 1991. 'The EMS, the EMU and the Transition to a Common Currency'. NBER Working Paper Series 3684, April.

FTC. 2020. *FTC to Examine Past Acquisitions by Large Technology Companies*. New York: Foreign Trade Commission.

Galbraith, J.K. 1967. *The New Industrial State*. New York: Signet.

Galen, D., N. Brand, L. Boucherle, R. Davis, N. Do, B. El-Baz, I. Kimura, K. Wharton, and J. Lee. 2018. 'Blockchain for Social Impact. Moving beyond the Hype'. Report, Stanford Graduate School of Business, Stanford, CA.

Garber, P.M., and M.C. Spencer. 1994. *The Dissolution of the Austro-Hungarian Empire: Lessons for Currency Reform*. Essays in International Finance, Vol. 191. Princeton: International Finance Section, Princeton University.

Garicano, L., C. Lelarge, and J. Van Reenen. 2013. 'Firm Size Distortions and the Productivity Distribution: Evidence from France'. NBER Working Paper Series 18841, February.

Garrigues, J. 2019. *Les Scandales de la République. De Panama à L'affaire Benalla*. Paris: Nouveau Monde.

Gasparotti, A., and M. Kullas. 2019. '20 Jahre Euro: Verlierer und Gewinner, Eine empirische Untersuchung'. cepStudie, CEP Centrum für Europäische Politik, Freiburg.

Gauchet, M. 2016. *Comprendre le malheur français*. Paris: Stock.

Gee, O. 2017. 'A Deeply Divided France: A Look at Marine Le Pen's and Emmanuel Macron's Voters'. *The Local*, 7 May.

Gendron, B. 2009. 'The Vocational Baccalaureate: A Gateway to Higher Education?' *European Journal of Vocational Training* 46 (1): 4–27.

Genieys, W. 2005. 'La constitution d'une Elite du Welfare dans la France des années 1990'. *Sociologie du travail* 47: 205–22.

– 2006. 'Nouveaux regards sur les élites du politique'. *Revue française de science politique* 56 (1): 121–47.

Genieys, W. 2010. *The New Custodians of the State, Programmatic Elites in French Society*. New York: Routledge.

Genieys, W., and J. Joana. 2015. 'Bringing the State Elites Back In? Les Gardiens des Politiques de l'État en Europe et aux États-Unis'. *Gouvernement et action publique* 3 (3): 57–80.

Gernelle, É. 2019. 'Macron ou la tentation de la "Pravda"'. *Le Point*, 4 February.

Ghoshray, A., J. Ordóñez, and H. Sala. 2016. 'Euro, Crisis and Unemployment: Youth Patterns, Youth Policies'. IZA Discussion Papers 9952, May.

Girard, R. 1978. *Des Choses Cachées depuis la Fondation du Monde*. Paris: Grasset.

Gobry, P.-E. 2019. 'The Failure of the French Elite'. *The Wall Street Journal*, 22 February.

Goldfarb, A., and C. Tucker. 2019. 'Digital Economics'. *Journal of Economic Literature* 57 (1): 3–43.

Gordon, R.J. 2000. 'Does the "New Economy" Measure Up to the Great Inventions of the Past?' *Journal of Economic Perspectives* 14 (4): 49–74.

Graham, R. 2003. 'French Secularism Unwraps Far More than Headscarves in the Classroom'. *Financial Times*, 20–21 December.

Grandjean, C., and N. Goulet. 2019. 'Lutter contre les fraudes aux prestations sociales, un levier de justice sociale pour une juste prestation'. Rapport de mission confée par le Premier Ministre Édouard Philippe, la Ministre de la Santé Agnès Buzyn et le Ministre de l'Action et des Comptes Publics, Gérald Darmanin, Assemblée nationale et Sénat, Paris, http://www.carolegrandjean. fr/wp-content/uploads/2019/11/LFPS-GRANDJEAN-GOULET-octobre-2019.pdf.

Granville, B. 1998. 'France in the Impasse'. In *The Politics of Economic Reform*, edited by R. Skidelsky, 29–37. London: Social Market Foundation, Centre for Post-Collectivist Studies.

– 2002. 'The IMF and the Ruble Zone: Response to Odling-Smee and Pastor'. *Comparative Economic Studies* XLIV (4): 59–80.

– 2013. *Remembering Inflation*. Princeton and Oxford: Princeton University Press.

Granville, B., and J. Martorell-Cruz. 2016. 'Squared Segmentation: How the Insider/Outsider Divide across Public/Private Employment Shapes Attitudes towards Markets'. Working Papers 78, Queen Mary, University of London, School of Business and Management, Centre for Globalisation Research.

Granville, B., and D. Nagly. 2015. 'Conflicting Incentives for the Public to Support the EMU'. *The Manchester School* 83: 142–57.

Granville, B., and C.S. Leonard. 2002. 'The Pharmaceutical Sector: The Generics Development Trajectory'. In *The Economics of Essential Medicines*, edited by B. Granville, 137–60. London and Washington, DC: Royal Institute of International Affairs.

Granville, B., J. Martorell-Cruz, and M. Prevezer. 2018. 'A Firm-level Measure of Institutional Specificity'. Mimeo.

Gravier, J.-F. 1972. *Paris et le désert français*. Paris: Flammarion.

GRECO. 2020. 'Evaluation Report 2, France'. Council of Europe, Strasbourg.

Greef-Madelin, M., and F. Paya. 2020. *Normes, réglementations … Mais laissez-nous vivre!* Paris: Plon.

Greenspan, A., and A. Wooldridge. 2018. *Capitalism in America: A History*. London: Allen Lane.

Grieu, E. 2011. 'Discovering Who God Is in Caritas'. In *Caritas, Love Received and Given: A Theological Reflection*, edited by O.C.R. Madariaga, 15–24. Luxembourg: Éditions St Paul.

Grislain-Letremy, C., and C. Trevien. 2014. 'The Impact of Housing Subsidies on the Rental Sector, the French Example'. INSEE Working Papers 08, July.

Grossman, E., and N. Sauger. 2017. *Pourquoi détestons-nous autant nos politiques?* Paris: Presses de Sciences Po.

Guay, T.R. 2014. *The Business Environment of Europe: Firms, Government and Institutions*. Cambridge: Cambridge University Press.

Guillot, J., G. Lecaplain, and S. de Rivet. 2019. 'Jean-Paul Delevoye, douzième ministre démissionnaire de l'ère Macron'. *Libération*, 16 December.

Guilluy, C. 2014. *La France périphérique. Comment on a sacrifié les classes populaires*. Paris: Flammarion.

– 2017. *Le crépuscule de la France d'en haut*. Paris: Flammarion.

– 2019. *Twilight of the Elites, Prosperity, the Periphery and the Future of France.* New Haven and London: Yale University Press.

Gumbel, P. 2010. *On achève bien les écoliers.* Paris: Grasset.

– 2013. *Elite Academy, Enquête sur la France malade de ses grandes écoles.* Paris: Denoel.

Gurfinkiel, M. 2007. 'Can France Be Saved?' *Commentary,* May, https://www.commentarymagazine.com/articles/michel-gurfinkiel/can-france-be-saved/.

– 2019. 'Chronicle of a Political Disaster Long Foretold'. Standpoint, 28 March, https://standpointmag.co.uk/chronicle-of-a-political-disaster-long-foretold/.

Gurr, T. 1970. *Why Men Rebel.* Princeton: Princeton University Press.

Gurría, A. 2017. 'Globalisation: Don't Patch It Up, Shake It Up'. Report, 6 June, OECD.

Haidt, J. 2012. *The Righteous Mind: Why Good People are Divided by Politics and Religion.* London: Penguin Books.

Harari, Y.N. 2015. *Sapiens: A Brief History of Humankind.* New York: HarperCollins.

Hardin, G. 1968. 'The Tragedy of the Commons'. *Science* 162 (3859): 1243–8.

Hartmann, M. 2000. 'Class-specific Habitus and the Social Reproduction of the Business Elite in Germany and France'. *The Sociological Review* 48 (2): 241–61.

Haskel, J., and S. Westlake. 2017. *Capitalism without Capital, the Rise of the Intangible Economy.* Princeton and Oxford: Princeton University Press.

Hazareesingh, S. 2015. *How the French Think: An Affectionate Portrait of an Intellectual People.* New York: Basic Books.

Heller, M.A., and R.S. Eisenberg. 1998. 'Can Patents Deter Innovation? The Anticommons'. *Biomedical Research Science* 280: 698–701.

Helliwell, J.F., and H. Huang. 2008. 'Well-being and Trust in the Workplace'. NBER Working Paper 14589, December.

Herreros, R. 2020. 'La popularité de Macron chute brutalement'. *HuffPost,* 10 January.

Hindman, M. 2018. *The Internet Trap. How the Digital Economy Builds Monopolies and Undermines Democracy.* Princeton and Oxford: Princeton University Press.

Hinnekint, Y., and C. Janin. 2019. *Mission relative à la lutte contre l'illettrisme.* Paris: Ministère du travail.

Hirschman, A. 1984. 'Against Parsimony: Three Easy Ways of Complicating Some Categories of Economic Discourse'. *American Economic Review* 74 (2): 89–96.

Hoffmann, S. 1993. *The Nation, Nationalism, and After: The Case of France*. The Tanner Lectures on Human Values. Princeton: Princeton University, 3–4 March.

Holm, U. 2012. 'The Implication of the Concept of the French State-Nation and "Patrie" for French Discourses on (Maghrebi) Immigration'. AMID Working Paper Series 6.

Honkapohja, S. 2014. 'The Euro Area Crisis: A View from the North'. *Journal of Macroeconomics* 39: 260–71.

Honneth, A. 2006. *La société du mépris. Vers une nouvelle théorie critique*. Paris: La Découverte.

Houellebecq, M. 2015. *Soumission*. Paris: Éditions Flammarion.

Hunter, S.T., K.E. Bedell, and M.D. Mumford. 2007. 'Climate for Creativity: A Quantitative Review'. *Creativity Research Journal* 19 (1): 69–90.

Hussey, A. 2014. *The French Intifada Review – The 'Long War between France and Its Arabs'*. New York: Farrar, Straus and Giroux.

Huxley, A. 2007. *Brave New World*. London: Vintage Books.

Hynes, W., K. Naumann, and A. Kirman. 2019. 'New analytical tools and techniques to better understand systems'. Report, September, OECD, https://www.oecd.org/naec/averting-systemic-collapse/SG-NAEC(2019)6_New_analytical_tools_and_techniques.pdf.

iFrap. 2005. *Le Dossier Noir de l'ENA*. Paris: Fondation iFrap.

IFOP en partenariat avec Valeurs. 2019. 'Les français et le référendum d'initiative citoyenne.' *IFOP*, 6 February, https://www.ifop.com/publication/les-francais-et-le-referendum-dinitiative-citoyenne/.

Inglehart, R., C. Haerpfer, A. Moreno, C. Welzel, K. Kizilova, J. Diez-Medrano, M. Lagos, P. Norris, E. Ponarin, B. Puranen, *et al.*, eds. 2014. 'World Values Survey: All Rounds – Country-Pooled Datafile Version'. Survery, JD Systems Institute, Madrid.

INSEE. 2018. *France, Social Portrait*. Paris: Institut national de la statistique et des études économiques.

– 2020a. *Ethnic-based Statistics*. Paris: Institut National de la Statistique et des études économiques.

– 2020b. *Tableaux de l'économie française. Édition 2020*. Paris: Institut nationale de la statitisque et des études économiques.

Jackson, J. 2018. *A Certain Idea of France: The Life of Charles de Gaulle*. London: Allen Lane.

James, H. 2012. *Making the European Monetary Union*. Cambridge, MA and London: Harvard University Press.

Jauvert, V. 2018. *Les Intouchables d'Etat*. Paris: Robert Laffont.

JDD. 2017. 'Cette carte des 64 ghettos de France qui n'existe pas'. *Le Journal du Dimanche*, 25 January.

Jobert, B., and B. Théret. 1994. 'France: la consécration républicaine du néo-libéralisme'. In *Le tournant néo-libéral en Europe. Idées et recettes dans les pratiques gouvernementales*, edited by B. Jobert, 21–85. Paris: L'Harmattan.

Kahn, L.M. 2015. 'The Structure of the Permanent Job Wage Premium: Evidence from Europe'. *Industrial Relations* 55 (1): 149–78.

Kahneman, D. 2012. *Thinking Fast and Slow*. New York: Penguin.

Kawalec, S., E. Pytlarczyk, and K. Kamiński. 2020. *The Economic Consequences of the Euro: The Safest Escape Plan*. London and New York: Routledge.

Kela. 2019. 'Basic Income Recipients Experienced Less Financial Insecurity'. *Kela*, 4 April, https://www.kela.fi/web/en/news-archive/-/asset_publisher/lNo8GY2nIrZo/content/basic-income-recipients-experienced-less-financial-insecurity.

Kepel, G. (with A. Jardin). 2015. *Terreur dans l'hexagone, Genèse du Djihad Français*. Paris: Gallimard.

Keynes, J.M. 1933. 'National Self-Sufficiency'. *An Irish Quarterly Review* 22 (86): 177–92.

– 1936. *The General Theory of Employment, Interest and Money*. New York: Harcourt, Brace & World.

King, S.D. 2017. *Grave New World: The End of Globalization, the Return of History*. New Haven and London: Yale University Press.

Kirman, A. 2010. *Complex Economics: Individual and Collective Rationality*. New York: Routledge.

Kissinger, H. 1994. *Diplomacy*. New York, London, Toronto, Sydney: Simon and Schuster.

Kluth, A. 2019. 'Emmanuel Macron Isn't Gaullist. He's Just Angry at Germany'. *Bloomberg Opinion*, 19 December.

Knausgård, K.O. 2015. 'Michel Houellebecq's "Submission"'. *New York Times*, 11 August.

Koolman, G. 1971. 'Say's Conception of the Role of the Entrepreneur'. *Economica* 38 (151): 269–86.

Kramarz, F., and D. Thesmar. 2013. 'Social Networks in the Boardroom'. *Journal of the European Economic Association* 11 (4), 780–807.

Krueger, A. 2012. 'The Rise and Consequences of Inequality'. Presentation Made to the Center for American Progress, 12 January.

Kucinskas, A. 2017. 'Pourquoi Macron méprise les journalistes français'. *L'Express*, 20 September.

Kuhn, R. 2015. 'Media Plurality in France'. In *Media Power and Plurality: From Hyperlocal to High-Level Policy*, edited by S. Barnett and J. Townend, 170–86, London: Palgrave Macmillan UK.

Kuper, S. 2017. 'They Don't Want Compassion. They Want Respect'. *Financial Times*, 10 May.

Laffer, A.B., and S. Moore. 2011. *Return to Prosperity: How Can America Regain Its Economic Superpower Status*. New York: Threshold Editions.

Laffont, C. 2018. 'Rapport Borloo, "une erreur de diagnostic"'. *L'Express*, 26 April.

Laffont, J.-J. 2000. 'Étapes vers un État moderne: une analyse économique.' In *État et gestion publique: Actes du Colloque du 16 décembre 1999*, edited by Pierre-Alain Muet, 117–49. Paris: La Documentation française.

Lambert, A., and J.-C. Boulard. 2013. *Rapport de la mission de lutte contre l'inflation normative*. Ministère de la réforme de l'état de la décentralisation et de la fonction publique.

Lazarus, J.V., S.C. Ratzan, A. Palayew, L.O. Gostin, H.J. Larson, K. Rabin, S. Kimball, and A. El-Mohandes. 2020. 'A Global Survey of Potential Acceptance of a COVID-19 Vaccine'. *Nature Medicine*, 20 October: 1–4.

Leandri, N., and L. Maurin. 2019. 'Pour la création d'un revenu minimum unique'. Tours: Observatoire des inégalités.

Le Boucher, É. 2005. 'Suivre le modèle suédois?' *Le Monde*, 26 November.

Lefebvre, A. 2018. *Macron le Suédois*. Paris: PUF.

Le Foulon, M.-L. 2006. *Le rebond du modèle scandinave*. Paris: Lignes de repères.

Le Monde with AFP. 2016. 'Les Suisses rejettent l'instauration d'un "revenu de base inconditionnel"'. *Le Monde*, 5 June.

LesObservateurs.ch. 2016. 'Valls: "La France va devoir vivre avec le terrorisme pour longtemps"'. *LesObservateurs.ch*, 17 July, https://lesobservateurs.ch/2016/07/17/valls-france-va-devoir-vivre-terrorisme-longtemps/.

Le Van-Lemesle, L. 1990. 'La participation dans l'entreprise: de la théorie à la pratique'. In *La Politique Sociale du Général de Gaulle*, edited by R. Vandenbussche, J.-F. Sirinelli, and M. Sadoun, 187–208. Lille: Publications de l'Institut de recherches historiques du Septentrion.

Linz, J.J., A. Stepan, and Y. Yadav. 2004. '"Nation State" or "State Nation"? Conceptual Reflections and Some Spanish, Belgian and Indian Data'. Occasional Paper 15, United Nations Development Programme, New York.

Liu, Z., and B. Laperche. 2015. 'The Knowledge Capital of SMEs: The French Paradox'. *Journal of Innovation Economics and Management* 17 (2): 27–48.

Lombard-Latune, M.-A. 2020. 'ENA: l'élite se rebiffe'. *L'Opinion*, 28 January.

Longhi, C., and A. Musolesi. 2007. 'European cities in the process of economic integration: Towards structural convergence'. *Annals of Regional Science* 41: 333–51.

L'Opinion. 2019. 'Tech: l'exécutif mobilise 5 milliards d'investissements institutionnels pour les jeunes pousses. *L'Opinion.* 18 September.

Loriol, M. 2019. 'Suicides chez les policiers: "On traite les conséquences plutôt que les causes"'. *Le Parisien,* 20 August.

Lucas, R.E. 2003. 'The Industrial Revolution: Past and Future'. Annual Report, May, Federal Reserve Bank of Minneapolis.

Maclean, M., C. Harvey, and J. Press. 2006. *Business Elites and Corporate Governance in France and the UK.* London: Palgrave Macmillan.

Macron, E. 2016. *Révolution.* Paris: XO.

Madec, P., P. Malliet, M. Plane, R. Sampognaro, and X. Timbeau. 2018. *Entre 2008 et 2016, les réformes sociales et fiscales ont pesé sur le revenu des ménages mais ont renforcé le rôle d'amortisseur social du système redistributif.* France, Portrait Social, INSEE.

Madelin, A., ed. 1997. *Aux sources du modèle libéral français.* Paris: Perrin.

Mallet, V., and M. Peel. 2019. '"Imperious" Macron Tests Patience of EU Partners'. *Financial Times,* 31 October.

Mallonee, L. 2015. '60-Year-Old French Apartments Look Like a Utopian Dream'. *Wired,* 11 December.

Mandrin, J. 1967. *L'énarchie, ou, Les mandarins de la société bourgeoise.* Paris: La Table Ronde.

Mankiw, G.N. 2019. 'Snake-Oil Economics. The Bad Math behind Trump's Policies'. *Foreign Affairs,* January/February: 176–80.

Marchand, B., and J. Salomon Cavin. 2007. 'Anti-urban Ideologies and Planning in France and Switzerland: Jean-François Gravier and Armin Meili'. *Planning Perspectives* 22: 29–53.

Maris, B. 2014. *Et si on aimait la France.* Paris: Grasset.

– 2016. *Souriez, vous êtes français!* Paris: Grasset.

Marzinotto, B., J. Pisani-Ferry, and A. Sapir. 2010. 'Two Crises, Two Responses'.*Policy Contribution Bruegel* 1: 1–8.

Mathieu, C., and H. Sterdyniak. 2019. 'Euro Area Macroeconomics: Where Do We Stand 20 Years Later?' *Revue de l'OFCE* 2 (6): 55–88.

Maurot, E. 2017. 'Christian Bobin dans une paisible clairière'. *La Croix,* 7 August.

McCloskey, D.N. 1998. *The Rhetoric of Economics.* Wisconsin: Wisconsin University Press.

– 2010. *Bourgeois Dignity: Why Economics Can't Explain the Modern World.* Chicago and London: University of Chicago Press.

– 2016. *Bourgeois Equality: How Ideas, Not Capital or Institutions, Enriched the World.* Chicago and London: University of Chicago Press.

McGregor, J.A., and N. Pouw. 2017. 'Towards an Economics of Well-being'. *Cambridge Journal of Economics* 41 (4): 1123–42.

McNamee, R. 2019. *Zucked. Waking Up to the Facebook Catastrophe.* London: HarperCollins.

Méda, D. 2016. 'The Future of Work: The Meaning and Value of Work in Europe'. Working Papers hal-01616579, HAL.

Mediapart. 2020. 'Masques: les preuves d'un mensonge d'Etat'. *Mediapart,* 2 April, https://www.mediapart.fr/journal/france/020420/masques-les-preuves-d-un-mensonge-d-etat?onglet=full.

Melchiorre, M. 2012. 'France's Anti-Business Orthodoxy'. Blog Post, 21 December, Competitive Enterprise Institute, https://cei.org/blog/frances-anti-business-orthodoxy.

Mercier, T. 2017. 'France: What to Expect from Labour Code Reform'. *Eco Conjoncture* September: 2–14.

Micco, A., E. Stein, G. Ordoñez, K.H. Midelfart, and J.-M. Viaene. 2003. 'The Currency Union Effect on Trade: Early Evidence from EMU'. *Economic Policy* 18 (37): 315–56.

Milanovic, B. 2015. 'Global Inequality of Opportunity: How Much of Our Income is Determined by Where We Live?' *Review of Economics and Statistics* 97 (2): 452–60.

– 2016. *Global Inequality: A New Approach for the Age of Globalization.* Cambridge, MA and London: Harvard University Press.

Mill, J.S. 1946. *On Liberty and Considerations of Representative Government.* Oxford: Blackwell.

– 1983. *On Liberty.* Harmondsworth: Penguin Books.

– 1994. *Principles of Political Economy and Chapters on Socialism.* Oxford: Oxford University Press.

Milward, A.S. 1994. *The European Rescue of the Nation State.* London and New York: Routledge.

– 2006. *The Reconstruction of Western Europe, 1945–51.* London and New York: Routledge.

Minenna, M. 2016. *The Incomplete Currency: The Future of the Euro and Solutions for the Eurozone.* Chichester: Wiley.

Miner, L. 2018. '"I'm Responsible, Let Them Come and Get Me!" Macron Challenges Critics'. *Euronews,* 25 July.

Miwa, Y., P. Wirtz, M. Mizuno, and M. Khenissi. 2016. 'Professional Asset
Managers and the Evolution of Corporate Governance in France and
Japan: Lessons from a Questionnaire Survey'. Working Papers hal-
01278443, HAL.

Mody, A. 2015. 'Did Politics Defy Economics When It Came to the Euro?'
World Economic Forum, 14 July.

Monin, J. 2019. 'Autoroutes: l'histoire secrète des privatisations'. *France
Inter*, 30 March.

Mongaillard, V. 2019. 'La conversation, un art bien de chez nous qui
pourrait entrer à l'Unesco'. *Le Parisien*, 16 April.

Moreau, G. 2019. 'La France d'en bas? Idées reçues sur les classes
populaires'. In *Aujourd'hui, même les ouvriers ne se syndiquent plus*, edited
by O. Masclet, S. Misset, and T. Poullaouec, 43–8. Paris: Le Cavalier
Bleu.

Morin, C. 2020. 'Opinion. Pourquoi les Français fantasment leur retraite'.
Les Echos, 9 January.

Moriset, B., O. Brette, O. Chareire, L. Grasland, A. Richaud, and
E. Thivant. 2012. 'The "Death of Distance" Fifteen Years On:
Information Technology and Knowledge-based Service Firms in Rural
Areas'. Working Papers 00728338, HAL.

Morvan, B. 2017. France: 'Comment Michèle Tribalat a été harcelée par
Hervé Le Bras pour ne pas donner les vrais chiffres de l'immigration'.
Les Observateurs.ch, 22 April.

Mulgan, G. 2018. *Big Mind: How Collective Intelligence Can Change Our
World*. Princeton and Oxford: Princeton University Press.

Mundell, R. 1961. 'A Theory of Optimum Currency Areas'. *American
Economic Review* 51: 557–65.

Munnell, A.H. 1986. 'Lessons from the Income Maintenance
Experiments: An Overview'. In *Lessons from the Income Maintenance
Experiments*, edited by A.H. Munnell, 1–21. Boston: Federal Reserve
Bank of Boston and the Brookings Institution.

Murphy, A. 2005. 'Corporate Ownership in France: The Importance of
History'. In *A History of Corporate Governance around the World: Family
Business Groups to Professional Managers,* edited by R.K. Morck, 185–222.
Cambridge, MA: National Bureau of Economic Research.

Nadau, L. 2019. 'Souverainisme = antisémitisme: le dernier délire de
Jacques Attali'. *Marianne*, 4 October.

Naidu, S., D. Rodrick, and G. Zucman. 2019. 'Economics for Inclusive
Prosperity: An Introduction'. Research Brief, February, Econfip.

Nelson, R., and S. Winter. 1982. 'The Schumpeterian Tradeoff Revisited'.
The American Economic Review 72 (1): 114–32.

Noé, J.-B. 2013. 'La vision de l'entreprise dans les manuels scolaires'. *Contrepoints*, 21 August.

Nouailhac, J. 2015. 'Nouailhac: le dossier noir de l'ENA'. *Le Point*, 12 February.

Obin, J.-P. 2020. *Comment on a laissé l'islamisme pénétrer l'école.* Paris: Hermann.

Observatoire des inégalités. 2018. *600 000 pauvres de plus en dix ans.* Tours: Observatoire des inégalités.

– 2019. *Un million de travailleurs pauvres en France.* Tours: Observatoire des inégalités.

Observatoire national du suicide. 2018. *Suicide enjeux éthiques de la prévention, singularités du suicide à l'adolescence.* Paris: Ministère des solidarités et de la Santé.

Odoxa. 2019. 'Les Français soutiennent toujours le mouvement mais demandent au moins une pause pour Noël'. Report, 19 December, Odoxa, http://www.odoxa.fr/sondage/francais-soutiennent-toujours-mouvement-demandent-pause-noel/.

– 2020. 'Des soignants cruellement touchés par le Covid-19, mais plus aimés que jamais par les Français'. *Le Figaro santé et France Info,* 17 April.

OECD. 2013. *Towards More Inclusive Growth in the Metropolitan Area of Aix-Marseille.* Paris: OECD Publishing.

– 2014. *OECD Reviews of Innovation Policy: France 2014.* Paris: OECD Publishing.

– 2015. *OECD Economic Surveys France 2015.* Paris: OECD Publishing.

– 2017a. *OECD Economic Surveys: France 2017.* Paris: OECD Publishing.

– 2017b. *Getting Skills Right: France.* Paris: OECD Publishing.

– 2017c. *Education at a Glance 2017: OECD Indicators.* Paris: OECD Publishing.

– 2019. *Tax Administration 2019: Comparative Information on OECD and Other Advanced and Emerging Economies.* Paris: OECD Publishing.

Onfray, M. 2017. *Décoloniser les Provinces. Contribution aux présidentielles.* Paris: Editions de l'Observatoire.

Organisation for the Prohibition of Chemical Weapons (OPCW). 2018. 'Report of the OPCW Fact-finding Mission in Syria Regarding an Alleged Incident in Saraqib, Syrian Arab Republic on 4 February 2018'. Note by the Technical Secretariat, 18 July, OPCW, The Hague.

O'Rourke, K., and A.M. Taylor. 2013. 'Cross of Euros'. *Journal of Economic Perspectives* 27 (3): 167–92.

Orsenna, E. 2019. *Beaumarchais, un aventurier de la liberté.* Paris: Stock.

Orwell, G. 1944. 'As I Please'. *Tribune,* 1 September, http://www.telelib.com/authors/O/OrwellGeorge/essay/tribune/AsIPlease19440901.html.

– 2004. *1984 Nineteen Eighty-Four*. London: Penguin Books.

Ostrom, E. 2015. *Governing the Commons: The Evolution of Institutions for Collective Action*. Cambridge: Cambridge University Press.

O'Sullivan, M. 2007. 'Acting Out Institutional Change: Understanding the Recent Transformation of the French Financial System'. *Socio-Economic Review* 5 (3): 389–436.

Ottenheimer, G. 2004. *Les Intouchables, grandeur et décadence d'une caste: l'inspection des finances*. Paris: Albin Michel.

Ouest France. 2018. 'Journalisme. Trois syndicats s'insurgent contre "un appel à l'autocensure" du Quai d'Orsay'. *Groupe Ouest France*, 17 March.

Pareto, V. 1964. *Œuvres complètes*. Genève: Librairie Droz.

Paris Match Rédaction. 2016. 'Exclusif: Emmanuel et Brigitte Macron, vacances en amoureux avant l'offensive'. *Paris Match,* 10 August.

Park, H.W. 2014. 'Transition from the Triple Helix to N-Tuple Helices? An Interview with Elias G. Carayannis and David F.J. Campbell'. *Scientometrics* 99 (9): 203–7.

Paskins, J. 2009. Vague Terrain: Bidonvilles, Run-down Housing, and the Stigmatisation of (Sub)urban Space In and Around Paris in the 1960s'. *Moveable Type* 5: 1–19.

Pasquier, D. 2019. 'Le numérique abolit les distances sociales'. In *La France d'en bas? Idées reçues sur les classes populaires*, edited by O. Masclet, S. Misset, and T. Poullaouec, 157–62. Paris: Le Cavalier Bleu.

Paya, F., and M. de Greef-Madelin. 2020. 'Agnès Verdier-Molinié: "Macron, le flou et l'incertitude permanents"'. *Valeurs Actuelles*, 2 January.

Pechberty, M. 2018. 'Emmanuel Macron à l'origine de la guerre entre Renault et Nissan.' *BFM Business*, 28 November.

Peillon, A. 2012. *Ces 600 milliards qui manquent à la France. Enquête au cœur de l'évasion fiscale*. Paris: Le Seuil.

Perona, M. 2019. 'La France Malheureuse'. Observatoire du Bien-être du CEPREMAP 2019-01, February.

Pérotin, V., and A. Robinson. 2002. 'Employee Participation in Profit and Ownership: A Review of the Issues and Evidence'. Report, European Parliament. Brussels.

Perotti, R. 2017. 'L'euro e il principio di autorità'. *Lavoce.info,* 12 May.

Peyrefitte, A. 2006. *Le Mal français*. Paris: Fayard.

– 2000. *C'était de Gaulle*. Paris: Gallimard.

Phelps, E. 2013. *Mass Flourishing*. Princeton and Oxford: Princeton University Press.

Philippon, T. 2007. *Le Capitalisme d'héritiers, la crise française du travail*. Paris: Seuil.

– 2019. *The Great Reversal. How America Gave Up on Free Markets*. Cambridge, MA and London: Belknap Press of Harvard University Press.

Pietralunga, C. 2014. 'Arnaud Montebourg retourne à l'école pour devenir "haut dirigeant"'. *Le Monde*, 31 October.

Piketty, T. 2001. *Les hauts revenus en France au XXe siècle. Inégalités et redistributions, 1901–1998*. Paris: Grasset.

– 2019. *Capital et Idéologie*. Paris: Seuil.

Pilkington, H., B. Blondel, N. Drewniak, and J. Zeitlin. 2014. 'Where Does Distance Matter? Distance to the Closest Maternity Unit and Risk of Foetal and Neonatal Mortality in France'. *European Journal of Public Health* 24 (6): 905–10.

Piquet, S. 2020. '"Le Président impressionne tout le monde autour de lui": va-t-on devoir déménager le siège de BFM à l'Élysée?' *Marianne*, 4 February.

Pisani-Ferry, J., A. Sapir, and G.B. Wolff. 2013. 'EU-IMF Assistance to Euro-area Countries: An Early Assessment'. Bruegel Blueprint 19, June.

Pistre, P. 2013. 'Renouveaux des campagnes françaises: évolutions démographiques, dynamiques spatiales et recomposition sociales'. *Carnets de géographes* 6: 1–6.

Poissonnier, H., and P.-Y. Sanséau. 2017. 'Les fondements culturels du pessimisme français au travail, entre histoire et école'. *The Conversation*, 15 October.

Pollin, J.-P., and J.-L. Gaffard. 2014. *The Barnier Proposal on Banking Regulation: Whence the Wrath? The Collective Blog of the French Observatory*. Paris: OFCE.

Porta, J. 2019. 'Le droit du travail en changement: Essai d'interprétations'. *Travail et emploi* 2 (158): 95–132.

Potts, J., J. Humphreys, and J. Clark. 2018. 'A Blockchain-based Universal Basic Income'. *Medium*, 14 February, https://medium.com/@jason. potts/a-blockchain-based-universal-basic-income-2cb7911e2aab.

Prasad, M. 2005. 'Why is France So French? Culture, Institutions, and Neoliberalism, 1974–1981'. *American Journal of Sociology* 111 (2): 357–407.

Pujol, P. 2016. *La fabrique du monstre, 10 ans d'immersion dans les quartiers nord de Marseille, la zone la plus pauvre d'Europe*. Paris: Editions des Arènes.

Rabreau, M. 2016. 'Les chiffres affolants de l'évasion fiscale dans le monde'. *Le Figaro*, 4 April.

Radcliffe, T. 2019. *Alive in God*. London: Bloomsbury.

Ranger, S. 2018. 'Startup Republic: How France reinvented itself for the 21st century by wooing entrepreneurs to Paris'. *TechRepublic*, 16 January.

Raymond, E.S. 2001. *The Cathedral and the Bazaar*. Sebastospol: O'Reilly Media Inc.

Raymond, G. 2014. 'Manifestations de patrons: "Pigeons", "Abeilles", "Poussins", dans la rue, sur Internet ou en slip'. *HuffPost*, 1 December.

Razemon, O. 2019. '10 choses apprises en lisant "Paris et le désert français"'. *L'interconnexion n'est plus assurée*, 22 March, https://www.lemonde.fr/blog/transports/2019/03/22/10-choses-paris-et-le-desert-francais/.

Rédaction du HuffPost. 2017. 'Les journalistes des Échos indignés après la "censure" d'une chronique évoquant François Ruffin'. *HuffPost*, 26 July.

Rey-Lefebvre, I. 2014. 'Au lycée Maillol de Perpignan, l'atelier Sciences Po insuffle un esprit nouveau'. *Le Monde*, 13 March.

Richard, F., J. Dellier, and G. Tommasi. 2014. 'Migration, environnement et gentrification rurale en Montagne limousine'. *Revue de Géographie Alpine* 102 (3): 1–16.

Richaud, N., and R. Bloch. 2018. 'Orange lance son système de vote sécurisé par la blockchain'. *Les Echos*. 13 December.

Riding, A. 1992. 'Turmoil in Europe; French Approve Unity Treaty, but Slim Margin Leaves Doubts'. *New York Times*, 21 September.

Robertson, D.H. 1956. *Economic Commentaries*. London: Staples Press.

Rodriguez, S. 2015. 'The Real Reason Everyone Calls Billion-Dollar Startups "Unicorns"'. *International Business Times*, 9 March.

Romer, C.D., and D. Romer. 2010. 'The Macroeconomic Effects of Tax Changes: Estimates Based on a New Measure of Fiscal Shocks'. *American Economic Review* 100 (3): 763–801.

Rosa, J.-J. 2006. *The Second Twentieth Century: How the Information Revolution Shapes Business, States and Nations*. Stanford, CA: Hoover Institution Press.

Rose, A.K. 2007. 'Checking Out: Exits from Currency Unions'. *Journal of Financial Transformation* 19 (April): 121–8.

Rose, M., and G. Jones. 2018. 'France's Macron warns of populism "leprosy", Italy hits back'. *Reuters*, 21 June.

Rossi, P.E., and A. Zellner. 1986. 'Evaluating the methodology of social experiments'. In *Lessons from the income maintenance experiments*, edited by A.H. Munnell, 131–57. Boston: Federal Reserve Bank of Boston and the Brookings Institution.

Rossi-Hansberg, E., P.-D. Sarte, and N. Trachter. 2018. 'Diverging Trends in National and Local Concentration'. NBER Working Paper 25066, September.

Rothman, J. 2016. 'How to Restore Your Faith in Democracy'. *The New Yorker*, 11 November.

Rouban, L. 2002. 'L'Inspection générale des Finances 1958–2000, quarante ans de pantouflage'. *Les cahiers du CEVIPOF* 31: 19–34.

– 2015. 'Les enjeux, L'ENA ou 70 ans de paradoxe'. Report, September, CEVIPOF.

– 2020. 'La fin de l'ENA et la recomposition du système élitaire français'. *The Conversation*, 20 February.

Rougier, L. 1955. 'Pourquoi les français sont-ils ingouvernables?' *Revue des Deux Mondes (1829–1971)* April: 654–64.

Roush, W. 2006. 'The Art of the Possible. Can Eric Bonabeau's Hunch Engine Expand Your Mind?' *MIT Technology Review*, 1 September.

Rueff, J. 1950. 'L'Europe se fera par la monnaie ou ne se fera pas'. *Synthèses* 45: 386–8.

Sabbagh, D. 2002. 'Affirmative Action at Sciences Po'. *French Politics, Culture & Society* 20 (3): 52–64.

Saby, O. 2012. *Promotion Ubu roi: mes 27 mois sur les bancs de l'ENA*. Paris: Flammarion.

Safran, W. 1991. 'Nation, National Identity and Citizenship: France as a Test Case'. *International Political Review* 12 (3): 219–38.

Saint-Exupéry, A. 1994. *Lettres non envoyées destinées au Général X. Ecrits de guerre, 1939–1944*. Paris: Gallimard, Folio.

Saint-Paul, G. 2010. 'Endogenous Indoctrination: Occupational Choice: The Evolution of Beliefs, and the Political Economy of Reform'. *The Economic Journal* 120 (544): 325–53.

Sala i Martin, X., and J. Sachs. 1991. 'Fiscal Federalism and Optimum Currency Areas: Evidence for Europe from the United States'. NBER Working Paper Series 3855, October.

Salin, P. 2000. *Libéralisme*. Paris: Odile Jacob.

Sapir, A. 2005. 'Globalization and the Reform of European Social Models'. Background Document for the Presentation at ECOFIN Informal Meeting in Manchester, Bruegel, Brussels, https://graspe.eu/SapirPaper.pdf.

Sapir, J. 2012. *Faut-il sortir de l'euro?* Paris: Seuil.

– 2017. 'A l'attention des français inquiets d'une sortie de l'euro ....' *Les Econoclastes, bienvenue dans l'économie réelle*, 27 March, https://leseconoclastes.fr/2017/03/a-lintention-des-francais-inquiets-dune-sortie-de-leuro/.

Scheidel, W. 2017. *The Great Leveler. Violence and the History of Inequality from the Stone Age to the Twenty-first Century*. Princeton and Oxford: Princeton University Press.

Schement, J., and L. Lievrouw. 1987. 'Introduction: The Fundamental Assumptions of Information Society Research'. In *Complex Visions, Complex Realities: Social Aspects of the Information Society*, edited by J. Schement, and L. Lievrow, 1–10. Norwood: Ablex.

Schleicher, A. 2019. 'Pisa 2018. Insights and Interpretations'. Report, OECD, Paris.

Schneider, V. 2017. *Ceux que l'on paie pour étudier: enquête sur les privilégiés de l'école.* Tours: Observatoire des inégalités.

Schumann, M., M. Couve de Murville, R. Massigli, R. Seydoux, and P. Modinos. 1981. 'Francois Seydoux'. *La Nouvelle Revue des Deux Mondes* October: 16–32.

Schumpeter, J.A. 1942. *Capitalism, Socialism, and Democracy*. New York and London: Harper & Brothers.

– 1997. *History of Economic Analysis*. London: Routledge.

Schwartz, A. 2018. 'Will Scandal Sink Emmanuel Macron?' *The New Yorker*, 2 August.

Sénat. 2018. 'Préconisations pour une réforme de la haute fonction publique – Position personnelle du rapporteur'. Report, Sénat, Paris, http://www.senat.fr/rap/r18-016-2/r18-016-24.html.

Senik, C. 2014. 'Why Are the French So Unhappy? The Cultural Dimension of Happiness'. *Journal of Economic Behavior and Organization* 106: 379–401.

Senik, C., and T. Verdier. 2011. 'Segregation, Entrepreneurship and Work Values'. *Journal of Population Economics* 24 (4): 1207–34.

Servais, O. 2006. 'Le "modèle scandinave": un concept problématique'. *La Revue Nouvelle* 12 (Décembre): 17–23.

Servière, S.-F. 2020a. 'Les plus aisés, grands gagnants du quinquennat? Pas si simple'. *Fondation iFrap*, 7 February, https://www.ifrap.org/budget-et-fiscalite/les-plus-aises-grands-gagnants-du-quinquennat-pas-si-simple.

– 2020b. 'ENA: rapport Thiriez, les bons et les mauvais points'. *Fondation iFrap*, 20 February, https://www.ifrap.org/fonction-publique-et-administration/ena-rapport-thiriez-les-bons-et-les-mauvais-points.

Service infographie, and C. Beyer. 2017. 'Écoles: les zones rurales, oubliées des politiques éducatives'. *Le Figaro*, 10 October.

SEWA Bharat. 2014. 'A Little More, How Much It Is … Piloting Basic Income Transfers in Madya Pradesh'. Report, UNICEF, New Delhi.

Seydoux, F. 1977. 'Le Mal français'. *La Nouvelle Revue Des Deux Mondes* 1977: 295–305.

Sinn, H.W. 2014. *The Eurotrap: On Bursting Bubbles, Budgets, and Beliefs*. Oxford: Oxford University Press.

Smith, A. 1982. *The Theory of Moral Sentiments*. Indianapolis: Liberty Fund.

Solano, T. 2019. 'David Dufresne: "Face aux gilets jaunes, la police est en roue libre"'. *L'Express*, 8 November.

Solow, R. 1998. 'The Productivity Paradox'. *Issues in Science and Technology* 15 (1): 9–10.

Spence, M., and D.W. Brady. 2020. 'COVID-19 and the Trust Deficit'. *Project Syndicate*, 22 April.

Spolaore, E. 2013. 'What Is European Integration Really About? A Political Guide for Economists'. *Journal of Economic Perspectives* 27 (3): 125–44.

Sraer, D., and D. Thesmar. 2007. 'Performance and Behavior of Family Firms: Evidence from the French Stock Market'. *Journal of the European Economic Association* 5 (4): 709–51.

Standard Eurobarometer. 2019. 'Public opinion in the European Union, first results'. Standard Eurobarometer 91, European Commission, Brussels.

Standing, G. 2011. '*The Precariat: The New Dangerous Class*'. New York: Bloomsbury Academic.

Statistics Time. 2020. 'Global Innovation Index 2019'. Report, Cornell, INSEAD, WIPO.

Stiglitz, J. 2000. 'Capital Account Liberalization, Economic Growth, and Instability'. *World Development* 28 (5): 1075–86.

Stille, A. 2014. 'Can the French Talk About Race?' *The New Yorker*, 11 July.

Sud Ouest. 2020. 'Coronavirus: En finir avec "l'esprit de jouissance"' *Sud Ouest*, 16 March, https://www.sudouest.fr/2020/03/16/en-finir-avec-l-esprit-de-jouissance-7334095-10142.php.

Suleiman, E.N. 1974. *Politics, Power and Bureaucracy in France: The Administrative Elite*. Princeton: Princeton University Press.

– 1976. *Les Hauts fonctionnaires et la politique*. Paris: Le Seuil.

– 1978. *Elites in French Society: The Politics of Survival*. Princeton: Princeton University Press.

– 1987. *Private Power and Centralization: The Notaires and the State*. Princeton: Princeton University Press.

Suleiman, E., F. Bournois, and Y. Jaïdi. 2017. *La Prouesse française: Le management du CAC 40 vu d'ailleurs*. Paris: Odile Jacob.

Summers, L. 2018. 'I Discovered the Rest of America on My Summer Holiday'. *Financial Times*, 8 October.

Sureau, F. 2019. *Sans la liberté*. Paris: Gallimard.

Szabo, N. 1997. 'Formalizing and Securing Relationships on Public Networks'. *First Monday* 2 (9), https://doi.org/10.5210/fm.v2i9.548.

Taleb, N.N. 2019. *Skin in the Game: Hidden Asymmetries in Daily Life*. London: Penguin Books.

Telegraph. 2001. 'Lively Exchange: Euro Quotes of the Year'. *The Telegraph*, 30 December.

Theobald, R. 1963. 'Automation and Profits'. *The Nation*, 11 May.

Thoenes, P. 1966. *Elite in the Welfare State*. London: Faber and Faber.

Tirole, J. 2016. *Economie du bien commun*. Paris: Presses Universitaire de France.

Tobin, J. 1968. 'Raising the Incomes of the Poor'. In *Agenda for the Nation*, edited by G. Kermit, 77–116. Washington, DC: Brookings Institution.

Tocqueville, A. 1985. *L'Ancien régime et la Révolution*. Paris: Gallimard.

Trabandt, M., and H. Uhlig. 2009. 'How Far Are We from the Slippery Slope? The Laffer Curve Revisited'. NBER Working Paper Series 15343, September.

Transparency International. 2015. *Lobbying in Europe: Hidden Influence, Privileged Access*. Berlin: Transparency International.

Tribalat, M. 2013. *La fin du modèle français*. Paris: Toucan.

Tribune. 2017. 'Le programme antieuropéen de Marine Le Pen dénoncé par 25 Nobel d'économie'. *Le Monde*, 18 April.

Trierweiler, V. 2014. *Merci pour ce moment*. Paris: Éditions Les Arènes.

Tronche, S. 2015. 'Attentat à *Charlie Hebdo*: pour Manuel Valls, "la France, ce n'est pas Michel Houellebecq"'. *Lelab Europe*, 8 January, http://lelab. europe1.fr/Attentat-a-Charlie-Hebdo-pour-Manuel-Valls-la-France-ce-n-est-pas-Michel-Houellebecq-20078.

Tung, L. 2020. 'Microsoft fait son mea culpa sur l'open source'. ZDN*et*, 18 May.

Union des fédéralistes européens. 1947. *Rapport du premier congrès annuel de l'UEF, 27–31 août 1947, Montreux (Suisse)*. Genève: UEF.

Valeursactuelles.com. 2018. 'L'ENA critique la médiocrité de ses candidats'. *Valeurs Actuelles*, 5 March.

– 2020. '"Louis XVI on l'a décapité, Macron on peut recommencer": la violence des mots dans les manifestations se multiplie'. *Valeurs Actuelles*, 25 January.

Valls, M. 2015. 'Creative France: "France is Changing, and Its Image Needs to Change Too"'. *Embassy of France*, 12 January, https://uk.ambafrance.org/Creative-France-France-is-changing-and-its-image-needs-to-change-too.

Van de Walle, S., B. Steijn, and S. Jilke. 2015. 'Extrinsic Motivation, PSM and Labour Market Characteristics: A Multilevel Model of Public

Sector Employment Preference in 26 Countries'. *International Review of Administrative Sciences* 81 (4): 833–55.

Varoufakis, Y. 2015. 'The Open Letter Sent to Me in 2015 by Paolo Savona & Giulio Tremonti, Two Former Italian Ministers, on Reforms to the EU that They Considered Necessary'. *Yanis Varoufakis,* 24 July, https://www.yanisvaroufakis.eu/2018/05/29/the-open-letter-sent-to-me-in-2015-by-paolo-savona-giulio-tremonti-two-former-italian-ministers-on-reforms-to-the-eu-that-they-considered-necessary/.

Verdier-Molinié, A. 2015. *On va dans le mur.* Paris: Albin Michel.

– 2018. *En marche vers l'immobilisme.* Paris: Albin Michel.

Verdugo, G. 2011. 'Public Housing and Residential Segregation of Immigrants in France, 1968–1999'. *Population* 66 (1): 169–93

Vermeren, P. 2018. 'Les ronds-points, symbole de la France moche et emblème du malaise français'. *Le Figaro,* 18 December.

Vesperini, J.-P. 2013. *L'Euro.* Paris: Dalloz.

Villeneuve, G. 2013. 'Mapping digital media: France'. Report, April, Open Society Foundations, https://www.opensocietyfoundations.org/publications/mapping-digital-media-france.

Vinocur, N. 2016. 'Where is the French Plan to Halt Radicalization?' *Politico,* 31 March.

Visser, J. 2013. Database on Institutional Characteristics of Trade Unions, Wage Setting, State Intervention and Social Pacts, 1960–2011 (ICTWSS). Report, Amsterdam Institute for Advance Labour Studies, The University of Amsterdam.

Wæver, O. 1995. 'Identity, Integration and Security: Solving the Sovereignty Puzzle in EU Studies'. *Journal of International Affairs* 48 (2): 389–431.

Walras, L. 1926. *Éléments d'économie politique pure ou théorie de la richesse sociale.* Paris and Lausanne: Pichon R and R. Durand-Auzias.

Weisbrot, M., and R. Ray. 2011. 'Latvia's Internal Devaluation: A Success Story?' Report, December, CEPR.

Williamson, V.S. 2017. *Read My Lips Why Americans Are Proud to Pay Taxes.* Princeton and Oxford: Princeton University Press.

Willsher, K. 2019. 'Black-clad Youths Clash with Police as *gilets jaunes* Mark Anniversary'. *The Guardian,* 16 November.

Wilson, D.S., and A. Kirman, eds. 2016. *Complexity and Evolution: Toward a New Synthesis for Economics.* Cambridge, MA: MIT Press.

World Health Organization (WHO). 2018. *Preventing Suicide, A Global Imperative.* Geneva, Switzerland: WHO.

Wuthnow, R. 2018. *The Left Behind, Decline and Rage in Rural America.* Princeton and Oxford: Princeton University Press.

Yaouancq, F., A. Lebrère, M. Marpsat, V. Régnier, S. Legleye, and M. Quaglia. 2013. 'L'hébergement des sans-domicile en 2012. Des modes d'hébergement différents selon les situations familiales'. *INSEE Premiere* 1455, July.

Yu, C., Y. Chai, and Y. Liu. 2018. 'Literature Review on Collective Intelligence: A Crowd Science Perspective'. *International Journal of Crowd Science* 2 (1): 64–73.

Index